TOKYO

TOP SIGHTS, AUTHENTIC EXPERIENCES

THIS EDITION WRITTEN AND RESEARCHED BY

Rebecca Milner
Simon Richmond

Lonely Planet's
Tokyo

Plan Your Trip
This Year in Tokyo 4
Need to Know 18
Top Days in Tokyo 20
Hotspots For 28
What's New 30
For Free 31
Family Travel 32

Top Experiences 35
Shinjuku Nightlife 36
Tsukiji Outer Market 40
Meiji-jingū 44
Shopping in Harajuku 46
Roppongi Art Triangle 50
Sushi in Tokyo 54
Tokyo National Museum 58
Walking Tour: Yanaka 64
Cherry-Blossom Viewing 66
Sumo at Ryōgoku Kokugikan............. 68
Day Trip: Mt Fuji 70
Walking Tour:
Omote-sandō Architecture 74
Sensō-ji 76
Onsen & Sentō....................................82
Kabukiza Theatre 88
Tokyo Cityscape 92
Ghibli Museum....................................96
Imperial Palace.................................. 98
Akihabara Pop Culture 102
Rikugi-en 106
Shibuya Crossing 108
Karaoke in Tokyo 110
Tokyo Bay 112

Dining Out 117
The Best 120
Marunouchi & Nihombashi 122

Ginza & Tsukiji 123
Roppongi & Akasaka........................... 126
Ebisu & Meguro................................... 127
Shibuya & Shimo-Kitazawa 129
Harajuku & Aoyama 133
Kōenji, Kichijōji & West Tokyo............135
Shinjuku & Ikebukuro 137
Kagurazaka, Kanda & Akihabara 138
Ueno & Yanesen 142
Asakusa & Ryōgoku 143

Treasure Hunt 147
The Best 150
Marunouchi & Nihombashi 152
Ginza & Tsukiji 153
Roppongi & Akasaka...........................155
Ebisu & Meguro...................................157
Shibuya & Shimo-Kitazawa.................159
Harajuku & Aoyama 159
Kōenji, Kichijōji & West Tokyo............. 160
Shinjuku & Ikebukuro 161
Kagurazaka, Kanda & Akihabara 164
Ueno & Yanesen 166
Asakusa & Ryōgoku 167

Bar Open 169
The Best 172
Marunouchi & Nihombashi 174
Ginza & Tsukiji 174
Roppongi & Akasaka...........................175
Ebisu & Meguro...................................176
Shibuya & Shimo-Kitazawa.................176
Harajuku & Aoyama 181
Kōenji, Kichijōji & West Tokyo............. 182
Ueno & Yanesen 182
Asakusa & Ryōgoku 182
Odaiba & Tokyo Bay 183

Ueno & Yanesen
Tokyo's most famous museum, a sprawling park and well-preserved historic neighbourhoods. *(Map p254)*

🏛 **Tokyo National Museum**

Ⓜ Ueno

Ⓐ **Sensō-ji**

Asakusa & Ryōgoku
Riverside district of ancient temples, old merchants' quarters and Tokyo's sumo stadium. *(Map p254)*

ⓞ **Ryōgoku Kokugikan**

agurazaka, anda & Akihabara
wathe of central okyo that includes a ormer geisha district nd a pop-culture ub. *(Map p254)*

◎ Rikugi-en

Imperial Palace ◎

Ⓜ Tokyo

Kabukiza Theatre ◎

untory useum of Art

rt m

◎ **Tsukiji Outer Market**

Tokyo Bay ◎

Marunouchi & Nihombashi
History meets modernity where the grounds of the Imperial Palace meet the skyscrapers of downtown. *(Map p250)*

gi & Akasaka
ary for its , this area he place for edge art and *(Map p252)*

Ginza & Tsukiji
Ginza is Tokyo's most polished neighbourhood; Tsukiji is synonymous with its famous food market. *(Map p250)*

Odaiba & Tokyo Bay
Waterside museums, amusement parks and shopping malls plus pleasure-boat cruises.

N 0 ——————— 2 km
0 ——————— 1 miles

Welcome to Tokyo

Yoking past and future, Tokyo dazzles with its traditional culture and passion for everything new.

Tokyo's neon-bright streets still look like a sci-fi film set – and that's a vision of the city from the 1980s. Tokyo has been building ever since, pushing the boundaries of what's possible on densely populated, earthquake-prone land, adding ever-taller, sleeker structures. Stand atop one of the city's skyscrapers and look out over the city at night to see it blinking like the control panel of a starship, stretching all the way to the horizon. Tokyo is a modern city built on old patterns, and in the shadows of those skyscrapers you can find quiet alleys, raucous traditional festivals and lantern-lit *yakitori* (grilled chicken) stands.

Speaking of food, Tokyo is one of the world's top dining destinations. Here you can splash out on the best sushi of your life, made by one of the city's legendary chefs using the freshest seasonal market ingredients. Or you can spend ¥800 on a bowl of noodles made with the same care and exacting attention to detail, from a recipe honed through decades of experience. Tokyo is also Japan's pop-culture laboratory, where new trends grow legs. See the newest anime and manga flying off the shelves in Akihabara, shop for your favourite character goods, or just pick up some style inspiration walking down the streets of Harajuku.

*Tokyo is a modern city built
on old patterns*

Omoide-yokochō (p137)
MAREMAGNUM / GETTY IMAGES ©

★ TOKYO ★

Shinjuku & Ikebukuro
Shinjuku has the world's busiest train station, city hall and nightlife galore; grittier Ikebukuro is a student haunt. *(Map p253)*

Kōenji, Kichijōji & West Tokyo
Neighbourhoods loved by locals, who appreciate the vintage mid-20th-century look and bohemian spirit.

Ghibli Museum
(6km)

Ⓡ Shinjuku

Shibuya & Shimo-Kitazawa
Shibuya is the heart of Tokyo's youth culture; Shimo-Kitazawa is a beloved, bohemian haunt. *(Map p246)*

◉ Meiji-jingu

National Art Center Tokyo 🏛

S M 🏛

🏛
Mori A Museu

Shibuya Crossing Ⓢ 🚉
Shibuya

Harajuku & Aoyama
Nexus of tradition and trends with Tokyo's grandest Shintō shrine, shoppers architecture. *(Map p246)*

Ebisu & Meguro
Broad collection of hip neighbourhoods with fashionable boutiques, (relatively) quiet streets and great dining. *(Map p246)*

Roppon
Legend nightlife is also cutting design.

Showtime 185

The Best **187**
Marunouchi & Nihombashi 188
Ginza & Tsukiji 188
Roppongi & Akasaka 189
Ebisu & Meguro 189
Shibuya & Shimo-Kitazawa 190
Harajuku & Aoyama 191
Kōenji, Kichijōji & West Tokyo 192
Shinjuku & Ikebukuro 194
Kagurazaka, Kanda & Akihabara 194
Ueno & Yanesen 195
Asakusa & Ryōgoku 195

Active Tokyo 197

The Best **199**
Spectator Sports 200
Amusement Parks 200
Courses 201
Tours 202

Rest Your Head **205**
Accommodation Types 208
Where to Stay 209

In Focus

Tokyo Today 212
History 214
Arts 219
Architecture 222
Pop Culture 224

Survival Guide

Directory A–Z 229
Transport 234
Language 238
Index 240
Tokyo Maps 245
Symbols & Map Key 257

CLOCKWISE FROM TOP LEFT: MATT MUNRO / LONELY PLANET ©; EASY CAMERA,
PSQXXX, TOPNATTHAPON / SHUTTERSTOCK ©; GEORGE PACHANTOURIS / 500PX
©; PHOTOGRAPHY BY ZHANGXUN / GETTY IMAGES ©; MATT MUNRO / LONELY
PLANET ©; TAKASHI YASUI / 500PX ©; TOM BONAVENTURE / GETTY IMAGES ©;
BIXPICTURE / SHUTTERSTOCK ©; ALESSANDRO CRUGNOLA / 500PX ©; OLIOPI /
SHUTTERSTOCK ©

Plan Your Trip
This Year in Tokyo

2018

Tokyo

From contemporary arts events to festivals that have been taking place for centuries, there is always something going on in Tokyo. Like elsewhere in Japan, the seasons have special meaning, with every new bloom a reason for celebration.

Clockwise from above: Sanja Matsuri (p10); Kōenji Awa Odori (p13); Cherry blossoms (p9)

2018

HIGH MOUNTAIN / SHUTTERSTOCK ©

★ Top Festivals & Events

Hatsu-mōde January (p6)

Cherry Blossoms April (p9)

Sanja Matsuri May (p10)

Sumida-gawa Fireworks July (p12)

Kōenji Awa Odori August (p13)

BOHISTOCK / GETTY IMAGES ©

Plan Your Trip
This Year in Tokyo

JOHN LEUNG / SHUTTERSTOCK ©

01

January

Tokyo is eerily quiet for O-shōgatsu (the first three days of the new year), but picks up as the month rolls on. Days are cold, but usually clear; sights are generally uncrowded.

🎎 Greeting the Emperor   2 Jan
The emperor makes a brief – and rare – public appearance in an inner courtyard of the Imperial Palace (p98) to make a ceremonial greeting.

🎎 Coming of Age Day   8 Jan
The second Monday of January is *seijin-no-hi*, the collective birthday for all who have turned 20 (the age of majority) in the past year; young women don gorgeous kimonos (pictured above) for ceremonies at Shintō shrines.

⚱ Setagaya Boro-ichi   15–16 Jan
Boro means 'old and worn'. At this market in residential Setagaya ward, hundreds of vendors converge to sell antiques and other sundry secondhand items. The market

🎎 Hatsu-mōde   1 Jan
Hatsu-mōde, the first shrine visit of the new year, starts just after midnight on 1 January and continues through O-shōgatsu. Meiji-jingū (pictured below) is the most popular spot in Tokyo; it can get very, very crowded, but that's part of the experience.

TAKASHI IMAGES / SHUTTERSTOCK ©

itself is also an antique: it's been happening for over 400 years. A second market is held 15 and 16 December.

February

February is the coldest month, though it rarely snows. Winter days are crisp and clear – the best time of year to spot Mt Fuji in the distance.

✿ Setsubun   3 Feb
The first day of spring on the traditional lunar calendar signalled a shift once believed to bode evil. As a precaution, people visit Buddhist temples, toss roasted beans and shout, *'Oni wa soto! Fuku wa uchi!'* ('Devil out! Fortune in!').

✿ Shimo-Kitazawa Tengu Matsuri   early Feb
On the weekend nearest to Setsubun, Shimo-Kitazawa hosts a parade with revellers dressed in *tengu* (devil) costumes.

🏃 Tokyo Marathon   25 Feb
Tokyo's biggest running event (www.marathon.tokyo; pictured above) sees tens of thousands hit the city streets. Sign up the summer before; competition for slots is fierce.

⊙ Plum Blossoms   late Feb
Ume (plum) blossoms, which appear towards the end of the month, are the first sign that winter is ending. Popular viewing spots include Koishikawa Kōrakuen and Yushima Tenjin.

02

Plan Your Trip
This Year in Tokyo

March

Spring begins in fits and starts. The Japanese have a saying: sankan-shion – three days cold, four days warm.

03

⚘ Hina Matsuri   3 Mar

On and around Girls' Day, public spaces and homes are decorated with *o-hina-sama* (princess) dolls in traditional royal dress.

🔒 Art Fair Tokyo   mid-Mar
Art Fair Tokyo (www.artfairtokyo.com) is the most important date for collectors on the Tokyo calendar. They come to scout contemporary and classical works, antiques, crafts and more.

☆ Anime Japan   late Mar
Anime Japan (www.anime-japan.jp) has events and exhibitions for industry insiders and fans alike, at Tokyo Big Sight.

☆ Tokyo Haru-sai   Mar–Apr
This month-long classical-music festival is held at venues around Ueno-kōen.

April

Warmer weather and blooming cherry trees make this quite simply the best month to be in Tokyo.

❀ Buddha's Birthday   8 Apr
In honour of the Buddha's birthday, Hana Matsuri (flower festival) celebrations take place at temples. Look for the parade of children in Asakusa, pulling a white papier-mâché elephant. Pictured above: Wooden and metal ladles used to sprinkle baby Buddha figurines.

❀ Kannon-ura Ichiyo Sakura-matsuri Festival   mid-Apr
The highlight of this annual spring event that takes place in the backstreets behind Sensō-ji is the Edo Yoshiwara Oiran-dōchū – a procession of women dressed in the finery of Edo-era (1603–1868) courtesans. There's also a flea market.

❀ Earth Day   21–22 Apr
Tokyo celebrates this international event with a weekend-long festival at Yoyogi-kōen with organic food stalls, live music and workshops for kids.

❂ Cherry Blossoms   early Apr
From the end of March through the beginning of April, the city's parks and riversides turn pink and Tokyoites toast spring in spirited parties, called *hanami*, beneath the blossoms.

❀ Naki-zumo   29 Apr
In Japan it's believed that crying babies grow big and strong. At this amusing festival, held at Sensō-ji, sumo wrestlers are brought in to pull faces at babies (in cute mini sumo outfits) to make them cry. The one who cries first, or loudest, is crowned the winner.

Plan Your Trip
This Year in Tokyo

May

05

There's a string of national holidays at the beginning of May, known as Golden Week, when much of the country makes travel plans. Festivals and warm days make this an excellent time to visit.

✤ Children's Day — 5 May
For the celebration also known as *otoko-no-hi* (Boys' Day), families fly *koinobori* (colourful banners in the shape of a carp; pictured above), a symbol of strength and courage.

✤ Design Festa — mid-May
Weekend-long Design Festa (www.design festa.com), held at Tokyo Big Sight in Odaiba, is Asia's largest art festival, featuring performances and thousands of exhibitors. There is a second event in November.

✤ Sanja Matsuri — 20 May
Arguably the grandest Tokyo *matsuri* (festival) of all, this event attracts around 1.5 million spectators to Asakusa-jinja

✤ Tokyo Rainbow Pride — early May
Usually over Golden Week, Japan's LGBT community comes together for the country's biggest pride event (www.tokyorainbowpride.com), some years followed by a parade. It's not London or Sydney, but it's a spirited affair just the same.

(p79). The highlight is the rowdy parade of *mikoshi* (portable shrines) carried by men and women in traditional dress.

2018

PAYLESSIMAGES / GETTY IMAGES ©

06

June

Early June is lovely, though by the end of the month tsuyu (the rainy season) sets in.

☉ Fireflies   Jun
June is the month for fireflies to light the night sky. The garden hotel Chinzan-so hosts evening events, as do parks and gardens on the outskirts of the city.

☉ Late Spring Blooms   Jun
Rainy season in Tokyo can be a drag, but it does result in some glorious late spring blooms. June sees irises bloom in gardens around Tokyo. Meiji-jingū Gyoen is the most famous viewing spot. You'll also spot starbursts of hydrangea (pictured above) around town.

🎋 Sannō Matsuri   mid-Jun
For a week in mid-June Hie-jinja puts on this major festival, with music, dancing and a procession of *mikoshi*. The parade takes place only every other year, but is set to happen in 2018.

🎋 Tsukiji Shishi Matsuri   mid-Jun
Tsukiji's Namiyoke-jinja predates the famous market; for centuries sailors and fishermen have come here to pray for safety (*namiyoke* means 'avoid the waves'). The highlight of the shrine's annual festival is the parading of a pair of giant lion heads carved from wood. Pictured below: Monks wearing reed gaiters.

DAMON COULTER / ALAMY STOCK PHOTO ©

Plan Your Trip
This Year in Tokyo

ANGIA / CONTRIBUTOR / GETTY IMAGES ©

07

July

When the rainy season passes in mid- to late July, suddenly it's summer – the season for lively street fairs and hanabi taikai (fireworks shows).

✿ Tanabata   7 Jul
On the day the stars Vega and Altar (stand-ins for a princess and cowherd who are in love) meet across the Milky Way, children tie strips of coloured paper bearing wishes around bamboo branches; look for decorations at youthful hang-outs such as Harajuku and Shibuya.

✿ Mitama Matsuri   13–16 Jul
Yasukuni-jinja celebrates O-Bon early with a festival of remembrance for the dead that sees 30,000 illuminated *bonbori* (paper lanterns) hung in and around the shrine.

☆ Rainbow Reel Tokyo   mid-Jul
Also known as the International Gay & Lesbian Film Festival (www.rainbowreeltokyo.com), this long-running event brings the works of international film makers to Tokyo, along with a whole host of fun related events.

✿ Ueno Summer Festival   Jul–Aug
From mid-July to mid-August various events, including markets and music performances, take place in Ueno-kōen (p59).

✿ Lantern Festivals   Jul–Aug
Toro nagashi (pictured above) is a photogenic summer tradition, connected to O-Bon, in which candle-lit paper lanterns are floated down rivers. It takes place from mid-July to mid-August; two big ones happen at Chidori-ga-fuchi, along the Imperial Palace moat, and at Sumida-kōen in Asakusa.

✿ Sumida-gawa Fireworks   28 Jul
The grandest of the summer fireworks shows features 20,000 pyrotechnic wonders. Head to Asakusa early in the day to score a good seat. Check events listings for other fireworks displays around town.

August

This is the height of Japan's sticky, hot summer; school holidays mean sights may be crowded.

🎎 Asagaya Tanabata   4 & 5 Aug
Asagaya holds a Tanabata festival with colourful lanterns strung up in its *shōtengai* (shopping arcade), Pearl Centre.

🎎 O-Bon   13–16 Aug
Several days in mid-August are set aside to honour the dead, when their spirits are said to return to the earth. Graves are swept, offerings are made, and *bon-odori* (folk dances; pictured above) take place. Many Tokyo residents return to their home towns; some shops may also close.

🎎 Asakusa Samba Carnival   25 Aug
Tokyo's Nikkei Brazilian community and local samba clubs turn Kaminarimon-dōri into one big party for the Asakusa Samba Carnival (www.asakusa-samba.org).

🎎 Kōenji Awa Odori   25 & 26 Aug
Kōenji Awa Odori (www.koenji-awaodori.com) is Tokyo's biggest *awa odori* (dance festival for O-Bon) with 12,000 participants in traditional costumes dancing their way through the streets.

Plan Your Trip
This Year in Tokyo

09

September

*Days are still warm – hot even –
though the odd typhoon rolls
through this time of year.*

☆ **Tokyo Jazz Festival**   early Sep
Enjoy three days of shows by international
and local stars at Tokyo's biggest jazz festival (www.tokyo-jazz.com).

☆ **Japan Media
Arts Festival**   mid-Sep
The year's top animation, manga and digital
installations go on display at the Japan
Media Arts Festival (www.j-mediaarts.jp).

☆ **Tokyo Game Show**   late Sep
Get your geek on when the Computer
Entertainment Suppliers Association hosts
Tokyo Game Show (http://tgs.cesa.or.jp;
pictured above), a massive expo at Maku-
hari Messe in late September.

☉ **Moon
Viewing**   25 Sep & 25 Oct
Full moons in September and October
call for *tsukimi*, moon-viewing gather-
ings. People eat *tsukimi dango* –
mochi (pounded-rice dumplings) that
are round like the moon.

October

Pleasantly warm days and cool evenings make this an excellent time to be in Tokyo. October is also the month that many of the city's biggest arts events take place.

⚑ Tokyo Grand Tea Ceremony　　mid-Oct
Held at Hama-rikyū Onshi-teien (p43), this is a big outdoor tea party (www.tokyo-grand-tea-ceremony.jp), with traditional tea ceremonies held in various styles; there is usually one with English translation.

☆ Roppongi Art Night　　mid-Oct
This weekend-long (literally, as venues stay open all night) arts event (www.roppongiartnight.com) sees large-scale installations and performances taking over the streets of Roppongi.

☆ Sancha de Daidogei　　mid-Oct
Artsy neighbourhood Sangenjaya hosts this weekend-long performance-art festival that sees a globally diverse range of artists staging entertaining shows on the street.

☆ Tokyo International Film Festival　　late Oct
Tokyo's principal film festival (www.tiff-jp.net) screens works from Japanese and international directors with English subtitles.

◉ Chrysanthemum Festivals　　late Oct
Chrysanthemums (pictured above) are the flower of the season (and of the royal family) and dazzling displays are put on from late October to mid-November in Hibiya-kōen and at shrines including Meiji-jingū (p44) and Yasukuni-jinja.

⚑ Halloween　　31 Oct
Tokyo has gone mad for Halloween with thousands of costumed celebrants converging on Shibuya Crossing (p108). Shinjuku Ni-chōme (p175) and Roppongi see action, too.

Plan Your Trip
This Year in Tokyo

November

Crisp and cool days, few crowds and a full calendar of traditional and contemporary arts events.

☆ F/T   Nov
Tokyo's contemporary theatre festival (www.festival-tokyo.jp) takes place all month at venues around the city, featuring works by local and international directors. Some events are subtitled.

⚜ Shichi-go-san   15 Nov
For this adorable festival parents dress girls aged seven *(shichi)* and three *(san)* and boys aged five *(go)* in wee kimonos and head to Shintō shrines for blessings.

☆ Tokyo Filmex   late Nov
Tokyo Filmex (www.filmex.net) focuses on emerging directors in Asia and screens many films with English subtitles.

☉ Autumn Leaves   late Nov
The city's trees undergo magnificent seasonal transformations during *kōyō* (autumn foliage season). Rikugi-en (p106; pictured above) and Koishikawa Kōrakuen have spectacular displays of flaming red

⚜ Tori-no-ichi   1, 13 & 25 Nov
On 'rooster' days in November, 'O-tori' shrines such as Hanazono-jinja hold fairs called Tori-no-ichi (*tori* means 'rooster'); the day is set according to the old calendar, which marks days by the zodiac. Vendors hawk *kumade* – rakes that literally symbolise 'raking in the wealth'.

maples. Tokyo's official tree, the *ichō* (gingko), turns a glorious shade of gold in late autumn; Ichō Namiki (Gingko Ave) in Gaienmae is the top viewing spot.

2018

12

December

Early December is pleasantly crisp, but as the month goes on the winter chill settles in. Commercial strips are decorated with pretty seasonal illuminations.

✥ Gishi-sai 14 Dec

Temple Sengaku-ji hosts a memorial service honouring the 47 *rōnin* (masterless samurai) who famously avenged their fallen master; locals dressed as the loyal retainers parade through nearby streets.

✗ Bōnenkai late Dec

During the last weeks of the year, restaurants and bars are filled with Tokyoites hosting *bōnenkai* (end-of-the-year parties) with friends or colleagues. The boisterous mood takes the sting out of the newly chilled air, though be warned that tables may be hard to come by this time of year.

✥ Joya-no-kane 31 Dec

Temple bells around Japan ring 108 times at midnight on 31 December, a purifying

✗ Toshikoshi Soba 31 Dec

Eating buckwheat noodles on New Year's Eve, a tradition called *toshi-koshi soba*, is said to bring luck and longevity – the latter symbolised by the length of the noodles.

ritual called *joya-no-kane* (pictured above). Sensō-ji (p76) draws the biggest crowds in Tokyo.

Plan Your Trip
Need to Know

Daily Costs

**Budget:
less than ¥8000**

- Dorm bed: ¥3000

- Free sights such as temples and markets

- Bowl of noodles: ¥750

- Happy-hour drink: ¥500

- 24-hour subway pass: ¥600

**Midrange:
¥8000–20,000**

- Double room at a business hotel: ¥14,000

- Museum entry: ¥1000

- Dinner for two at an *izakaya* (Japanese pub-eatery): ¥6000

- Live music show: ¥3000

**Top End:
more than ¥20,000**

- Double room in a four-star hotel: ¥35,000

- Sushi-tasting menu: ¥15,000

- Box seat for kabuki: ¥21,000

- Taxi ride back to the hotel: ¥3000

Advance Planning

Three months before
Purchase tickets for the Ghibli Museum; book a table at your top splurge restaurant.

One month before Book any tickets for sumo, kabuki and Giants games online, and a spot on the Imperial Palace tour; scan web listings for festivals, events and exhibitions.

On arrival Look for free copies of *Time Out Tokyo* and *Metropolis* magazines at airports and hotels.

Useful Websites

- **Go Tokyo** (www.gotokyo.org) The city's official website includes information on sights, events and suggested itineraries.

- **Lonely Planet** (www.lonelyplanet.com/tokyo) Destination information, hotel bookings, traveller forum and more.

- **Time Out Tokyo** (www.timeout.jp) Arts and entertainment listings.

- **Tokyo Food Page** (www.bento.com) City-wide restaurant coverage.

- **Tokyo Cheapo** (www.tokyocheapo.com) Hints on how to do Tokyo on the cheap.

Currency

Japanese yen (¥)

Language

Japanese

Visas

Visas are generally not required for stays of up to 90 days.

Money

Post offices and most convenience stores have international ATMs. Credit cards are accepted at major establishments, though it's best to keep cash on hand.

Mobile Phones

Purchase prepaid data-only SIM cards (for unlocked smartphones only) online or at airport kiosks or electronics stores. For voice calls, rent a pay-as-you-go mobile.

Time

Japan Standard Time (GMT/UTC plus nine hours)

Tourist Information

Tokyo Tourist Information Center (p233) Has English-language information and publications.

For more, see the **Survival Guide** (p228)

When to Go

Spring and autumn are the best times to visit; August is hot and humid, but is also the month for summer festivals.

Tokyo

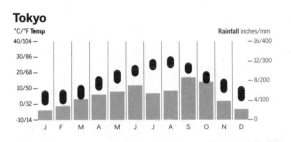

Arriving in Tokyo

Narita Airport An express train or highway bus to central Tokyo costs around ¥3000 (one to two hours). Both run frequently from 6am to 10.30pm, pick up tickets at kiosks inside the arrivals hall (no advance reservations required). Taxis start at ¥20,000.

Haneda Airport Frequent trains and buses (¥400 to ¥1200, 30 to 45 minutes) to central Tokyo run frequently from 5.30am to midnight; times and costs depend on your destination in the city. There are only a couple of night buses. Budget between ¥5000 and ¥8000 for a cab.

Tokyo Station Connect from the *shinkansen* (bullet train) terminal here to the JR Yamanote line or the Marunouchi subway to destinations around central Tokyo.

Getting Around

○ **Subway** The quickest and easiest way to get around central Tokyo. Runs from 5am to midnight.

○ **Train** Japan Rail (JR) Yamanote (loop) and Chūō-Sōbu (central) lines service major stations. Runs from 5am to midnight.

○ **Taxi** The only transport option that runs all night; unless you're stuck, taxis only make economical sense for groups of four.

○ **Cycling** A fun way to get around, though traffic can be intense. Rentals available; some hostels and ryokan lend bicycles.

○ **Walking** Subway stations are close in the city centre; save cash by walking if you only need to go one stop.

What to Take

○ Tokyo hotels can be tiny, so bring as small a suitcase as possible.

○ You'll likely find yourself taking your shoes on and off a lot and sitting on the floor, so it helps to have shoes that don't need lacing up. You might also want to pack socks even during sandal season (and think twice about that short skirt).

What to Wear

○ Casual clothes are fine, but you'll feel out of place if you're dressed as if you're heading to the gym.

○ Some high-end restaurants and bars do have a dress code, but this usually just means no sleeveless shirts or sandals for men.

○ There are no dress requirements for entering traditional Japanese religious sites.

Plan Your Trip
Top Days in Tokyo

West Side Highlights

The neighbourhoods of Harajuku, Shibuya and Shinjuku, on the western edge of central Tokyo, make for a strong first impression: this is the Tokyo of towers illuminated with giant screens and liquid-crystal light, of bold fashion statements and of intoxicating nightlife.

❶ Meiji-jingū (p44)

Tokyo's most famous Shintō shrine is shrouded in woods. It's a peaceful haven that feels worlds away from the city, even though it is right in the thick of it. Get here early to beat the crowds.

➲ Meiji-jingū to Omote-sandō

🕈 The broad boulevard Omote-sandō starts just across the street from the shrine entrance.

❷ Omote-sandō Architecture (p74)

Make your way up Omote-sandō, before the shopping starts in earnest – the better to see the striking contemporary buildings, created by Japan's leading architects, that line this boulevard.

➲ Omote-sandō to d47

🚇 It's one stop on the Ginza subway line from Omote-sandō to Shibuya. You can also walk to the restaurant in about 15 minutes.

Day 01

❸ Lunch at d47 (p129)

Ease your way into hectic Shibuya with lunch at the fantastic d47 Shokudō, which serves local specialities from all over Japan. Get a seat by the window for views over the neighbourhood.

➲ d47 to Shibuya Crossing

✈ Exit the Hikarie building on the 2nd floor and follow the above-ground tunnel to Shibuya Station, then take the Hachiko exit.

❹ Shibuya Crossing (p108)

This epic intersection, lit by giant screens, has become synonymous with Tokyo. From here, the pedestrian traffic flows onto Shibuya Center-gai, the neighbourhood's lively main artery, lined with shops, cheap eateries and bars. Stick around Shibuya until dusk to see the crossing all lit up.

➲ Shibuya Crossing to the Tokyo Metropolitan Government Building

🚃 Take the JR Yamanote line three stops north to Shinjuku, then walk 10 minutes to the government building from the west exit.

❺ Tokyo Metropolitan Government Building (p94)

The government building has observatories at 202m high that stay open until 11pm, so you can come for twinkling night views over the city. Bonus: entry is free.

➲ Tokyo Metropolitan Government Building to Shinjuku nightlife district

✈ On opposite sides of Shinjuku, it's a 15-minute walk from the government building to the bright lights of the nightlife area.

❻ Shinjuku Nightlife (p36)

Head out to explore the crackling neon canyons of Tokyo's biggest and most colourful nightlife district, where the vivacity and sheer volume of dining, drinking and entertainment options is something to behold.

From left: Prada store on Omote-sandō (p75); Tokyo Metropolitan Government Building (p94)

Top Days in Tokyo

F11PHOTO / SHUTTERSTOCK ©

Classic Sights of Central Tokyo

Spend your second day exploring Tokyo's more polished side in the central districts of Tsukiji, Ginza and Marunouchi. This area is home to many big ticket attractions – the Imperial Palace, Tsukiji Outer Market and the theatre, Kabukiza – as well as fine dining and shopping options.

❶ Tsukiji Outer Market (p40)

Skip breakfast and head to Tokyo's iconic food market, where you can cobble together a morning meal of snacks and coffee from the market vendors. There are also stalls selling kitchen tools, tea and more.

● Tsukiji Outer Market to Hama-rikyū Onshi-teien

🏃 It's an easy 10-minute walk from the market to the garden.

❷ Hama-rikyū Onshi-teien (p43)

From the bustling market head to the quiet scenery of this classic landscape garden on the bay. There's a teahouse here, on an island in the middle of a placid pond, where you can have a pick-me-up bowl of bitter *matcha* tea.

● Hama-rikyū Onshi-teien to Kyūbey

🚕 Hop in a taxi; it should cost about ¥1000. Otherwise, it's a 15-minute walk.

Day

02

❸ Lunch at Kyūbey (p57)

Splurge on lunch at this classy sushi counter, where you can indulge in a full tasting course of seasonal seafood. Be sure to reserve well in advance. A late seating will power you through the rest of the day.

➲ Kyūbey to the Ginza Mitsukoshi

🚶 Work off lunch with a 10-minute stroll up Ginza's main drag, Chūō-dōri, to the department store.

❹ Ginza Mitsukoshi (p155)

Ginza Mitsukoshi is a quintessential Tokyo department store, with floors for pretty Japanese-style homewares, gourmet food products, and local and international fashion brands. It's the perfect place to start a shopping (or window-shopping) spree through stylish Ginza.

➲ Ginza Mitsukoshi to the Imperial Palace

🚶 It's a leisurely 15-minute walk from the department store to Hibiya, then alongside the moat to the palace grounds.

❺ Imperial Palace (p98)

The majority of the compound, encased in a broad moat, remains off-limits to the general public, as it's the home of Japan's emperor. However, in the Imperial Palace East Garden you can admire the remains of the mammoth stone walls that once constituted Edo-jō, the largest fortress in the world.

➲ Imperial Palace to Kabukiza Theatre

🚃 Take the Hibiya line from Hibiya Station two stops to Higashi-Ginza for the theatre.

❻ Kabukiza Theatre (p88)

Kabuki, a form of stylised traditional Japanese theatre, features stories based on popular legend and an all-male cast in dramatic make-up and decadent costumes. Catch a performance (or just a single act) at Kabukiza, Tokyo's principal kabuki theatre.

From left: Tsukiji Outer Market (p40); Kabukiza Theatre (p88)

Plan Your Trip
Top Days in Tokyo

The Historic East Side

Welcome to Tokyo's historic east side, which includes Ueno, long the cultural heart of Tokyo, with its park and museums; Yanaka, with its high concentration of traditional wooden buildings; and Asakusa, with its ancient temple and old-Tokyo atmosphere.

Day

03

❶ Tokyo National Museum (p58)

Start with a morning at Japan's premier museum, which houses the world's largest collection of Japanese art and antiquities, including swords, gilded screens, kimonos and colourful *ukiyo-e* (woodblock prints). You'll need about two hours to hit the highlights.

○ Tokyo National Museum to Ueno-kōen

🏃 The museum is on the edge of the park.

❷ Ueno-kōen (p59)

After the museum, take an hour or two to explore Ueno-kōen. Wend your way southward past the temples and shrines in the park, which include some of Tokyo's oldest standing buildings, to the large pond, Shinobazu-ike, choked with lotus flowers. There are cafes here, too.

○ Ueno-kōen to Hantei

🏃 The restaurant is just a few minutes on foot from the northwestern edge of the park.

BESTFORLATER91 / GETTY IMAGES ©

❸ Lunch at Hantei (p142)

Hantei, in a century-old heritage house, is one of the city's most charming lunch spots. On the menu are crumbed and fried skewers of meat, fish and seasonal vegetables.

➡ Hantei to Yanaka

✈ The Yanaka district starts just north of the restaurant.

❹ Yanaka (p64)

Yanaka is a neighbourhood with a high concentration of vintage wooden structures and more than a hundred temples. It's a rare pocket of Tokyo that miraculously survived the Great Kantō Earthquake and the allied firebombing of WWII to remain largely intact. It's a wonderful place to stroll.

➡ Yanaka to Sensō-ji

🚊 Take the Yamanote line from Nippori to Ueno then transfer for the Ginza subway line for Asakusa.

❺ Sensō-ji (p76)

The spiritual home of Tokyoites' ancestors, Sensō-ji was founded more than 1000 years before Tokyo got its start. Today the temple retains an alluring, lively atmosphere redolent of Edo (old Tokyo under the shogun). There are lots of shops selling traditional crafts and foodstuffs around here, too. Don't miss Sensō-ji all lit up from dusk.

➡ Sensō-ji to Oiwake

✈ It's a 10-minute walk from the temple to the club.

❻ Oiwake (p195)

Get a taste of entertainment old-Tokyo style at Oiwake, one of Tokyo's few remaining folk-music pubs. Here talented performers play *tsugaru-jamisen* (a banjo-like instrument) and other traditional instruments.

From left: Tokyo National Museum (p58); Yanaka Ginza (p63)

Plan Your Trip
Top Days in Tokyo

Icons of Art & Pop Culture

On the agenda for your final day: culture, shopping and, most importantly, fun. This is a packed schedule, with a bit of running around, but it makes sure that you get in all the highlights – and some great souvenirs and photo ops in the process.

Day
04

❶ Ghibli Museum (p96)

Take the train to the western suburb of Mitaka for a visit to the magical Ghibli Museum, created by famed animator Miyazaki Hayao (reservations necessary; we recommend getting in early at 10am). Afterwards walk through woodsy Inokashira-kōen to Kichijōji.

➲ Ghibli Museum to Harajuku

🚃 Take the JR Chūō line from Kichijōji to Shinjuku and transfer to the JR Yamanote line for Harajuku.

❷ Shopping in Harajuku (p46)

Harajuku is Tokyo's real-life catwalk, where the ultra-chic come to browse and be seen. Work your way through the snaking side alleys of Ura-Hara (the nickname for the side streets on either side of Omote-sandō), where the fashion, and the fashionistas, are edgier than on the main drag. There are lots of great lunch spots and cafes here, too.

➲ Harajuku to Akihabara

🚃 Take the JR Yamanote line one stop north to Yoyogi and transfer to the JR Sōbu line for Akihabara.

FRANK DEIM / GETTY IMAGES ©

❸ Akihabara Pop Culture (p102)

In Akiba you can shop for anime and manga; play retro video games at Super Potato Retro-kan; and ride go-karts – while dressed as video-game characters – through the streets (reserve ahead; international driving licence required).

◗ Akihabara to Mori Art Museum

🚇 Take the Hibiya subway line from Akihabara to Roppongi, the nearest stop for the museum.

❹ Mori Art Museum (p51)

The excellent Mori Art Museum stages contemporary exhibits that include superstars of the art world from both Japan and abroad. Unlike most Tokyo museums, this one stays open until 10pm. Your ticket includes admission to Tokyo City View, the observatory on the 52nd floor of Mori Tower – if you want to get a last look of the city from this impressive vantage point.

◗ Mori Art Museum to SuperDeluxe

🚶 The club is just a few minutes' walk down the street from the museum.

❺ SuperDeluxe (p175)

Come back to ground level, then go one step deeper, into this basement performance space/club, a favourite hang-out spot for local and expat creatives. Events include avant-garde musical performances, live painting and talk programs.

◗ SuperDeluxe to Gogyō

🚶 It's a 10-minute walk to the restaurant from the club.

❻ Dinner at Gogyō (p136)

End your last night with a time-honoured Tokyo tradition: a late-night bowl of ramen. This local favourite all-night noodle shop serves bowls of hot flaming ramen (literally).

From left: Ghibli Museum (p96); Mori Art Museum (p51)

Plan Your Trip
Hotspots For...

CULTURE VULTURES

FUN LOVERS

🍷 **Shinjuku Nightlife** Eat and drink the night away in Tokyo's biggest nightlife district. (p137)

🌸 **Cherry Blossoms** When the cherry trees bloom, Tokyoites head to the parks for sake-drenched picnics. (p66)

👁 **Akihabara Pop Culture** Sip tea in a maid cafe or drive a go-kart through the city streets. (p102)

🍷 **Karaoke** Sing your heart out and see why Japan is nuts for karaoke. (p110)

👁 **Ghibli Museum** Unleash your inner kid in this wonder-filled museum. (p96)

👁 **Tokyo National Museum** Home to the world's largest collection of Japanese art. (p58)

☆ **Kabukiza Theatre** Go in for a visual and dramatic feast at Tokyo's premier kabuki theatre. (p88)

👁 **Rikugi-en** Tokyo's most beautiful landscape garden, evoking scenes from classical literature. (p106; pictured above)

👁 **Roppongi Art Triangle** A trio of fantastic museums, with galleries in between. (p50)

🍷 **SuperDeluxe** Preferred gathering spot for Tokyo's artsy crowd. (p175)

FOODIES

◉ **Tsukiji Outer Market** A pilgrimage site for chefs and home cooks alike, with lots of food to sample. (p40)

🛍 **Akomeya** Shop for packaged foods from around Japan at this beautiful food-stuffs boutique. (p154)

✕ **Sushi** (p54) Go for broke on a chef's tasting course, take lessons, or experience the wonder of the conveyor-belt sushi restaurant.

✕ **Kagari** The current darling of the Tokyo ramen scene. (p136)

☕ **Tokyo Cooking Studio** Soba-making lessons from a seasoned pro. (p202)

GLITZ & GLAMOUR

✕ **Kikunoi** Splurge on the meal of a lifetime at this famed *kaiseki* (haute cuisine) restaurant. (p127)

♨ **Spa LaQua** Soak away your troubles in this chic onsen (hot spring) complex. (p86)

🍷 **Two Rooms** Sundown cocktails on the terrace here are a must. (p181)

✕ **Kozue** Gaze over the city from this sky-high Japanese restaurant. (p138)

🛍 **Shopping in Harajuku** See the latest looks bubbling out of Harajuku's back streets. (p46)

HISTORY BUFFS

◉ **Edo-Tokyo Museum** Discover how a fishing village evolved into a sprawling, modern metropolis. (p80; pictured above)

◉ **Sensō-ji** Tokyo's oldest and most famous Buddhist temple. (p76)

🛍 **Ameya-yokochō** Tokyo's last open-air market dates to the tumultuous days after WWII. (p62)

✕ **Komagata Dozeu** Landmark restaurant serving *dojō-nabe* (loach hotpot) for 200 years. (p144)

↻ **Haunted Tokyo Tours** Hear about the ghosts of Tokyo's past. (p202)

Plan Your Trip
What's New

KAMETARO / SHUTTERSTOCK ©

Tokyo's Tourism Push

More and more English is popping up, in the form of navigational signs, apps, menus and brochures; more restaurants and shops are hiring English-speaking staff, too. Free city wi-fi, though still clunky, is improving.

Ginza Shopping

New mall openings in Ginza include Ginza Six (p154) and Tōkyū Plaza Ginza.

Go-Karting

The latest Tokyo craze is racing around the city streets in go-karts – dressed like your favourite video game character. Operators include Akiba Kart (p105).

Artsy East Tokyo

Kuramae (p165), near Asakusa, is shaping up to be a hot spot for contemporary artisan studios and boutiques.

Sumida Hokusai Museum

In 2016, east Tokyo neighbourhood Ryōgoku got a striking new museum (p80) devoted to this woodblock print master.

Tennōzu Isle Art & Architecture

This warehouse district on Tokyo Bay is suddenly happening, with the opening of the gallery Archi-Depot (p113) and the arts-supply store Pigment (p114).

Tsukiji Market Moving

At the time of writing, the impending market move to new facilities in Toyosu was still on hold.

Cafes, Cafes, Cafes

The coffee third wave has shown no signs yet of cresting in Tokyo, with another new cafe belt forming in Kiyosumi.

Above: Ginza Six (p154)

Plan Your Trip
For Free

Temples & Shrines

Shintō shrines are usually free in Tokyo and most Buddhist temples charge only to enter their *honden* (main hall) – meaning that two of the city's top sights, Meiji-jingū (p44) and Sensō-ji (p76), are free.

Parks & Gardens

Spend an afternoon people-watching in one of Tokyo's excellent public parks, such as Yoyogi-kōen (p66) or Inokashira-kōen (p97). Grab a *bento* (boxed meal) from a convenience store for a cheap and easy picnic.

Markets

Tsukiji (p40) is the most famous of Tokyo's many markets. There's also the old-fashioned open-air market Ameya-yokochō (p62) and a weekend farmers market in Aoyama.

Festivals & Events

Throughout the year festivals take place at shrines and temples. In the warmer months, festivals and markets, often hosted by Tokyo's ethnic communities and with live music, set up in Yoyogi-kōen. And where there are festivals, there are always street-food vendors. See Go Tokyo (www.gotokyo.org) for a list of festivals.

Walking Tours

Tokyo SGG Club (www.tokyosgg.jp) offers regular free tours of Asakusa, Ueno-kōen and the Imperial Palace East Garden. No advance reservation required (though places are limited).

Discount Cards & Coupons

The Grutto Pass (¥2000; www.rekibun.or.jp/grutto) gives you free or discounted admission to 79 attractions around town within two months. If you plan on visiting more than a few museums, it's excellent value. All participating venues sell them. Also check hotel lobbies and TICs for discount coupons to city attractions.

Above: Yoyogi-kōen (p66)

Plan Your Trip
Family Travel

Need to Know

o **Activities** Tokyo Mothers Group (www.tokyomothersgroup.com) suggests activities and family-friendly spots.

o **Babysitting** Babysitters (www.babysitters.jp) partners with many Tokyo hotels to provide English-speaking childcare workers.

o **Nappy Changing & Nursing** Department stores and shopping malls always have nappy-changing facilities; newer ones have nursing rooms.

Sights & Activities

Local families love Odaiba, an island on Tokyo Bay. At the **National Museum of Emerging Science & Innovation** (Miraikan; p112) kids can meet humanoid robot ASIMO, see a planetarium show and interact with hands-on exhibits. **Ōedo Onsen Monogatari** (p86) and **Tokyo Joypolis** (p113) are here, too. As the attractions here are indoors, this is good for rainy days. (Also good for rainy days: karaoke).

Another option is **Tokyo Dome City** (p200), where there are thrill rides and play areas; catch a baseball game here at **Tokyo Dome** (p200). Restaurants at both Odaiba and Tokyo Dome City are kid friendly.

Unfortunately few museums go out of their way to appeal to the little ones; however, kids might enjoy the samurai armour and swords at the **Tokyo National Museum** (p58). **Ueno Zoo** (p59) is nearby.

Older kids and teens should get a kick out of Tokyo's pop culture and neon streetscapes. Take them to explore the magical world of famed animator Miyazaki Hayao (Ponyo, Spirited Away) at the **Ghibli Museum** (p96) and to spot (and shop for) all their favourite characters at stores such as **Pokemon Center Mega Tokyo** (p162) and **KiddyLand** (p49). Snap souvenir family photos at **Purikura no Mecca** (p201).

Japanese kids love trains and chances are yours will too. A platform ticket to see the shinkansen (bullet train) costs ¥140. Another popular train-spotting location is Shinjuku Station's southern terrace,

COWARDLION / SHUTTERSTOCK ©

overlooking the multiple tracks that feed the world's busiest train station.

Eating

In terms of room to move, big chain restaurants (such as Jonathan's, Royal Host and Gusto) are the most family-friendly eating options: they have large booths, high chairs, non-smoking sections and children's menus. Local restaurants can be teeny and won't fit a stroller (and are unlikely to have high chairs). That said, smaller restaurants serve up plenty of dishes that kids will love, including *gyōza* (dumplings), noodles, sushi, *onigiri* (rice-ball snacks) and *yakitori* (grilled chicken on a skewer). For dessert, tempt their taste buds with *mochi* (sweet rice cakes), *kakigōri* (flavoured shaved ice), crêpes and fresh fruit.

Getting Around

You won't get much sympathy if you get on a crowded train during morning rush hour (7am to 9.30am) with a pram. If

Best Activities for Kids

Tokyo Disney Resort (p115)
Ōedo Onsen Monogatari (p86)
Tokyo Joypolis (p113)
Mokuhankan (p201)
Super Potato Retro-kan (p105)

you must, children under 12 can ride with mums in the less-crowded women-only carriages. Otherwise the subway system is fairly child friendly: priority seats exist for passengers who are pregnant or travelling with small children; most train stations and buildings in larger cities have lifts; and children between the ages of six and 11 ride for half-price on trains (under-sixes ride for free). Beware that side streets often lack pavements, though fortunately traffic is generally orderly in Tokyo.

From left: *Shinkansen* (bullet trains); National Museum of Emerging Science & Innovation (Miraikan; p112)

Shinjuku Nightlife....................36

Tsukiji Outer Market..............40

Meiji-jingū...............................44

Shopping in Harajuku 46

Roppongi Art Triangle...........50

Sushi in Tokyo........................54

Tokyo National Museum 58

Walking Tour: Yanaka............64

Cherry-Blossom Viewing 66

Sumo at
Ryōgoku Kokugikan...............68

Day Trip: Mt Fuji.....................70

Walking Tour:
Omote-sandō Architecture 74

Sensō-ji....................................76

Onsen & Sentō........................82

Kabukiza Theatre....................88

Tokyo Cityscape.....................92

Ghibli Museum........................96

Imperial Palace.......................98

Akihabara Pop Culture.........102

Rikugi-en...............................106

Shibuya Crossing..................108

Karaoke in Tokyo..................110

Tokyo Bay..............................112

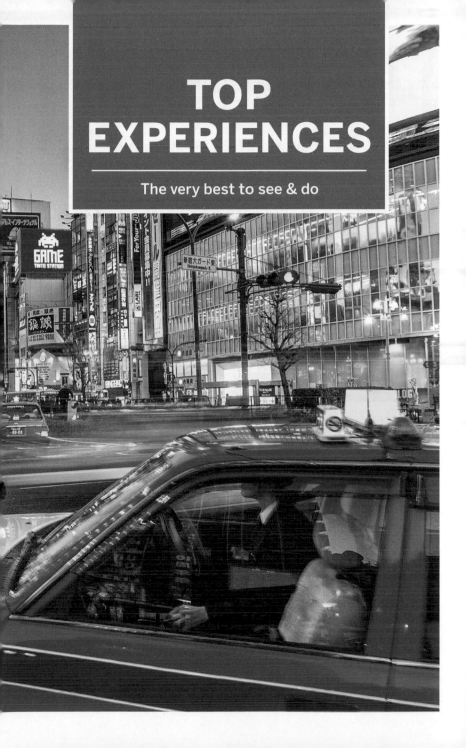

TOP
EXPERIENCES

The very best to see & do

Kabukichō

SEAN PAVONE / SHUTTERSTOCK ©

Shinjuku Nightlife

Shinjuku is the biggest nightlife district in the land of the rising neon sun. The options are dizzying, the lights spellbinding and the whole show continues past dawn.

Omoide-yokochō

Start the evening with *yakitori* (grilled chicken skewers) in Omoide-yokochō (p137). This alley near the train tracks has been around for over half a century. Several stalls have English menus.

Kabukichō

A flashing red *torii* (gate) marks the entrance to **Kabukichō** (歌舞伎町; Map p253; ⊠JR Yamanote line to Shinjuku, east exit), Tokyo's biggest red-light district. It was famously named for a kabuki theatre that was never built, and today is infamously known for an urban theatre of a different sort. It's a strange mix of 'hostess bars' (staffed by sexily clad young women) and their inverse, 'host bars' (where pretty boys wait on the gals); 'information centres' (which match customers with establishments that suit

Great For...

☑ **Don't Miss**

The enormous Godzilla statue in Kabukichō, atop the Shinjuku TOHO building.

Robot Restaurant

ANDREAS MANN / SHUTTERSTOCK ©

ⓘ Need to Know

Shinjuku Station (train and subway) and Shinjuku-sanchōme Station (subway) are the most convenient.

✕ Take a Break

For an upscale start to the evening, book for a *kaiseki* meal at Michelin-starred Nakajima (p137).

★ Top Tip

Look for discount tickets for Robot Restaurant at hotels around town.

1-10-10 Kabukichō, Shinjuku-ku; ◷6pm-6am; 🏠; 🚃JR Yamanote line to Shinjuku, east exit), around the corner.

Golden Gai

Golden Gai, a warren of tiny alleys and narrow, two-storey wooden buildings, began as a black market following WWII. Now those same buildings are filled with more than a hundred closet-sized bars. Each is as unique and eccentric as the 'master' or 'mama' who runs it. That Golden Gai – prime real estate – has so far resisted the kind of development seen elsewhere in Shinjuku is a credit to these stubbornly bohemian characters.

The best way to experience Golden Gai is to stroll the lanes and pick a place that suits your mood. Bars here usually have a theme – from punk rock to photography – and draw customers with matching expertise and obsessions. Some establishments may give tourists a cool reception; others expressly welcome them. If there is no sign on the door to indicate otherwise, expect to pay a cover charge (usually ¥500 to ¥1500).

their particular, uh, needs); 'love hotels' (hotels for amorous encounters); and otherwise ordinary bars and restaurants.

Robot Restaurant

In the heart of Kabukichō is one of Tokyo's most popular spectacles, **Robot Restaurant** (ロボットレストラン; Map p253; ☎03-3200-5500; www.shinjuku-robot.com; 1-7-1 Kabukichō, Shinjuku-ku; tickets ¥8000; ◷shows at 4pm, 5.55pm, 7.50pm & 9.45pm; 🚃JR Yamanote line to Shinjuku, east exit). It's wacky Japan at its finest, with giant robots operated by bikini-clad women and enough neon to light all of Shinjuku. Reservations aren't necessary, but are recommended. There are a couple of robots parked outside for photo-ops.

You can also grab a drink (and a taste of Robot Restaurant's game-show-set aesthetic) at new sister bar **Ren** (蓮; Map p253;

Late Night Eats

Nagi   Ramen ¥

(凪; Map p253; www.n-nagi.com; 2nd fl, Golden Gai G2, 1-1-10 Kabukichō, Shinjuku-ku; ramen from ¥850; ◷24hr; ⌖; ⊠JR Yamanote line to Shinjuku, east exit) Nagi, once an upstart, has done well and now has branches around the city – and around Asia. This tiny shop, one of the originals, up a treacherous stairway in Golden Gai, is still our favourite. (It's many people's favourite and often has a line.) The house speciality is *niboshi* ramen (egg noodles in a broth flavoured with dried sardines).

Donjaca   Izakaya ¥

(呑者家; Map p253; ☎03-3341-2497; 3-9-10 Shinjuku, Shinjuku-ku; dishes ¥350-850; ◷5pm-7am; ⌖; ⊠Marunouchi line to Shinju-ku-sanchōme, exit C6) The platonic ideal of a Shōwa-era *izakaya*, Donjaca, in business since 1979, has red pleather stools, paper-lantern lighting and hand-written menus on the wall. The food is equal parts classic (fried chicken) and inventive: house specialities include *natto gyoza* (dumplings stuffed with fermented soy beans) and *mochi* gratin. Excellent sake is served in convenient tasting sets.

Shinjuku Asia-yokochō   Asian ¥

(新宿アジア横丁; Map p253; ☎03-3207-7218; rooftop, 2nd Toa Hall bldg, 1-21-1 Kabukichō, Shinjuku-ku; dishes ¥450-1250; ◷5pm-midnight Tue-Thu & Sun, 5pm-5am Fri & Sat; ⌖; ⊠JR Yamanote line to Shinjuku, east exit) A rooftop night market that spans the Asian continent, with vendors dishing out everything from Korean *bibimbap* to Vietnamese *pho*.

Omoide-yokochō (p137)

It's noisy, a bit chaotic and particularly fun in a group.

Great Bars

BenFiddich   Cocktail Bar
(ベンフィディック; Map p253; ☑03-6279-4223; 9th fl, 1-13-7 Nishi-Shinjuku, Shinjuku-ku; ☺6pm-3am Mon-Sat; 🚇 JR Yamanote line to Shinjuku, west exit) Step into the magical space that is BenFiddich. It's dark, it's tiny, and vials of infusions line the shelves, while herbs hang drying from the ceiling. The barman, Kayama Hiroyasu, in a white suit, moves like a magician. There's no menu,

> ### ❶ Need to Know
> Just a warning – men walking through Kabukichō may be solicited; women (especially those going alone) may be harassed.

URA WONS / SHUTTERSTOCK ©

but cocktails run about ¥1500; service charge is 10%.

Zoetrope   Bar
(ゾートロープ; Map p253; http://homepage2.nifty.com/zoetrope; 3rd fl, 7-10-14 Nishi-Shinjuku, Shinjuku-ku; ☺7pm-4am Mon-Sat; 🔘; 🚇 JR Yamanote line to Shinjuku, west exit) A must-visit for whisky fans, Zoetrope has some 300 varieties of Japanese whisky behind its small counter – including hard-to-find bottles from cult favourite Chichibu Distillery. The owner speaks English and can help you pick from the daunting menu. Cover charge ¥1000; whisky by the glass from ¥400 to ¥19,000.

Jazzy Joints

Shinjuku Pit Inn   Jazz
(新宿ピットイン; Map p253; ☑03-3354-2024; www.pit-inn.com; basement, 2-12-4 Shinjuku, Shinjuku-ku; from ¥3000; ☺matinee 2.30pm, evening show 7.30pm; Ⓢ Marunouchi line to Shinjuku-sanchome, exit C5) This is not the kind of place you come to talk over the music. It's the kind of place you come to sit in thrall of Japan's best jazz performers (as Tokyoites have been doing for half a century now). Weekday matinees feature up-and-coming artists and cost only ¥1300.

Samurai   Bar
(サムライ; Map p253; http://jazz-samurai.seesaa.net; 5th fl, 3-35-5 Shinjuku, Shinjuku-ku; ☺6pm-1am; 🔘; 🚇 JR Yamanote line to Shinjuku, southeast exit) Never mind the impressive record collection, this eccentric jazz *kissa* (cafe where jazz records are played) is worth a visit just for the owner's overwhelming collection of 2500 *maneki-neko* (beckoning cats). Look for the sign next door to Disc Union and take the elevator. There's a ¥300 cover charge (¥500 after 9pm); drinks from ¥650.

> ### ❶ Need to Know
> For more on Shinjuku Ni-chōme, see p175.

Tsukiji Outer Market

Don't mourn Tsukiji yet: while the seafood market may very well move, the lively outer market isn't going anywhere. And it's here that you can wander the stalls snacking on treats from food stalls, shop for professional quality kitchen tools, listen to the banter of the merchants and their regular customers, and bask in the energy of a storied, old-style, open-air market.

Great For...

❶ Need to Know

場外市場; Jōgai Shijō; Map p250; 6-chōme Tsukiji, Chūō-ku; ⏱5am-2pm; Ⓢ Hibiya line to Tsukiji, exit 1

★ **Top Tip**

Pick up a market map in English from the **Information Centre Plat Tsukiji** (ぷらっと築地; Map p250; www.tsukiji.or.jp; 4-16-2 Tsukiji, Chūō-ku; ⊙8am-2pm Mon-Sat, 10am-2pm Sun; ⑤Hibiya line to Tsukiji, exit 1).

History

For more than 80 years, Tsukiji Market has been the place where top chefs, fishmongers, department stores and hotels have sourced their ingredients. While the Inner Market, Tokyo's largest wholesale market, was purpose-built (in 1935), the Outer Market sprang up organically, with vendors gathering to sell other ingredients – such as seaweed and dried fish – that chefs might need. Small restaurants, too, were established to feed the market workers. As Tsukiji has grown to become one of Tokyo's most popular attractions, the outer market has expanded to include shops targeting both local home cooks and foreign visitors.

The Inner Market is slated to move to a new facility on Toyosu, an artificial island on Tokyo Bay – though this is still up in the air; the Outer Market will remain in Tsukiji.

Street Food

Come hungry, as there are plenty of snack foods sold here, including fat slices of *tamago-yaki* (sweet and savoury rolled omelettes) on a stick from **Yamachō** (山長; Map p250; ☎03-3248-6002; 4-16-1 Tsukiji; omelette slices ¥100; ☯6am-3.30pm), delicious fish-paste treats from **Tsukugon** (つくごん; Map p250; www.tsukugon.co.jp; 4-12-5 Tsukiji, Chūō-ku; snacks from ¥210; ☯6.30am-2pm Tue-Sun) and *maguro-yaki* (tuna-shaped pancakes, filled with sweet beans) from **Sanokiya** (さのきや; Map p250; 4-11-9 Tsukiji, Chūō-ku; pancakes ¥200-220; ☯8.30am-2pm Thu-Tue). Most shops open early (from 5am) and close early (by 2pm).

A *tamago-yaki* demonstration at the Tsukiji Market

Shopping

Tsukiji's Outer Market is a fantastic place to pick up gourmet goods such as green tea and *nori* (laver; edible seaweed sheets). It's also well stocked with crockery, fine-quality kitchen knives and other tools of the trade, like bamboo mats for rolling sushi. Try Tsukiji Hitachiya (p154) for a great selection of useful kitchen implements.

The Inner Market

The **Seafood Intermediate Wholesalers' Market** (水産仲卸業者売場; Map p250; ☑03-3261-8326; www.tsukiji-market.or.jp; 5-2-1 Tsukiji, Chūō-ku; ☺10-11am; ⓢHibiya line to

> ☑ **Don't Miss**
>
> Tsukiji's signature three-wheeled trucks, called turrets. Watch your step as these are going about their work.

Tsukiji, exit 1) opens to the public at 10am. This is where you can see all manner of sea creatures lain out in boxes and styrofoam crates, though admittedly much has been packed away and sold by the time the gates open to everyone. For information on the tuna auction, which starts here at 5am, see the market website. Large groups and small children are not permitted.

Should the Inner Market move, access will change.

Market Tours

The **Tsukiji Market Information Centre** (Map p250; ☑03-3541-6521; www.tsukijitour. jp; 4-7-5 Tsukiji, Chūō-ku; tour per person from ¥8800; ☺9am-3pm market days; ⓢHibiya line to Tsukiji, exit 2) runs popular 2½-hour tours of Tsukiji Market for a minimum of two people. It starts with a video and finishes up with a sushi lunch in the area. When the market moves, it will continue tours in the Outer Market area and will likely include a sushi-making class at a local restaurant.

What's Nearby?

Hama-rikyū Onshi-teien   Gardens (浜離宮恩賜庭園; Detached Palace Garden; Map p250; www.tokyo-park.or.jp/park/format/index028.html; 1-1 Hama-rikyū-teien, Chūō-ku; adult/child ¥300/free; ☺9am-5pm; ⓢŌedo line to Shiodome, exit A1) This beautiful garden, one of Tokyo's finest, is all that remains of a shogunal palace that once extended into the area now occupied by Tsukiji Market. There's a large duck pond with an island that's home to a charming tea pavilion, **Nakajima no Ochaya** (中島の御茶屋; tea set ¥500; ☺9am-4.30pm), as well as some wonderful old trees (black pine, Japanese apricot, hydrangeas etc).

> ✕ **Take a Break**
>
> Grab a latte from nearby **Turret Coffee** (Map p250; http://ja-jp.facebook.com/turretcoffee; 2-12-6 Tsukiji, Chūō-ku; ☺7am-6pm Mon-Sat, noon-6pm Sun; ⓓ; ⓢHibiya line to Tsukiji, exit 2), named after the market's turret trucks.

BIXPICTURE / SHUTTERSTOCK ©

Meiji-jingū

Tokyo's largest and most famous Shintō shrine feels a world away from the city. The grounds are vast, enveloping the classic wooden shrine buildings and a landscaped garden in a thick coat of green.

Great For...

☑ **Don't Miss**

The kiosks near the main shrine for *ema* (wooden plaques on which prayers are written) and *omamori* (charms).

Meiji-jingū is dedicated to the Emperor Meiji and Empress Shōken, whose reign (1868–1912) coincided with Japan's transformation from isolationist, feudal state to modern nation. It's also a place for traditional festivals and rituals; if you're lucky you may even catch a wedding procession, with the bride and groom in traditional dress. Note that the shrine is undergoing renovation in preparation for its centennial in 2020 – some structures may be under wraps, but as a whole it will remain open.

The Gates

Several wooden *torii* (gates) mark the entrance to Meiji-jingū. The largest, created from a 1500-year-old Taiwanese cypress, stands 12m high. It's the custom to bow

Wedding procession leaving the shrine

MATT MUNRO / LONELY PLANET ©

◉ *Meiji-jingu*

Meiji-dōri

Yoyogi-kōen

Takeshita-dōri

Harajuku Ⓡ
Ⓢ Meiji-jingūmae

❶ Need to Know

明治神宮; Map p246; www.meijijingu.or.jp; 1-1
Yoyogi Kamizono-chō, Shibuya-ku; ⏱dawn-
dusk; 🚆JR Yamanote line to Harajuku, Omote-
sandō exit; FREE

✕ Take a Break

Coffee shop **Mori no Terrace** (杜のテ
ラス; Map p246; 📞03-3379-9222; 1-1 Yoyogi
Kamizono-chō, Shibuya-ku; ⏱9am-dusk) is
right on the gravel path leading into the
shrine grounds.

★ Top Tip

Time your visit for 8am or 2pm to
catch the twice-daily *nikkusai*, the ceremonial offering of food and prayers
to the gods.

upon passing through a *torii,* which marks
the boundary between the mundane world
and the sacred one.

The Font

Before approaching the main shrine,
visitors purify themselves by pouring water
over their hands at the *temizuya* (font). Dip
the ladle in the water and first rinse your
left hand and then your right. Pour some
water into your left hand and rinse your
mouth, then rinse your left hand again.
Make sure none of this water gets back into
the font!

The Main Shrine

Constructed in 1920 and destroyed in WWII
air raids, the shrine was rebuilt in 1958;
however, unlike so many of Japan's postwar
reconstructions, Meiji-jingū has an authen-
tic old-world feel. The main shrine is made
of cypress from the Kiso region of Nagano.
To make an offering, toss a ¥5 coin in the
box, bow twice, clap your hands twice and
then bow again.

The Gardens

The shrine itself occupies only a small
fraction of the sprawling forested grounds,
which contain some 120,000 trees collected from all over Japan. Along the path
towards the main shrine is the entrance
to **Meiji-jingū Gyoen** (明治神宮御苑; Inner
Garden; Map p246; ¥500, ⏱9am-4.30pm, to
4pm Nov-Feb), a landscaped garden. It once
belonged to a feudal estate; however, when
the grounds passed into imperial hands,
the emperor himself designed the iris
garden to please the empress.

Laforet (p48)

Shopping in Harajuku

Harajuku is the gathering point for Tokyo's eccentric fashion tribes: the teens who hang out on Takeshita-dōri, the polished divas who strut up and down the wide pavements of Omote-sandō and the trendsetters and peacocks who haunt the side streets (known as Ura-Hara). Simply put, for shopping (and people-watching), there's no better spot in Tokyo than Harajuku.

Great For...

ⓘ Need to Know

The JR Yamanote line stops at Harajuku. Meiji-jingūmae subway station (Chiyoda and Fukutoshin lines) is also convenient.

★ **Top Tip**

For serious shopping, avoid weekends, when Harajuku gets very crowded.

Top Shops

Dog   Fashion, Vintage

(ドッグ; Map p246; www.dog-hjk.com/index.html; basement fl, 3-23-3 Jingūmae, Shibuya-ku; ⌚noon-8pm; 🚉JR Yamanote line to Harajuku, Takeshita exit) Club kids and stylists love the showpiece items at legendary Ura-Hara boutique Dog. The store itself, which is decorated to look like a derelict carnival funhouse, is much of the appeal: it looks like an art installation.

Laforet   Fashion & Accessories

(ラフォーレ; Map p246; www.laforet.ne.jp; 1-11-6 Jingūmae, Shibuya-ku; ⌚11am-8pm; 🚉JR Yamanote line to Harajuku, Omote-sandō exit) Laforet has been a beacon of cutting-edge Harajuku style for decades and lots of quirky, cult-favourite brands still cut their teeth here. A range of looks are represented, from *ame-kaji* (American casual) to gothic.

Musubi   Arts & Crafts

(むす美; Map p246; http://kyoto-musubi.com; 2-31-8 Jingūmae, Shibuya-ku; ⌚11am-7pm Thu-Tue; 🚉JR Yamanote line to Harajuku, Takeshita exit) *Furoshiki* are versatile squares of cloth that can be folded and knotted to make shopping bags and gift wrap. This shop sells pretty ones in both traditional and contemporary patterns. There is usually an English-speaking clerk who can show you how to tie them, or pick up one of the English-language books sold here.

6% Doki Doki   Fashion & Accessories

(ロクパーセントドキドキ; Map p246; www.dokidoki6.com; 2nd fl, 4-28-16 Jingūmae, Shibuya-ku; ⌚noon-8pm; 🚉JR Yamanote line to Harajuku, Omote-sandō exit) Tucked away on an Ura-Hara backstreet, this bubblegum-pink store sells acid-bright accessories that are part

Takeshita-dōri (p49)

raver, part schoolgirl and, according to the shop's name, 'six percent exciting'.

Pass the Baton — Vintage

(パスザバトン; Map p246; www.pass-the-baton.com; 4-12-10 Jingūmae, Shibuya-ku; ⏰11am-9pm Mon-Sat, to 8pm Sun; ⑤Ginza line to Omote-sandō, exit A3) There are all sorts of treasures to be found at this consignment shop, from 1970s designer duds to delicate teacups to dead stock from long-defunct retailers. It's in the basement of Omote-sandō Hills, but you'll need to enter from a separate street entrance on Omote-sandō.

☑ Don't Miss

The narrow streets on either side of Omote-sandō, known as Ura-Hara ('back' Harajuku). For more shopping in Harajuku see p159.

KiddyLand — Toys

(キデイランド; Map p246; www.kiddyland.co.jp/en/index.html; 6-1-9 Jingūmae, Shibuya-ku; ⏰10am-9pm; ⒭JR Yamanote line to Harajuku, Omote-sandō exit) This multistorey toy emporium is packed to the rafters with character goods, including all your Studio Ghibli, Sanrio and Disney faves. It's not just for kids either; you'll spot plenty of adults on a nostalgia trip down the Hello Kitty aisle.

Bedrock — Fashion & Accessories

(ベッドロック; Map p246; 4-12-10 Jingūmae, Shibuya-ku; ⏰11am-9pm, to 8pm Sun; ⑤Ginza line to Omote-sandō, exit A2) Walking into Bedrock is like stepping into Keith Richards' boudoir, or the costume closet for *Pirates of the Caribbean* – all leather, feathers and lace. Enter through a secret staircase in the back of the Forbidden Fruit juice bar.

Boutique Byways

Takeshita-dōri — Area

(竹下通り; Map p246; ⒭JR Yamanote line to Harajuku, Takeshita exit) This is Tokyo's famously outré fashion bazaar, where trendy duds sit alongside the trappings of decades of fashion subcultures (plaid and safety pins for the punks, Victorian dresses for the Gothic Lolitas). Be warned: this pedestrian alley is a pilgrimage site for teens from all over Japan, which means it can get packed.

Cat Street — Area

(キャットストリート; Map p246; ⒭JR Yamanote line to Harajuku, Omote-sandō exit) Had enough of crowded Harajuku? Exit, stage right, for Cat Street, a winding road lined with a mishmash of boutiques and more room to move. The retail architecture is also quite a spectacle, as this is where smaller brands strike their monuments to consumerism if they can't afford to do so on the main drag.

✕ Take a Break

Grab a plate of delicious *gyōza* (dumplings) at Harajuku Gyōza-rō (p133).

Roppongi Art Triangle

The area nicknamed 'Roppongi Art Triangle' is anchored by three of Tokyo's leading art museums: Mori Art Museum, Suntory Museum of Art and the National Art Center Tokyo. Smaller art spaces and ambitious building projects exist in their midst.

Great For...

  📷

☑ **Don't Miss**

The Mori Art Museum at night, when it doubles as a sky-high observatory.

Legendary for its nightlife, Roppongi has reinvented itself in the last 15 years as a polished cultural destination (though the nightlife is still here). This transformation is largely due to the addition of two chic complexes, Roppongi Hills (home to the Mori Art Museum) and Tokyo Midtown (home to the Suntory Museum of Art and 21_21 Design Sight).

Roppongi Hills

Roppongi Hills (六本木ヒルズ; Map p252; www.roppongihills.com/en; 6-chōme Roppongi, Minato-ku; ⏱11am-11pm; Ⓢ Hibiya line to Roppongi, exit 1) sprawls more than 11 hectares, an urban maze containing dozens of shops and restaurants – even a formal garden. Among the architects who worked on the structures were Jon Jerde and Fumihiko Maki.

National Art Center Tokyo (p52)

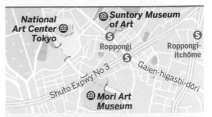

❶ Need to Know

The Hibiya and Ōedo subway lines stop in Roppongi.

✕ Take a Break

Start the day with breakfast or brunch at Lauderdale (p126), just off leafy Keyaki-zaka.

★ Top Tip

Save your ticket stub from any of the three major museums to get discounted admission at the other two.

Mori Art Museum

The **Mori Art Museum** (森美術館; Map p252; www.mori.art.museum; 52nd fl, Mori Tower, Roppongi Hills, 6-10-1 Roppongi, Minato-ku; adult/child/student ¥1600/600/1100; ⊙10am-10pm Wed-Mon, to 5pm Tue, inside Sky Deck 10am-10pm; ⑤Hibiya line to Roppongi, exit 1) occupies the 52nd and 53rd floors of Mori Tower in Roppongi Hills. There's no permanent exhibition; instead, large-scale, original shows introduce major local and global artists and movements. Past exhibitions have focused on the works of Chinese artist and dissident Ai Weiwei and native son Murakami Takashi.

Tokyo Midtown

Sleek complex **Tokyo Midtown** (東京ミッドタウン; Map p252; www.tokyo-midtown.com/en;

9-7 Akasaka, Minato-ku; ⊙11am-11pm; ⑤Ōedo line to Roppongi, exit 8) is the yin to nearby Roppongi Hills' yang. Escalators ascend alongside artificial waterfalls of rock and glass, bridges in the air are lined with backlit *washi* (Japanese handmade paper), and planters full of soaring bamboo draw your eyes through skylights to the lofty heights of the towers above.

Suntory Museum of Art

Since its original 1961 opening, the **Suntory Museum of Art** (サントリー美術館; Map p252; ☏03-3479-8600; www.suntory.com/sma; 4th fl, Tokyo Midtown, 9-7-4 Akasaka, Minato-ku; admission varies, child free; ⊙10am-6pm Sun-Wed, to 8pm Fri & Sat; ⑤Ōedo line to Roppongi, exit 8) has subscribed to an underlying philosophy of lifestyle art. Rotating exhibitions focus on the beauty of useful things: Japanese ceramics, lacquerware, glass, dyeing, weaving and such. Its current digs, inside Tokyo Midtown and designed by architect Kuma Kengō, are both understated and breathtaking.

21_21 Design Sight

21_21 Design Sight (21_21 デザインサイト; Map p252; ☎03-3475-2121; www.2121design sight.jp; Tokyo Midtown, 9-7-6 Akasaka, Minato-ku; admission varies; ⏰11am-8pm Wed-Mon; Ⓢ Ōedo line to Roppongi, exit 8) is an exhibition and discussion space dedicated to all forms of design. The striking concrete and glass building, bursting out of the ground at sharp angles, was designed by Pritzker Prize–winning architect Andō Tadao.

National Art Center Tokyo

Kurokawa Kishō designed the architectural beauty that is the **National Art Center Tokyo** (国立新美術館; Map p252; ☎03-5777-8600; www.nact.jp; 7-22-1 Roppongi, Minato-ku; admission varies by exhibition; ⏰10am-6pm Wed, Thu & Sat-Mon, to 8pm Fri; Ⓢ Chiyoda line to Nogi-zaka, exit 6). It has no permanent collection, but boasts the country's largest exhibition space for visiting shows. Apart from exhibitions, a visit here is recommended to admire the building's awesome undulating glass facade, its cafes atop giant inverted cones and the great gift shop, Souvenir from Tokyo (p156).

Complex 665

Opened in October 2016, **Complex 665** (Map p252; 6-5-24 Roppongi, Minato-ku; ⏰11am-7pm Tue-Sat; Ⓢ Hibiya line to Roppongi, exit 1) pulls together three major commerical art galleries into one building: **Taka Ishii** (www.takaishiigallery.com), **ShugoArts** (www.shugoarts.com) and **Tomio Koyama Gallery** (www.tomiokoyamagallery.com). The free shows gather up an eclectic selection

21_21 Design Sight

of Japanese contemporary works and are generally worth a look.

Mohri Garden

This landscaped **garden** (Map p252; ⑤Hibiya line to Roppongi, exit 1) is modelled after those popular during the Edo period. When juxtaposed with the gleaming towers, it creates a fascinating study of luxury then and now. Look for the cherry trees in spring.

What's Nearby?

Tokyo Garden Terrace   Landmark
(www.tgt-kioicho.jp.e.yu.hp.transer.com; 1-2 Kioi-chō, Chiyoda-ku; ⑤Namboku line to Nagatachō,

> ### ☑ Don't Miss
>
> One of Louise Bourgeois' giant Maman spider sculptures in the open-air plaza at Roppongi Hills.

K SHUN / SHUTTERSTOCK ©

exit 9A) This new mixed-use development is best visited for its pleasant surrounding gardens and public art, including *White Deer* by Nawa Kōhei and the giant metallic flowers of Ōmaki Shinji. Opened in 2016, on the former site of the Akasaka Grand Prince Hotel, the only remaining piece of the old complex is the restored Kitashirakawa Palace. Originally built in 1930 for the Korean Crown Prince Yi Un, this baronial-style mansion is now a restaurant and bar.

**Canadian Embassy
Stone Garden**   Gardens
(www.canadainternational.gc.ca/japan-japon/index.aspx?lang=eng; 7-3-38 Akasaka, Minato-ko; ⊙garden 10am-5.30pm Mon-Fri; ⑤Ginza line to Aoyama-itchōme, exit 4) **FREE** Bring photo ID, sign in and take the escalator up to the entrance to the **Canadian Embassy** (カナダ大使館; ☎03-5412-6200), which is fronted by this stark and brilliant stone sculpture garden. Designed by the Zen priest Shunmyō Masuno, natural and cut stones from the Hiroshima region are used to represent Canada's geological character. Over the balcony, the trees of the Akasaka Palace and the distant skyscrapers provide *shakkei*, the 'borrowed scenery' that's a key principle of Japanese garden design.

**Hotel New
Ōtani Gardens**   Gardens, Museum
(ホテルニューオータニ; www.newotani.co.jp; 4-1 Kioi-chō, Chiyoda-ku; ⊙6am-10pm; ⑤Ginza line to Akasaka-mitsuke, exit D) **FREE** The New Ōtani was a showplace hotel when it opened in 1964 to coincide with the Tokyo Olympics. Nonguests are welcome to visit its beautiful 400-year-old Japanese garden, which once belonged to a Tokugawa regent. Including vermilion arched bridges, koi (carp) ponds and a mini Niagara waterfall, it is one of Tokyo's most enchanting outdoor spaces.

> ### ★ Top Tip
>
> Unlike most museums, Mori Art Museum is open late – until 10pm every day except Tuesday.

Sushi in Tokyo

Sushi – raw fish and rice seasoned with vinegar – comes in many forms: classic and nouveau, breathtakingly expensive and surprisingly good value. Whatever you go for (and we recommend it all), odds are it will taste better here than any you've had before. After all, Tokyo moves more seafood than any other city in the world, drawing the best ingredients and top chefs.

Great For...

ℹ Need to Know

Many of Tokyo's top sushi restaurants are in Ginza. Tsukiji has many popular casual joints.

★ **Top Tip**
If you prefer your sushi without wasabi,
order it 'wasabi-nuki'.

Edo-mae Sushi

Sushi (寿司 or 鮨) was originally a way to make fish last longer – the vinegar in the rice was a preserving agent. The dish took a turn, however, in 19th century Tokyo (then called Edo). Tokyo Bay provided a steady stream of fresh fish, making preservation less crucial. A style emerged – of bite-sized slivers of fish hand-pressed onto pedestals of rice – that could be made quickly and eaten right away. It was known as 'Edo-mae' ('in the style of Edo') sushi or, more commonly today, as *nigiri-zushi*.

Ordering

If you visit one of Tokyo's top sushi counters, most likely you'll be served a belly-busting set course of seasonal *nigiri-zushi*. This is called *omakase,* meaning

everything is left up to the chef, who puts together a tasting menu of the day's best haul. If there is something you can't eat, be sure to tell the staff when you sit down (most places are accommodating). You can also order à la carte, though this usually works out to be more expensive.

Dos & Don'ts

All but the most extreme type-A chefs will say they'd rather have foreign visitors enjoy their meal than agonise over getting the etiquette right. Still, there's nothing that makes a Japanese chef grimace more than out-of-towners who over-season their food – a little soy sauce and wasabi go a long way. Many chefs serve *nigiri-zushi* pre-seasoned (you'll likely be instructed by the staff when to use soy sauce). You

Kaiten-zushi (conveyor-belt sushi restaurant)

also might be surprised to learn that it is perfectly acceptable (nay, encouraged) to eat *nigiri-zushi* with your hands. The pickled ginger (called *gari*) served with sushi is to cleanse your palate between pieces.

A Meal of a Lifetime

Open since 1936, **Kyūbey** (久兵衛; Map p250; ☑03-3571-6523; www.kyubey.jp; 8 7-6 Ginza, Chūō-ku; lunch/dinner from ¥4000/10,000; ☺11.30am-2pm & 5-10pm Mon-Sat; ⓓ; ⓢGinza line to Shimbashi, exit 3) is an excellent place to splash out on an *omakase* meal. The

---

> ☑ **Don't Miss**
>
> Seasonal delicacies: leave the ordering up to the chef and you're guaranteed to get a taste of whatever is in season. For more sushi options, see p121.

BLUEHARD / SHUTTERSTOCK ©

quality and presentation is always faultless and the service is never stern or fussy. The friendly owner Imada-san speaks excellent English as do some of his team of talented chefs, who will make and serve your sushi, piece by piece. Lunch is excellent value.

Kaiten-zushi

For an experience at the opposite extreme, try a *kaiten-zushi* (回転寿司), where ready-made plates of sushi are sent around the restaurant on a conveyor belt. The best thing about these restaurants is that you don't have to worry about ordering: just grab whatever looks good as it goes by. Plates are colour-coded by price and if you don't see what you want, you can order off the menu. Numazukō (p138) is one of Tokyo's best kaiten-zushi restaurants.

Kaisen-don

A popular dish at many casual sushi restaurants, especially at lunch, is *kaisen-don* (海鮮丼) – a heaping serving of raw fish on a bowl of vinegared rice. **Sushikuni** (鮨國; Map p250; ☑03-3545-8234; 4-14-15 Tsukiji, Chūō-ku; seafood rice bowls from ¥3000; ☺10am-3pm & 5-9pm Thu-Tue; ⓓ; ⓢHibiya line to Tsukiji, exit 1), near Tsukiji Market, is an excellent place to try it.

Make your own sushi

Learn the art of sushi making at **Tokyo Sushi Academy** (Map p250; ☑03-3362-2789; http://sushimaking.tokyo; 2nd fl, Tsukiji KY Bldg, 4-7-5 Tsukiji, Chūō-ku; per person ¥5400; ☺9am-3pm Sat; ⓢHibiya line to Tsukiji, exit 1). English-speaking sushi chefs will give you a 30-minute crash course, after which you'll have an hour in which to make (and eat) as much of your favourite type of sushi as you like. Classes are held on Saturdays.

> ✕ **Take a Break**
>
> After a sushi lunch in Ginza or Tsukiji have tea at Cha Ginza (p123).

JAVIER LARREA / AGE FOTOSTOCK ©

Tokyo National Museum

This is the world's largest collection of Japanese art, home to gorgeous silk kimonos, evocative scroll paintings done in charcoal ink, earthy tea-ceremony pottery and haunting examples of samurai armour and swords.

Great For...

☑ **Don't Miss**

The 2nd floor of the Honkan building, which traces the history of Japanese art.

Honkan (Japanese Gallery)

The museum is divided into several buildings, the most important of which is the Honkan, which houses the collection of Japanese art. Visitors with only an hour or two should hone in on the galleries here, starting with the 2nd floor. Be sure to pick up the brochure *Highlights of Japanese Art* here. Note that exhibits rotate to protect works and present seasonal displays, so there's no guarantee that a particular work will be on show.

Gallery of Hōryū-ji Treasures

Next on the priority list is the enchanting **Gallery of Hōryū-ji Treasures** (法隆寺宝物館; Map p254), which display masks, scrolls and gilt Buddhas from Hōryū-ji (in Nara Prefecture, dating from 607). The spare,

Honkan (Japanese Gallery)

❶ Need to Know

東京国立博物館, Tokyo Kokuritsu Hakubutsukan; Map p254; ☎03-3822-1111; www.tnm.jp; 13-9 Ueno-kōen, Taitō-ku; adult/child & senior/student ¥620/free/410; ⏱9.30am-5pm Tue-Sun year-round, to 8pm Fri Mar-Dec, to 6pm Sat & Sun Mar-Aug; ☒JR lines to Ueno, Ueno-kōen exit

---

★ Top Tip

Allow two hours to take in the highlights, a half-day to do the Honkan in depth or a whole day to take in everything.

---

elegant, box-shaped building (1999) was designed by Taniguchi Yoshio.

Tōyōkan

Visitors with more time can explore the three-storied **Tōyōkan** (Gallery of Asian Art), with its collection of delicate Chinese ceramics and Buddhist sculptures from around Asia.

Heiseikan

The **Heiseikan** (平成館; Map p254), accessed via a passage on the 1st floor of the Honkan, houses the Japanese Archaeological Gallery, full of pottery, talismans and articles of daily life from Japan's paleolithic and neolithic periods.

The museum also regularly hosts temporary exhibitions (which cost extra), on the 2nd floor of the Heiseikan; these can be fantastic, but sometimes lack the English signage found throughout the rest of the museum.

The Grounds

To the west of the main gate is the **Kuromon** (Black Gate; Map p254), transported from the Edo-era mansion of a feudal lord. On weekends it opens for visitors to pass through. For a couple of weeks in spring and autumn, the back garden, home to five vintage **teahouses**, opens to the public.

Ueno-kōen

The Tokyo National Museum sits at the edge of **Ueno-kōen** (上野公園; Map p254; http://ueno-bunka.jp; Ueno-kōen, Taitō-ku; ☒JR lines to Ueno, Ueno-kōen & Shinobazu exits), which is home to several other museums, shrines, temples, and Tokyo's zoo, **Ueno Zoo** (上野動物園, Ueno Dōbutsu-en; Map p254; ☎03-3828-5171; www.tokyo-zoo.net; 9-83 Ueno-kōen, Taitō-ku; adult/child ¥600/free; ⏱9.30am-5pm Tue-Sun; ☒JR lines to Ueno, Ueno-kōen exit).

Tokyo National Museum

HISTORIC HIGHLIGHTS

It would be a challenge to take in everything the sprawling Tokyo National Museum has to offer in a day. Fortunately, the Honkan (Japanese Gallery) is designed to give visitors a crash course in Japanese art history from the Jōmon era (13,000–300 BC) to the Edo era (AD 1603–1868). The works on display here are rotated regularly, to protect fragile ones and to create seasonal exhibitions, so you're always guaranteed to see something new.

Buy your ticket from outside the main gate then head straight to the Honkan with its sloping tile roof. Stow your coat in a locker and take the central staircase up to the 2nd floor, where the exhibitions are arranged chronologically. Allow two hours for this tour of the highlights.

The first room on your right starts from the beginning with **ancient Japanese art ❶**. Be sure to pick up a copy of the brochure *Highlights of Japanese Art* at the entrance.

Continue to the **National Treasure Gallery ❷**. 'National Treasure' is the highest distinction awarded to a work of art in Japan. Keep an eye out for more National Treasures, labelled in red, on display in other rooms throughout the museum.

Moving on, stop to admire the **courtly art gallery ❸**, the **samurai armour and swords ❹** and the **ukiyo-e and kimono ❺**.

Next, take the stairs down to the 1st floor, where each room is dedicated to a different decorative art, such as lacquerware or ceramics. Don't miss the excellent examples of **religious sculpture ❻** and **folk art ❼**.

Finish your visit with a look inside the enchanting **Gallery of Hōryū-ji Treasures ❽**.

Ukiyo-e & Kimono (Room 10)
Chic silken kimono and lushly coloured *ukiyo-e* (woodblock prints) are two icons of the Edo-era (AD 1603–1868) *ukiyo* – the 'floating world', or world of fleeting beauty and pleasure.

Japanese Sculpture (Room 11)
Many of Japan's most famous sculptures, religious in nature, are locked away in temple reliquaries. This is a rare chance to see them up close.

MUSEUM GARDEN
Don't miss the garden if you visit in spring and autumn during the few weeks it's open to the public.

Heiseikan & Japanese Archaeology Gallery

Research & Information Centre

Hyōkeikan

Kuro-mon

Main Gate

Gallery of Hōryū-ji Treasures
Surround yourself with miniature gilt Buddhas from Hōryū-ji, one of Japan's oldest Buddhist temples, founded in 607. Don't miss the graceful Pitcher with Dragon Head, a National Treasure.

Courtly Art (Room 3-2)

Literature works, calligraphy and narrative picture scrolls are displayed alongside decorative art objects, which allude to the life of elegance led by courtesans a thousand years ago.

Samurai Armour & Swords (Rooms 5 & 6)

Glistening swords, finely stitched armour and imposing helmets bring to life the samurai, those iconic warriors of Japan's medieval age.

Honkan (Japanese Gallery) 2nd Floor

National Treasure Gallery (Room 2)

A single, superlative work from the museum's collection of 88 National Treasures (perhaps a painted screen, or a gilded, hand-drawn sutra) is displayed in a serene, contemplative setting.

Museum Garden & Teahouses

Honkan (Japanese Gallery)

Tōyōkan (Gallery of Asian Art)

Honkan (Japanese Gallery) 1st Floor

GIFT SHOP

The museum gift shop, on the 1st floor of the Honkan, has an excellent collection of Japanese art books in English.

Dawn of Japanese Art (Room 1)

The rise of the imperial court and the introduction of Buddhism changed the Japanese aesthetic forever. These clay works from previous eras show what came before.

Folk Culture (Room 15)

See artefacts from Japan's historical minorities – the indigenous Ainu of Hokkaidō and the former Ryūkyū Empire, now Okinawa.

Ueno Tōshō-gū — Shintō Shrine

(上野東照宮; Map p254; ☎03-3822-3455; www.
uenotoshogu.com; 9-88 Ueno-kōen, Taitō-ku;
¥500; ⏱9am-5.30pm Mar-Sep, to 4.30pm Oct-
Feb; ⓡJR lines to Ueno, Shinobazu exit) This
shrine inside Ueno-kōen was built in honour of Tokugawa Ieyasu, the warlord who
unified Japan. Resplendent in gold leaf and
ornate details, it dates from 1651 (though
it has had recent touch-ups). You can get
a pretty good look from outside the gate, if
you want to skip the admission fee.

Kiyōmizu
Kannon-dō — Buddhist Temple

(清水観音堂; Map p254; ☎03-3821-4749; 1-29
Ueno-kōen, Taitō-ku; ⏱9am-4pm; ⓡJR lines to
Ueno, Shinobazu exit) Ueno-kōen's Kiyōmizu Kannon-dō is one of Tokyo's oldest
structures: established in 1631 and in its
present position since 1698, it has survived
every disaster that has come its way. It's a
miniature of the famous Kiyomizu-dera in
Kyoto and is a pilgrimage site for women
hoping to conceive as it enshrines Koso-
date Kannon, the protector of childbearing
and child-raising.

What's Nearby?
Ameya-yokochō — Market

(アメヤ横町; Map p254; www.ameyoko.net; 4
Ueno, Taitō-ku; ⏱10am-7pm, some shops close
Wed; ⓡJR lines to Okachimachi, north exit)
Step into this partially open-air market
paralleling and beneath the JR line tracks,
and ritzy, glitzy Tokyo feels like a distant
memory. It got its start as a black market,
after WWII, when American goods were sold
here. Today, it's packed with vendors selling
everything from fresh seafood and exotic

Ueno Tōshō-gū

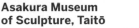

cooking spices to jeans, sneakers and elaborately embroidered bomber jackets.

Nezu-jinja
Shintō Shrine

(根津神社; Map p254; ☑03-3822-0753; www.nedujinja.or.jp; 1-28-9 Nezu, Bunkyō-ku; ☺24hr; Ⓢ Chiyoda line to Nezu, exit 1) Not only is this one of Japan's oldest shrines, it is also easily the most beautiful in a district packed with attractive religious buildings. The opulently decorated structure, which dates from the early 18th century, is one of the city's miraculous survivors and is offset by a long corridor of small red *torii* (gates) that make for great photos.

☑ **Don't Miss**

The enchanting Gallery of Hōryū-ji Treasures, filled with dozens of spot-lit Buddha statues dating from the 7th century.

Asakura Museum of Sculpture, Taitō
Museum

(朝倉彫塑館; Map p254; www.taitocity.net/taito/asakura; 7-16-10 Yanaka, Taitō-ku; adult/student ¥500/250; ☺9.30am-4.30pm Tue, Wed & Fri-Sun; Ⓡ JR Yamanote line to Nippori, north exit) Sculptor Asakura Fumio (artist name Chōso; 1883–1964) designed this atmospheric house himself. It combined his original Japanese home and garden with a large studio that incorporated vaulted ceilings, a 'sunrise room' and a rooftop garden with wonderful neighbourhood views. It's now a reverential museum with many of the artist's signature realist works, mostly of people and cats, on display.

Yanaka Ginza
Area

(谷中銀座; Map p254; Ⓡ JR Yamanote line to Nippori, north exit) Yanaka Ginza is pure, vintage mid-20th-century Tokyo, a pedestrian street lined with butcher shops, vegetable vendors and the like. Most Tokyo neighbourhoods once had stretches like these (until supermarkets took over). It's popular with locals as well as Tokyoites from all over the city, who come to soak up the nostalgic atmosphere.

SCAI the Bathhouse
Gallery

(スカイザバスハウス; Map p254; ☑03-3821-1144; www.scaithebathhouse.com; 6-1-23 Yanaka, Taitō-ku; ☺noon-6pm Tue-Sat; Ⓢ Chiyoda line to Nezu, exit 1) FREE This 200-year-old bathhouse has for several decades been an avant-garde gallery space, showcasing Japanese and international artists in its austere vaulted space.

✖ **Take a Break**

The museum complex itself has restaurants in the Gallery of Hōryū-ji Treasures and in the Tōyōkan. There's also a cafe in the **Kuroda Memorial Hall** annexe (黒田記念室; Map p254; ☑03-5777-8600; www.tobunken.go.jp/kuroda/index_e.html; 13-9 Ueno-kōen, Taitō-ku; ☺9.30am-5pm Tue-Sun; Ⓡ JR lines to Ueno, Ueno-kōen exit) FREE.

Walking Tour: Yanaka

Yanaka is a charming part of Tokyo where it feels like time stopped several decades ago. There are dozens of temples here, and it's the favourite district of local artists.

Start Tokyo National Museum
Distance 3km
Duration 2 hours

NISHI-NIPPORI

FINISH
7 Yanaka Ginza

Classic photo Yanaka Ginza from the Yūyake Dandan 'Sunset Stairs'.

7 The classic mid-20th-century shopping street **Yanaka Ginza** (p63) has food vendors and craft stores.

2 See the works of long-time Yanaka resident and painter Allan West at his studio, **Edokoro** (p166).

3 This ancient, thick-trunked **Himalayan cedar tree** is a local landmark.

4 At **Enju-ji** (延寿寺), Nichika-sama, the 'god of strong legs', is enshrined; it's popular with runners.

â (N) 0 — 200 m
0 — 0.1 miles

Goten-zaka

6

Sakura-dōri

5

YANAKA

1

START

Kototoi-dōri

UENO-
SAKURAGI

6 The **Asakura Museum of Sculpture Taitō** (p63) was the home studio of an early 20th-century sculptor and is now an attractive museum.

5 Yanaka-reien (谷中霊園) is one of Tokyo's most atmospheric and prestigious cemeteries (also a favourite sunning spot of Yanaka's many stray cats).

1 SCAI the Bathhouse (p63) is a classic old public bathhouse turned contemporary art gallery.

Take a break...
Enjoy a quick pit-stop in the rustic surrounds of **Kayaba Coffee** (p132).

Yoyogi-kōen

LOTTIE DAVIES / LONELY PLANET ©

Cherry-Blossom Viewing

Come spring, thousands of cherry trees around the city burst into white and pink flowers. Tokyoites gather in parks and along river banks for sake-fuelled cherry-blossom-viewing parties called hanami.

Great For...

☑ **Don't Miss**

The cherry blossoms in full bloom (called 'mankai') – said to be the most beautiful sight of the season.

Hanami is a centuries-old tradition that celebrates the fleeting beauty of life, symbolised by the blossoms, which last only a week or two. It's the one time of year you'll see Tokyoites let their hair down en masse, as a carnival spirit envelopes the city.

Yoyogi-kōen

Grassy **Yoyogi-kōen** (代々木公園; Map p246; www.yoyogipark.info; ◉ JR Yamanote line to Harajuku, Omote-sandō exit), one of the city's largest parks, is where you'll find some of the most spirited and elaborate bacchanals – complete with barbecues and turntables. Many revellers stay long past dark for *yozakura* (night-time cherry blossoms).

Ueno-kōen

Ueno-kōen (p59) is Tokyo's classic *hanami* spot. Blossom-viewing parties here appear

AODAADAOAAOD / SHUTTERSTOCK ©

exit 1), formerly an imperial retreat, has wide grassy lawns that make it a popular blossom-viewing spot, especially for families.

Aoyama Rei-en

A cemetery may seem an unlikely destination for a celebration of spring, but **Aoyama Rei-en** (青山霊園; Map p252; 2-32-2 Minami-Aoyama, Minato-ku; Ⓢ Chiyoda line to Nogizaka, exit 5 or Ginza line to Gaienmae, exit 1B) has lots of cherry trees and is a local favourite.

Meguro-gawa

One of the city's best parties takes place along the **Meguro-gawa** (目黒川; Map p246; Ⓢ Hibiya line to Naka-Meguro) in Naka-Meguro. Here vendors line the canal selling more upmarket treats than you'll find anywhere else. Rather than stake out a space to sit, visitors stroll under the blossoms, hot wine in hand.

on *ukiyo-e* (woodblock prints) from the 19th century. While many do grab spots under the trees, this park is better for strolling as it doesn't have a lawn. You'll spot many food vendors here.

Chidori-ga-fuchi

The Chidori-ga-fuchi moat surrounding Kitanomaru-kōen (p100) explodes with cherry blossoms in spring. You can also rent pedal boats here to view the blossoms from the water.

Shinjuku-gyoen

Shinjuku-gyoen (新宿御苑; Map p253; ☎ 03-3350-0151; www.env.go.jp/garden/shinjukugyoen; 11 Naito-chō, Shinjuku-ku; adult/child ¥200/50; ⊙ 9am-4.30pm Tue-Sun; Ⓢ Marunouchi line to Shinjuku-gyoenmae,

Sumida Park

Sumida Park, running along both sides of the river around Asakusa, is a cherry-blossom-viewing hot spot in spring and also gets packed for the grand fireworks festival in summer.

Sumo at Ryōgoku Kokugikan

The purifying salt sails into the air; the two giants leap up and crash into each other; a flurry of slapping and heaving ensues: from the ancient rituals to the thrill of the quick bouts, sumo is a fascinating spectacle.

Great For...

☑ Don't Miss

The ceremonial entrance of the top-ranking wrestlers, which takes place around 3.45pm.

Tournaments

Tournaments take place in Tokyo three times a year, for 15 days each January, May and September. Doors open at 8am, but the action doesn't heat up until the senior wrestlers hit the ring around 2pm. Tickets can be bought online one month before the start of the tournament. Around 200 general-admission tickets (¥2200) are sold on the day of the match from the box office in front of the stadium. You'll have to line up very early (say 6am) on the last couple of days of the tournament to snag one.

The Ritual of Sumo

Sumo was originally part of a ritual prayer to the gods for a good harvest. While it has obviously evolved, it remains deeply connected to Japan's Shintō tradition. You'll see a roof suspended over the *dōyo* (ring)

ⓘ Need to Know

両国国技館; Ryōgoku Sumo Stadium; Map
p254; ☑03-3623-5111; www.sumo.or.jp; 1-3-
28 Yokoami, Sumida-ku; ¥2200-14,800; ☒JR
Sōbu line to Ryōgoku, west exit

✕ Take a Break

During tournaments, the basement ban-
quet hall in the stadium serves *chanko-
nabe* (the protein-rich stew eaten by the
wrestlers) for just ¥300 a bowl.

★ Top Tip

Rent a radio (¥100 fee, plus ¥2000
deposit) to listen to commentary in
English.

that resembles that of a shrine. Before
bouts, *rikishi* (wrestlers) rinse their mouths
with water and toss salt into the ring – both
are purification rituals.

Rising through the Ranks

Morning matches take place between the
lower-ranking wrestlers. The pageantry
(and the stakes) begin in earnest in the
afternoon, when the *makuuchi* (top-tier)
wrestlers enter the ring, followed by that
of the *yokozuna* (the top of the top), complete with sword-bearing attendants. The
yokozuna wrestle in the final, most exciting,
bouts of the day.

In order to achieve the rank of *yokozuna*
a wrestler must win two consecutive tournaments and be considered, in the eyes of
the Sumo Association, to embody certain
traditional values. While sumo is very

Japanese in origin, in fact many of the top
wrestlers are foreign-born (Mongolia is a
sumo powerhouse). You'll also see portraits
of past champions hanging around the
stadium and at the **Sumo Museum** (相撲博
物館; 10am-4.30pm Mon-Fri) attached to the
stadium.

Sumo Practice

Not in town for a sumo tournament? You can
still catch an early-morning practice session
at a 'stable' – where the wrestlers live and
practise. Overseas visitors are welcome
at **Arashio Stable** (荒汐部屋, Arashio-beya;
☑03-3666-7646; www.arashio.net/tour_e.html;
2-47-2 Hama-chō, Nihombashi, Chūō-ku; ⑤Toei
Shinjuku line to Hamachō, exit A2) **FREE**, so long
as they mind the rules (check the website).
Visit between 7.30am and 10am – you can
watch through the window or on a bench
outside the door. There is no practice during tournaments.

Day Trip: Mt Fuji

Catching a glimpse of Mt Fuji (富士山; 3776m), Japan's highest and most famous peak, will take your breath away. Climbing it and watching the sunrise from the summit is one of Japan's superlative experiences (though it's often cloudy).

Great For...

☑ Don't Miss

Watching the sunrise from the summit – a profound, once-in-a-lifetime experience.

Climbing Mt Fuji

The Japanese proverb 'He who climbs Mt Fuji once is a wise man, he who climbs it twice is a fool' remains as valid as ever. While reaching the top brings a great sense of achievement, it's a gruelling climb not known for its beautiful scenery.

The mountain is divided into 10 'stations' from base (First Station) to summit (Tenth), but most hikers start from one of the four Fifth Stations. The vast majority of visitors hike the **Kawaguchi-ko Trail** from the Fuji Subaru Line Fifth Station (aka Kawaguchi-ko Fifth Station), as it's easy to reach from Tokyo. During the climbing season, Keiō Dentetsu Bus runs direct buses (¥2700, 2½ hours; reservations necessary) from the Shinjuku Bus Station to Fuji Subaru Line Fifth Station. From here, allow five to six hours to reach the top (though some

View of Mt Fuji during cherry blossom season

TOKYO

Mt Fuji

Tokyo Bay

❶ Need to Know

The official climbing season runs from 1 July to 31 August.

✕ Take a Break

Mountain huts offer hikers simple hot meals in addition to a place to sleep. Most huts allow you to rest inside as long as you order something.

★ Top Tip

Check summit weather conditions before planning a climb at www. snow-forecast.com/resorts/Mount-Fuji/6day/top. Free wi-fi is also now available at Fifth Station access points and the summit, for 72 hours after you've acquired an access card at one of the Fifth Station information centres.

climb it in half the time) and about three hours to descend, plus 1½ hours for circling the crater at the top.

Know Before You Climb

Mt Fuji is a serious mountain, high enough for altitude sickness, and weather and visibility can change instantly and dramatically. At a minimum, bring clothing appropriate for cold and wet weather, including a hat and gloves, at least two litres of water, a map, snacks and cash for other necessities, such as toilets (¥200). If you're climbing at night, bring a torch (flashlight) or headlamp and spare batteries.

When to Climb

To time your arrival for dawn you can either start up in the afternoon, stay overnight in

a mountain hut and continue early in the morning, or climb the whole way at night. You do not want to arrive on the top too long before dawn, as it will be very cold and windy, even at the height of summer. It's a very busy mountain during the two-month climbing season; to avoid the worst of the crush head up on a weekday, or start earlier during the day.

Authorities strongly caution against climbing outside the regular season, when the weather is highly unpredictable and first-aid stations on the mountain are closed. Once snow or ice is on the mountain, Fuji becomes a very serious and dangerous undertaking and should only be attempted by those with winter-mountaineering equipment and plenty of experience. Do not climb alone; a guide will be invaluable.

Mountain Huts

Conditions in mountain huts are spartan (a blanket on the floor sandwiched between other climbers), but reservations are recommended and are essential on weekends. It's also important to let huts know if you decide to cancel at the last minute; be prepared to pay to cover the cost of your no-show.

Two of the Eighth Station huts usually have English-speaking staff: **Taishikan** (太子館; ☏0555-22-1947; www.mfi.or.jp/w3/home0/taisikan; per person incl 2 meals from ¥8500), with vegetarian or halal meals possible with advance request; and **Fujisan Hotel** (富士山ホテル; ☏0555-22-0237; www.fujisanhotel.com; per person excl/incl 2 meals from ¥5950/8350), one of the largest and most popular huts.

Tours

Discover Japan Tours　　Tours
(www.discover-japan-tours.com/en; 2-day Mt Fuji tours per person ¥10,000) Reputable company offering guided tours from Tokyo for groups of two or more and specialising in less-frequented routes.

Fuji Mountain Guides　　Walking
(☏042-445-0798; www.fujimountainguides.com/; 2-day Mt Fuji tours per person ¥44,000) Aimed at foreign visitors, these excellent tours are run both in and out of season by highly experienced and very professional American bilingual guides.

Fuji Five Lakes

Outside the climbing season, you can hunt for views of Mt Fuji in the Fuji Five Lake

Kawaguchi-ko in the Fuji Five Lake region

region, where placid lakes, formed by ancient eruptions, serve as natural reflecting pools. Kawaguchi-ko is the most popular lake, with plenty of accommodation, eating and hiking options around it. The other lakes are Yamanaka-ko, Sai-ko, Shōji-ko and Motosu-ko.

Buses run year-round to Kawaguchi-ko (¥1750, 1¾ hours) from the Shinjuku Bus Terminal in Tokyo; from Kawaguchi-ko, local buses run to the other lakes (though renting a car is an easier option).

Fuji-Spotting

Mt Fuji has many different personalities depending on the season. Winter and spring months are your best bet for seeing it in all its clichéd glory; however, even during these times the snowcapped peak may be visible only in the morning before it retreats behind its cloud curtain. Its elusiveness, however, is part of the appeal, making sightings all the more special.

Several hiking trails through the foothills offer rewarding vistas (with fewer crowds). Ask for a map at the **Kawaguchi-ko Tourist Information Center** (📞0555-72-6700; ⏱8.30am-5.30pm Sun-Fri, to 7pm Sat).

Some of our top spots for viewing in the Fuji Five Lake region include the north side of **Kawaguchi-ko**, where Fuji looms large over its shimmering reflection; the northwest side of **Motosu-ko**, from where the famous view depicted on the ¥1000 bill can be seen; the end of the **Panorama-dai** hiking trail, which rewards with a magnificent front-on view of the mountain; and the **Kōyō-dai** lookout, from where Mt Fuji views are particularly stunning in autumn.

Kawaguchi-ko to Fifth Station

From roughly mid-April to early December (weather permitting), buses travel from Kawaguchi-ko to the Fuji Subaru Line Fifth Station (one way/return ¥1540/2100, one hour), so even if you can't climb you can still get up close to the hulking volcano.

ⓘ Need to Know

Climbing Mt Fuji (www17.plala.or.jp/climb_fujiyama) and the Official Web Site for Mt Fuji Climbing (www.fujisan-climb.jp) are good online resources. The *Climbing Mt Fuji* brochure, available at the Fuji-Yoshida or Kawaguchi-ko Tourist Information Centers, is also worth picking up.

Walking Tour: Omote-sandō Architecture

Omote-sandō, a broad, tree-lined boulevard running through Harajuku, is known for its parade of upmarket boutiques designed by the who's who of (mostly) Japanese contemporary architects.
Start Tokyū Plaza
Distance 1.5km
Duration 1 hour

2 Andō Tadao's deceptively deep **Omotesandō Hills** (表参道ヒルズ; 2003) is a high-end shopping mall spiralling around a sunken central atrium.

Meiji-dōri

HARAJUKU

START

Omote-sandō

Cat St

1 Tokyū Plaza (東急プラザ; 2012), is a castle-like structure by up-and-coming architect Nakamura Hiroshi. There's a spacious roof garden on top.

Omote-Sandō Hills

3 The flagship boutique for **Dior** (2003), designed by Pritzker Prize–winner SANAA (composed of Sejima Kazuyo and Nishizawa Ryūe), has a filmy, white exterior that seems to hang like a dress.

4 Meant to evoke a stack of clothes trunks, Aoki Jun's design for **Louis Vuitton** (2002) features offset panels of tinted glass behind sheets of metal mesh of varying patterns.

6 The patchwork, uncentred design of Maki Fumihiko's postmodernist **Spiral Building** (スパイラルビル; 1985) is a nod to Tokyo's own mismatched landscape.

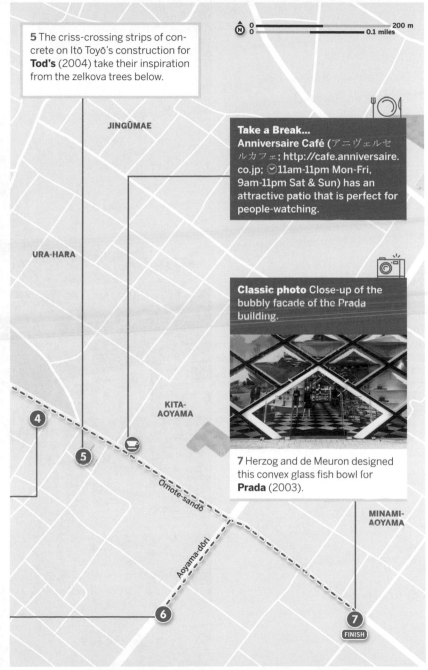

5 The criss-crossing strips of concrete on Itō Toyō's construction for **Tod's** (2004) take their inspiration from the zelkova trees below.

0 — 200 m
0 — 0.1 miles

JINGŪMAE

Take a Break...
Anniversaire Café (アニヴェルセ
ルカフェ; http://cafe.anniversaire.
co.jp; ⊙11am-11pm Mon-Fri,
9am-11pm Sat & Sun) has an
attractive patio that is perfect for
people-watching.

URA-HARA

Classic photo Close-up of the
bubbly facade of the Prada
building.

KITA-
AOYAMA

7 Herzog and de Meuron designed
this convex glass fish bowl for
Prada (2003).

Omote-sandō

MINAMI-
AOYAMA

Aoyama-dōri

6

7
FINISH

Sensō-ji

Sensō-ji is the capital's oldest temple, far older than Tokyo itself. Today the temple stands out for its old-world atmosphere – a glimpse of a bygone Japan rarely visible in Tokyo today.

Great For...

❶ Need to Know

浅草寺; Map p254; ☎03-3842-0181; www. senso-ji.jp; 2-3-1 Asakusa, Taitō-ku; ⊙24hr; Ⓢ Ginza line to Asakusa, exit 1 FREE

★ **Top Tip**
The minutes just before the sun sinks make for some of the best pictures of this photogenic sanctuary.

According to legend, in AD 628, two fishermen brothers pulled out a golden image of Kannon (the Bodhisattva of compassion) from the nearby Sumida-gawa. Sensō-ji was built (and rebuilt several times since) to enshrine it.

Kaminari-mon

The temple precinct begins at the majestic **Kaminari-mon** (雷門; Thunder Gate; Map p254), which means Thunder Gate. An enormous *chōchin* (lantern), which weighs 670kg, hangs from the centre. On either side are a pair of ferocious protective deities: Fūjin, the god of wind, on the right; and Raijin, the god of thunder, on the left. Kaminari-mon has burnt down countless times over the centuries; the current gate dates to 1970.

Nakamise-dōri

Beyond Kaminari-mon is the bustling shopping street, Nakamise-dōri. With its lines of souvenir stands it is very touristy, though that's nothing new: Sensō-ji has been Tokyo's top tourist sight for centuries, since travel was restricted to religious pilgrimages during the feudal era. In addition to the usual T-shirts, you can find Edo-style crafts and oddities (such as wigs done up in traditional hairstyles). There are also numerous snack vendors serving up crunchy *sembei* (rice crackers) and *age-manju* (deep-fried *anko* – bean-paste – buns).

Hōzō-mon

At the end of Nakamise-dōri is **Hōzō-mon** (宝蔵門; Map p254), another gate with fierce

Nakamise-dōri shopping street

guardians. On the gate's back side are a pair of 2500kg, 4.5m-tall *waraji* (straw sandals) crafted for Sensō-ji by some 800 villagers in northern Yamagata Prefecture. These are meant to symbolise the Buddha's power and it's believed that evil spirits will be scared off by the giant footwear.

Hondō (Main Hall)

The grand Hondō was constructed in 1958, replacing the one destroyed in WWII air raids. The style is similar to the previous one, though the tiles on the dramatic sloping roof are made of titanium. The Kannon image (a tiny 6cm) is cloistered away from

> ☑ **Don't Miss**
> The tasty, traditional snack foods sold along Nakamise-dōri.

TAKASHI IMAGES / SHUTTERSTOCK ©

view deep inside (and admittedly may not exist at all). Nonetheless, a steady stream of worshippers visits the temple to cast coins, pray and bow in a gesture of respect. Do feel free to join in.

Fortune Telling

Don't miss getting your fortune told by an *omikuji* (paper fortune). Drop ¥100 into the slots by the wooden drawers at either side of the approach to the Main Hall, grab a silver canister and shake it. Extract a stick and note its number (in kanji). Replace the stick, find the matching drawer and withdraw a paper fortune (there's English on the back). If you pull out 大凶 (*dai-kyō*, Great Curse), never fear. Just tie the paper on the nearby rack, ask the gods for better luck and try again!

Five-Storey Pagoda

Off the courtyard stands a 53m-high **Five-Storey Pagoda** (五重塔; Map p254), a 1973 reconstruction of a pagoda built by Tokugawa Iemitsu, just renovated in 2017. The current structure is the second-highest pagoda in Japan.

Asakusa-jinja

On the east side of the temple complex is **Asakusa-jinja** (浅草神社; Map p254; ☑03-3844-1575; www.asakusajinja.jp/english; ☺9am-4.30pm), built in honour of the brothers who discovered the Kannon statue that inspired the construction of Sensō-ji. (Historically, Japan's two religions, Buddhism and Shintō, were intertwined and it was not uncommon for temples to include shrines and vice versa.) This section of Sensō-ji survived WWII and Asakusa-jinja's current structure dates to 1649.

Next to the shrine is the temple complex's eastern gate, **Niten-mon** (二天門; Map p254), standing since 1618. Though it

> ✕ **Take a Break**
> Just off Nakamise-dōri, Daikokuya (p144) serves delicious tempura.

appears minor today, this gate was the point of entry for visitors arriving in Asakusa via boat – the main form of transport during the Edo period.

Awashima-dō

Sensō-ji includes many other smaller temples. One to visit is **Awashima-dō** (あわしま堂; Map p254), on the western edge of the temple grounds, which dates to the late 17th century. The deity enshrined here is a guardian of women and the temple is the site of a curious ancient ritual: *hari-kuyō* (the needle funeral). Annually on 8 February, monks perform last rites for broken or old sewing needles. Kimono makers and seamstresses express their thanks to the needles by sticking them in a block of soft tofu.

Festivals

During the first three days of the New Year more than 2.5 million people visit Sensō-ji to pray for the year to come. Asakusa-jinja is the epicentre of one of Tokyo's most important festivals, May's Sanja Matsuri, which draws another 1.5 million visitors.

What's Nearby?

Edo-Tokyo Museum   Museum

(江戸東京博物館; Map p254; ☎03-3626-9974; www.edo-tokyo-museum.or.jp; 1-4-1 Yokoami, Sumida-ku; adult/child ¥600/free; ⊗9.30am-5.30pm, to 7.30pm Sat, closed Mon; ⒭JR Sōbu line to Ryōgoku, west exit) This history museum, in a cavernous building, does an excellent job laying out Tokyo's miraculous transformation from feudal city to modern capital, through city models, miniatures of real buildings, reproductions of old maps and *ukiyo-e* (woodblock prints). It starts with a bang as you cross the life-sized partial replica of the original Nihombashi bridge and gaze down on facades of a kabuki theatre and Meiji-era bank. There is English signage throughout and a free audio guide available (¥1000 deposit).

Sumida Hokusai Museum   Museum

(すみだ北斎美術館; Map p254; ☎03-6658-8931; http://hokusai-museum.jp; 2-7-2 Kamezawa, Sumida-ku; adult/child/student ¥1200/400/900; ⊗9.30am-5.30pm Tue-Sun; ⒮Oedo line to Ryōgoku, exit A4) The artist Katsushika Hokusai was born and died near the location of this new museum, opened in 2016. The striking aluminium-clad building is designed by Pritzker Prize–winning architect Kazuyo Sejima. The museum's collection numbers more than 1500 pieces and includes some of the master's most famous images, such as *The Great Wave off Kanagawa* from his series *Thirty-six Views of Mount Fuji*.

Asakusa-jinja (p79)

Chingo-dō
Buddhist Temple

(鎮護堂; Map p254; www.senso-ji.jp/guide/
chingodo_e.html; 2-3-1 Asakusa, Taitō-ku; ⊙6am-
5pm; Ⓢ Ginza line to Asakusa, exit 1) This small,
peaceful temple is actually part of Sensō-ji
but has a separate entrance on Dembō-in-
dōri. It pays tribute to the *tanuki* (racoon-
like folkloric characters), who figure in
Japanese myth as mystical shape-shifters
and merry pranksters. They are also said to
protect against fire and theft, which is why
you'll often see *tanuki* figurines in front of
restaurants.

Super Dry Hall
Architecture

(フラム ドール; Flamme d'Or; Map p254; www.
asahibeer.co.jp/aboutus/summary/#headQuarter;
1-23-1 Azuma-bashi, Sumida-ku; Ⓢ Ginza line to
Asakusa, exit 4) Also known as Asahi Beer

Hall, the headquarters of the brewery was
designed by Philippe Starck and completed
in 1989. It remains one of the city's most
distinctive buildings. The tower, with its
golden glass facade and white top floors,
is supposed to evoke a giant mug of beer,
while the golden blob atop the lower jet-
black building is the flame (locals, however,
refer to it as the 'golden turd').

☑ **Don't Miss**

Asakusa-jinja – painted a deep shade
of red, it's a rare example of early Edo
architecture.

ⓘ **Did You Know?**

The incense smoke from the caul-
drons in front of the Hondō is believed
by some to bestow health; you'll see
people wafting it over their bodies.

Ōedo Onsen Monogatari (p86)

Onsen & Sentō

Don't be shy! Many Japanese would argue that you couldn't possibly understand their culture without taking a dip in an onsen (natural hot-spring bath). The blissful relaxation that follows can turn a sceptic into a convert.

Great For...

❶ Need to Know

Bathhouses can be identified by *noren* (half-length curtains over the doorway), printed with the hiragana (ゆ; *yu*) for hot water (or sometimes the kanji: 湯).

★ **Top Tip**

Know your kanji: 女 means women and 男 means men.

Known as *hadaka no tsukiai*, meaning 'naked friendship', communal bathing is seen in Japan as a great social leveller.

Konyoku (mixed bathing) was the norm in Japan until the Meiji Restoration, when the country sought to align itself with more 'civilised' Western ideas and outlawed the practice. Within Tokyo's central 23 wards you won't encounter it, but in the countryside and on the Izu Islands (where baths may be no more than a pool in a riverbed blocked off with stones, or a tidal basin beside crashing waves), *konyoku* is more common.

Onsen or Sentō?

What sets an onsen apart from a *sentō* (public bath) is the nature of the water. Onsen water comes naturally heated from a hot spring and often contains a number of minerals; *sentō* water comes from the tap and is mechanically heated. Onsen are reputed to makes one's skin *sube-sube* (smooth), while the chemical composition of particular waters is also believed to help alleviate such ailments as high blood pressure and poor circulation.

The old-school public *sentō* don't have the mineral-rich waters, but they do have lots of local charm. They date back to the era when many private homes in Japan did not have baths. Most do now and *sentō* numbers are dwindling (down to around 1000, from a high of over 2500).

Onsen spas are used to foreign visitors and usually have dos and don'ts posted in multiple languages. Here you'll get to try out lots of different baths. *Sentō*, mostly

frequented by neighbourhood regulars, can be a little intimidating, but can also be a great local experience. Spas provide everything you need, while sentō expect you to bring your own towel and toiletries. (You can, however, show up empty handed and rent a towel and purchase soap, shampoo etc for a small price.)

Many larger spa complexes refuse entry to people with tattoos because of the association of tattoos with the yakuza (Japanese mafia). However, most sentō are open to all.

> **ⓘ Need to Know**
>
> See Tokyo Sentō (www.1010.or.jp/index.php) for more info on local bathhouses.

Bathing Etiquette

Upon entering an onsen or sentō, the first thing you'll encounter is a row of lockers for your shoes. After you pay your admission and head to the correct changing room, you'll find either more lockers or baskets for your clothes. Take everything off here and enter the bathing room with only the small towel.

That little towel performs a variety of functions: you can use it to wash (but make sure to give it a good rinse afterwards) or to cover yourself as you walk around. It is not supposed to touch the water though, so leave it on the side of the bath or – as the locals do – folded on top of your head.

Park yourself on a stool in front of one of the taps and give yourself a thorough wash. Make sure you rinse off all the suds. When you're done, it's polite to rinse off the stool for the next person. At more humble bathhouses you might have little more than a ladle to work with; in that case, crouch low and use it to scoop out water from the bath and pour over your body – taking care not to splash water into the tub – and scrub a bit with the towel.

In the baths, keep splashing to a minimum and your head above the water. Before heading back to the changing room, wipe yourself down with the towel to avoid dripping on the floor.

Best Baths

Rokuryu Kōsen   Bathhouse

(六龍鉱泉; Map p254; ☑03-3821-3826; 3-4-20 Ikenohata, Taitō-ku; ¥460; ☺3.30-11pm Tue-Sun; ⑤Chiyoda line to Nezu, exit 2) Dating from 1931, this gem of a neighbourhood sentō has a beautiful mural of the wooden arched bridge Kintai-kyo in Iwasaki on the bathhouse wall. The amber-hued water is

> **ⓘ Local Knowledge**
>
> The most important thing to know to avoid a major etiquette breach is to wash yourself before getting into the bath.

packed with minerals that are reputed to be excellent for your skin, if you can stand the water temperature – a scalding-hot 45°C in the cooler of the two pools!

Ōedo Onsen Monogatari   Onsen

(大江戸温泉物語; www.ooedoonsen.jp; 2-6-3 Aomi, Kōtō-ku; adult/child ¥2280/980, surcharge Sat & Sun ¥200; ☺11am-9am, last entry 7am; ⋒Yurikamome line to Telecom Center, Rinkai line to Tokyo Teleport with free shuttle bus) Just to experience the truly Japanese phenomenon that is an amusement park centred on bathing is reason enough to visit. The baths here, which include gender-divided indoor tubs and outdoor *rotemburo* (outdoor baths), are filled with real hot-spring water, pumped from 1400m below Tokyo Bay. Come after 6pm for a ¥500 discount. Visitors with tattoos will be denied admission.

Upon entering, visitors change their clothes for a choice of colourful *yukata* (light cotton kimonos) to wear while they stroll around the complex, which is a lantern-lit re-creation of an old Tokyo downtown area, with food stalls and carnival games.

There's a huge variety of baths here, including jet baths, pools of natural rock and, on the ladies' side, personal bucket-shaped baths made of cedar. These are segregated by gender, but there's also a communal outdoor foot bath, set in a garden, where mixed groups and families can hang out together (the town area is also communal).

You can also crash here overnight, sleeping on reclining chairs in the lounge, bathing at whim if you want to dig deep into the onsen experience; there's a surcharge of ¥2000 per person if you stay between 2am and 5am.

Spa LaQua   Onsen

(スパ ラクーア; ☎03-5800-9999; www.laqua. jp; 5th-9th fl, Tokyo Dome City, 1-1-1 Kasuga, Bunkyō-ku; weekday/weekend ¥2635/2960; ☺11am-9am; ⑤Marunouchi line to Kōrakuen, exit 2) One of Tokyo's few true onsen, this chic spa complex relies on natural hot-spring water from 1700m below ground. There are indoor and outdoor baths, saunas and a bunch of add-on options, such as *akasuri* (Korean-style whole-body exfoliation). It's a fascinating introduction to Japanese health and beauty rituals.

Jakotsu-yu   Bathhouse

(蛇骨湯; Map p254; ☎03-3841-8645; www. jakotsuyu.co.jp; 1-11-11 Asakusa, Taitō-ku; adult/ child ¥460/180; ☺1pm-midnight Wed-Mon; ⑤Ginza line to Tawaramachi, exit 3) Unlike most *sentō*, the tubs here are filled with pure hot-spring water, naturally the colour of weak tea. Another treat is the lovely, lantern-lit, rock-framed *rotemburo* (outdoor bath). Jakotsu-yu is a welcoming place; it has English signage and doesn't have a policy against tattoos. It's an extra ¥200 for the sauna and ¥140 for a small towel.

Ōedo Onsen Monogatari

Thermae-yu
Onsen

(テルマー湯; Map p253; ☏03-5285-1726; www.thermae-yu.jp; 1-1-2 Kabukichō, Shinjuku-ku; weekdays/weekends & holidays ¥2360/2690; ⏰11am-9am; 🚆JR Yamanote line to Shinjuku, east exit) The best (and most literal) example to date that red-light district Kabukichō is cleaning up its act: the 2016 opening of this gleaming onsen complex. The tubs, which include several indoor and outdoor ones (sex-segregated), are filled with honest-to-goodness natural hot-spring water. There are several saunas, including a hot-stone sauna (*ganbanyoku*, ¥810 extra). Sorry, no tattoos allowed.

Shimizu-yu
Sento

(清水湯; Map p246; ☏03-3401-4404; http://shimizuyu.jp/; 3-12-3 Minami-Aoyama, Minato-ku; with/without sauna ¥1000/460; ⏰noon-midnight Mon-Thu, to 11pm Sat & Sun; 🚆Ginza line to Omote-sandō, exit A4) Not all *sentō* are historical relics: Shimizu-yu has ultramodern tubs of glistening white tile, jet baths and a sauna. It's just as likely to be filled with young shoppers – perhaps transitioning to a night out – as local grandmas. You can rent a towel (¥300) and purchase soap and shampoo (¥310) at the counter.

☑ Don't Miss
A soak in a *rotemburo* (outdoor bath).

✗ Take a Break
Beer is considered the ultimate after-bath indulgence; many bathhouses sell it.

JAVIER LARREA / AGE FOTOSTOCK ©

Kabukiza Theatre

Dramatic, intensely visual kabuki is Japan's most recognised art form. Kabuki developed in Tokyo, then known as Edo, during the 18th and 19th centuries; an afternoon at the theatre has been a favourite local pastime ever since. Descendants of the great actors of the day still grace Tokyo stages, drawing devoted fans. Established in 1889 (and rebuilt in 2013), Kabukiza is Tokyo's premier kabuki theatre.

Great For...

❶ Need to Know

歌舞伎座; Map p250; ☎03-3545-6800; www.kabuki-bito.jp/eng; 4-12-15 Ginza, Chūō-ku; tickets ¥4000-21,000, single-act tickets ¥800-2000; 🚇Hibiya line to Higashi-Ginza, exit 3

★ Top Tip

Rent a headset for explanations in English; the recording begins 10 minutes before each act, with background information about the play.

History

Kabuki got its start in Kyoto: around the year 1600, a charismatic shrine priestess led a troupe of female performers in a new type of dance people dubbed 'kabuki', a slang expression that meant 'cool' or 'in vogue' at the time. The dancing – rather ribald and performed on a dry riverbed for gathering crowds – was also a gateway to prostitution, which eventually led the shogunate to ban the female performers. Adolescent men took their place, though they too attracted amorous admirers. Finally, in 1653, the authorities mandated that only adult men with shorn forelocks could perform kabuki, which gave rise to one of kabuki's most fascinating elements, the *onnagata* (actors who specialise in portraying women).

When kabuki arrived in Edo, it developed hand in hand with the increasingly affluent merchant class, whose decadent tastes translated into the breathtaking costumes, dramatic music and elaborate stagecraft that have come to characterise the art form. It is this intensely visual nature that makes kabuki accessible to foreign audiences – you don't really have to know the story to enjoy the spectacle.

Understanding Kabuki

There is no pretence of reality in kabuki; it's ruled by aesthetics and plays to the senses rather than the intellect. Kabuki has been likened to a moving woodblock print, and when the actors pause in dramatic poses (called *mie*) the whole stage really does look fit to be framed. The kabuki stage

Traditional kabuki dance

employs a number of unique devices, including the *hanamichi* (the walkway that extends into the audience), which is used for dramatic entrances and exits. Naturally the best seats are those that line the *hanamichi*.

The plays draw from a repertoire of popular themes, such as famous historical accounts and stories of love-suicide. But kabuki is driven less by plot and more by its actors, who train for the profession from childhood. The leading families of modern kabuki (such as Bando and Ichikawa) go back many generations, as sons follow their fathers into the *yago* (kabuki acting

> ☑ **Don't Miss**
>
> The flamboyant costumes and outrageous make-up. (Tip: if you opt for the cheap seats, bring binoculars.)

house). The audience takes great interest in watching how different generations of one family perform the same part. At pivotal moments in a performance, enthusiastic fans shout out the actor's *yago* – an act called *kakegoe*.

Performances

A full kabuki performance comprises three or four acts (usually from different plays) over an afternoon or an evening (typically 11am to 3.30pm or 4.30pm to 9pm), with long intervals between the acts. It's tradition to eat a *bentō* (boxed meal) at the theatre during the intermission. Purchase one (around ¥1000) inside the theatre or at stalls outside. Tickets go on sale about one month in advance; book early (online) for good seats.

If four-plus hours sounds too long, 90 sitting and 60 standing tickets are sold on the day for each single act. You'll be at the back of the auditorium, but the views are still good. Some acts tend to be more popular than others, so ask ahead which to catch and arrive at least 1½ hours before the start of the performance.

The Theatre

Kabukiza's current incarnation, designed by architect Kuma Kengo, has a flamboyant facade (and an office tower peeking out the back). If you have a ticket to see a show at the theatre you get a ¥100 discount on entry to the small **Kabuki-za Gallery** (歌舞伎座ギャラリー; adult/child/student ¥600/free/500; 10am-5.30pm) on the 5th floor, displaying stage props, scenery and costumes used in the plays. There's also a lovely rooftop garden on the same floor.

KAZUHIRO NOGI / STAFF / GETTY IMAGES ©

> ✕ **Take a Break**
>
> Offering a view of Kabukiza's roof garden is the tea salon Jugetsudo (p123); here you can sample various Japanese green teas paired with sweets.

View from the Mori Tower (p95)

Tokyo Cityscape

There's nothing quite like gazing out over the Tokyo cityscape from a few hundred metres in the air. From this vantage point, the city is endless, stretching all the way to the horizon. By night, Tokyo appears truly beautiful, as if the sky were inverted, with the glittering stars below. Take in the view from an observatory or a stylish hotel lounge atop one of the city's many towers.

Great For...

ⓘ Need to Know

Most of Tokyo's top-tier hotels have top-floor bars – you can take your pick, really.

★ **Top Tip**

Admission to the Mori Art Museum (p51) also gets you into the Mori Tower observatory, Tokyo City View (p95).

MATT MUNRO / LONELY PLANET ©

Observatories

Tokyo Metropolitan Government Building

Notable Building

(東京都庁; Tokyo Tochō; Map p253; http://www.metro.tokyo.jp/english/offices/observat.htm; 2-8-1 Nishi-Shinjuku, Shinjuku-ku; ⊘observatories 9.30am-11pm; ⑤Ōedo line to Tochō-mae, exit A4) FREE Tokyo's seat of power, designed by Tange Kenzō and completed in 1991, looms large and looks somewhat like a pixelated cathedral (or the lair of an animated villain). Take an elevator from the ground floor of Building 1 to one of the twin 202m-high observatories for panoramic views over the never-ending cityscape (the views are virtually the same from either tower).

Tokyo Sky Tree

Tower

(東京スカイツリー; Map p254; www.tokyo-skytree.jp; 1-1-2 Oshiage, Sumida-ku; 350m/450m observation decks ¥2060/3090; ⊘8am-10pm; ⑤Hanzōmon line to Oshiage, Sky Tree exit) Tokyo Sky Tree opened in May 2012 as the world's tallest 'free-standing tower' at 634m. Its silvery exterior of steel mesh morphs from a triangle at the base to a circle at 300m. There are two observation decks, at 350m and 450m. You can see more of the city during daylight hours – at peak visibility you can see up to 100km away.

The upper observatory, the **Tembō Galleria**, beneath the digital broadcasting antennas, features a circular glass corridor for more vertiginous thrills. The elevator between the two has a glass front, so you

Tembō Galleria, Tokyo Sky Tree

can see yourself racing up the tower as the city grows smaller below.

The ticket counter is on the 4th floor. You'll see signs in English noting the wait and the current visibility. Try to avoid visiting on the weekend, when you might have to wait in line.

Tokyo City View   Viewpoint

(東京シティビュー; Map p252; ☑03-6406-6652; www.roppongihills.com/tcv/en; 52nd fl, Mori Tower, Roppongi Hills, 6-10-1 Roppongi, Minato-ku; adult/child/student ¥1800/600/1200; ☺10am-11pm Mon-Thu & Sun, to 1am Fri & Sat; Ⓢ Hibiya line to Roppongi, exit 1) This observatory wraps itself around the 52nd floor of

---

☑ **Don't Miss**

Looking west for Mt Fuji (although you'll need a clear day).

Mori Tower, 250m off the ground. Weather permitting, you can also pop out to the external rooftop **Sky Deck** (additional adult/child ¥500/300; 11am to 8pm) for alfresco views.

Bars with a View

New York Bar   Bar

(ニューヨークバー; Map p253; ☑03-5323-3458; http://tokyo.park.hyatt.com; 52nd fl, Park Hyatt, 3-7-1-2 Nishi-Shinjuku, Shinjuku-ku; ☺5pm-midnight Sun-Wed, to 1am Thu-Sat; Ⓓ; Ⓡ Ōedo line to Tochōmae, exit A4) Head to the Park Hyatt's 52nd floor to swoon over the sweeping nightscape from the floor-to-ceiling windows at this bar (of *Lost in Translation* fame). There's a cover charge of ¥2400 if you visit or stay past 8pm (7pm Sunday); go earlier and watch the sky fade to black. Note: dress code enforced and 20% service charge levied.

Asahi Sky Room   Bar

(アサヒスカイルーム; Map p254; ☑03-5608-5277; http://r.gnavi.co.jp/a1/0000/menu10, 22F, Asahi Super Dry Bldg, 1-23-1 Azuma-bashi, Sumida-ku; beer ¥720; ☺10am-9pm; Ⓓ; Ⓢ Ginza line to Asakusa, exit 4) This bar on the 22nd floor of the golden-tinged Asahi Super Dry Building has spectacular views over the Sumida River, especially at sunset.

Peter: the Bar   Cocktail Bar

(Map p250; ☑03-6270-2763; http://tokyo.peninsula.com/en/fine-dining/peter-lounge-bar; 24th fl, 1-8-1 Yūrakuchō, Chiyoda-ku; ☺noon-midnight, to 1am Fri & Sat; Ⓢ Hibiya line to Hibiya, exits A6 & A7) The Peninsula hotel's Peter: the Bar distinguishes itself with dress-circle views across the Imperial Palace (p81), Hibiya Park and Ginza as well as a generous happy hour (5pm to 8pm Sunday to Thursday), when drinks and snacks are all ¥800. You can also sample the Peninsula's famous afternoon tea up here.

✕ **Take a Break**

There's good ramen at Rokurinsha (p144), at the base of Tokyo Sky Tree.

STEP MOREU / SHUTTERSTOCK ©

Ghibli Museum

Even those uninitiated in the magical world of master animator Miyazaki Hayao will be enchanted by this museum dedicated to him and his works. Fans won't want to leave.

Great For...

☑ Don't Miss

The small theatre where original animated shorts – which can only be seen here! – are screened.

Get to Know Ghibli

If you've seen a Ghibli movie, odds are it was 2001's *Spirited Away,* which won the Academy Award for Best Animated Feature (and remains the only Japanese animated film and only hand-drawn film ever to win). Here's a chance to further explore Ghibli's world: inside the museum is an imagined workshop filled with the kinds of books and artworks that inspire Ghibli's creator Miyazaki Hayao, as well as vintage machines from animation's history. Miyazaki designed this museum himself, and it's redolent of the dreamy, vaguely steampunk atmosphere that makes his animations so enchanting.

Meet Old Friends & New

The Ghibli Museum rewards curiosity and play: peer through a small window,

❶ Need to Know

ジブリ美術館; www.ghibli-museum.jp; 1-1-83 Shimo-Renjaku, Mitaka-shi; adult ¥1000, child ¥100-700; ⏱10am-6pm, closed Tue; 🚃JR Sōbu-Chūō line to Mitaka, south exit

✕ Take a Break

Takeaway-tea spot Uni Stand (p137) is a short walk from the museum.

★ Top Tip

Shuttle buses (round trip/one way ¥320/210; every 20 minutes) depart for the museum from bus stop no 9 outside the south exit of Mitaka Station.

for example, and you'll see little soot sprites (as seen in *Spirited Away*). A spiral staircase leads to a purposefully overgrown rooftop terrace with a 5m-tall statue of the Robot Soldier from *Laputa* (Castle in the Sky; 1986). A highlight for children (sorry grown-ups!) is a giant, plush replica of the cat bus from the classic *My Neighbor Totoro* (1988) that kids can climb on.

Getting Tickets

Tickets must be purchased in advance and you must choose the exact time and date you plan to visit. They are limited and go fast (especially during the summer school holidays). You can purchase them up to three months in advance from a travel agent. Otherwise get them up to a month in advance from the (somewhat tricky, Japanese-only) kiosks inside Lawson convenience stores. Both options are explained in detail on the website, where you will also find a useful map. Tickets are non-transferable; you may be asked to show ID.

Inokashira-kōen

The Ghibli Museum is on the western edge of **Inokashira-kōen** (井の頭公園; www.kensetsu.metro.tokyo.jp/seibuk/inokashira/index.html; 1-18-31 Gotenyama, Musashino-shi; 🚃JR Sōbu-Chūō line to Kichijōji, Kōen exit), one of Tokyo's best parks. You can walk through the park to or from the museum in about 30 minutes, using Kichijōji Station (one stop before Mitaka on the JR Sōbu-Chūō). Inokashira-kōen has a big pond flanked by woodsy strolling paths. Don't miss the shrine here to the goddess Benzaiten, one of Japan's eight lucky gods. There are a few cafes and restaurants in the park, too.

TOOYKRUB / SHUTTERSTOCK ©

Imperial Palace

Take a tour of the leafy grounds of the imperial family's residence, or stroll along the ancient moat and climb an old castle keep in the garden.

The Imperial Palace is home to Emperor Akihito and Empress Michiko. The sprawling grounds occupy the site of the original Edo-jō, the Tokugawa shogunate's castle when they ruled the land. In its heyday this was the largest fortress in the world.

Palace Tours

Most of the 3.4 sq km of the complex are off-limits, as this is the emperor's home, but you can join one of the free tours organised by the Imperial Household Agency to see a small part of the inner compound. Tours (lasting around 1¼ hours) run at 10am and 1.30pm usually Tuesday through to Saturday, but not on public holidays nor afternoons from late July through to the end of August. See the website for a more detailed schedule.

Great For...

☑ Don't Miss

Climbing on the castle ruins in the Imperial Palace East Garden.

Statue of Kusunoki Masashige

AOR_SKYNOTLIMIT / SHUTTERSTOCK ©

❶ Need to Know

皇居; Kōkyo; Map p250; ☎03-5223-8071; http://sankan.kunaicho.go.jp/english/guide/koukyo.html; 1 Chiyoda, Chiyoda-ku; tours usually 10am & 1.30pm Tue-Sat; Ⓢ Chiyoda line to Ōtemachi, exits C13b & C10) FREE

✕ Take a Break

Not far from Nijū-bashi, Rose Bakery Marunouchi (p122) does light lunches, coffee and cake.

★ Top Tip

If you're joining the tour, remember to bring your passport and to pick up the free English audio headset.

Reservations are taken – via the website, phone or by post – up to a month in advance. Alternatively, show up at least 30 minutes before the tour at the tour office at the **Kikyō-mon** (桔梗門; Map p250) – if there is space you'll be able to register and take part. Bring photo ID.

Imperial Palace Plaza

If you're not on the tour, head instead to **Imperial Palace Plaza** (Map p250; Ⓢ Hibiya line to Hibiya, exit B6), a grassy park that is open to the public. This is the spot from which to take in the famous view of two palace bridges: **Megane-bashi** and **Nijū-bashi**. Behind the bridges rises the Edo-era **Fushimi-yagura** (伏見櫓; Map p250) watchtower, part of the original castle.

Imperial Palace East Garden

Crafted from part of the original castle compound, the **Imperial Palace East Garden** (東御苑; Kōkyo Higashi-gyoen; Map p250; ☻9am-4pm Nov-Feb, to 4.30pm Mar–mid-Apr, Sep & Oct, to 5pm mid-Apr–Aug, closed Mon & Fri year-round) FREE has been open to the public since 1968. Here you can get up-close views of the massive stones used to build the castle walls and even climb the ruins of one of the keeps, off the upper Honmaru lawn. Entry is free, but the number of visitors at any one time is limited, so it never feels crowded.

Free two-hour guided walking tours of the East Garden are offered on Wednesday, Saturday and Sunday; meet at the JNTO Tourist Information Center (p233) before 1pm.

Cycling the Grounds

Every Sunday (bar rainy days), 150 free bicycles are provided for use along the 3.3km **Imperial Palace cycling course** (パレスサイクリングコース; Map p250; www.jbpi.or.jp/english/pc1.html; Babasakimon Police Box; ⏰10am-3pm Sun; Ⓢ Chiyoda line to Nijūbashi-mae, exit 2) between Iwaida Bridge and Hirakawa-mon. Bikes are given on a first-come, first-served basis and can be picked up next to the Babasakimon police box.

Kitanomaru-koen

Split from the Imperial Palace and the East Garden by part of the moat and the city expressway, leafy **Kitanomaru-kōen** (北の丸公園; Map p250; www.env.go.jp/garden/kokyogaien/english/index.html; Ⓢ Hanzōmon line to Kudanshita, exit 2) is home to several

museums. The park's northern gate **Tayasu-mon** (田安門; Map p250), dates from 1636, making it the oldest existing gate to the old castle.

National Museum of Modern Art (MOMAT)   Museum

(国立近代美術館; Kokuritsu Kindai Bijutsukan; Map p250; ☎03-5777-8600; www.momat.go.jp/english; 3-1 Kitanomaru-kōen, Chiyoda-ku; adult/student ¥430/130, extra for special exhibitions; ⏰10am-5pm Tue-Thu, Sat & Sun, to 8pm Fri; Ⓢ Tōzai line to Takebashi, exit 1b) The museum has regularly changing displays from its superb collection of more than 12,000 works by local and international artists; these are shown on floors 2 to 4. Special exhibitions are mounted on the ground floor. All pieces date from the Meiji period onward and impart a sense of how modern Japan has

Kitanomaru-kōen

developed through portraits, photography, contemporary sculptures and video works.

Crafts Gallery · Museum

(東京国立近代美術館 工芸館; Map p250; www.momat.go.jp/english; 1 Kitanomaru-kōen, Chiyoda-ku; adult/child ¥210/70, 1st Sun of month free; ⊙10am-5pm Tue-Sun; ⓈTōzai line to Takebashi, exit 1b) Housed in a vintage red-brick building, this annexe of MOMAT stages excellent changing exhibitions of *mingei* (folk crafts): ceramics, lacquerware, bamboo, textiles, dolls and much more. The building was once the headquarters of the imperial guards and was rebuilt after its destruction in WWII.

What's Nearby?

Intermediatheque · Museum

(Map p250; ☑03-5777-8600; www.inter mediatheque.jp; 2nd & 3rd fl, JP Tower, 2-7-2 Marunouchi, Chiyoda-ku; ⊙11am-6pm Sun & Tue-Thu, to 8pm Fri & Sat; ⓇJR Yamanote line to Tokyo, Marunouchi exit) **FREE** Dedicated to interdisciplinary experimentation, Intermediatheque cherry picks from the vast collection of the University of Tokyo (Tōdai) to craft a fascinating, contemporary museum experience. Go from viewing the best ornithological taxidermy collection in Japan to a giant pop-art print or the beautifully encased skeleton of a dinosaur.

Tokyo International Forum · Architecture

(東京国際フォーラム; Map p250; ☑03-5221-9000; www.t-i-forum.co.jp; 3-5-1 Marunouchi, Chiyoda-ku; ⓇJR Yamanote line to Yūrakuchō, central exit) **FREE** This architectural marvel designed by Rafael Viñoly houses a convention and arts centre, with eight auditoriums and a spacious courtyard in which concerts and events are held. The eastern wing looks like a glass ship plying the urban waters; take the lift to the 7th floor and look down on the tiny people below. Also look out for the statue of Ōta Dōkan, the samurai who first built the Edo Castle in 1457.

Tokyo Station · Landmark

(東京駅; Map p250; www.tokyostationcity.com/en; 1-9 Marunouchi, Chiyoda-ku; ⓇJR lines to Tokyo Station) Tokyo Station celebrated its centenary in 2014 with a major renovation and expansion. Kingo Tatsuno's original elegant brick building on the Marunouchi side has been expertly restored to include domes faithful to the original design, decorated inside with relief sculptures.

WIBOWO RUSLI / GETTY IMAGES ©

> ☑ **Don't Miss**
> The National Museum of Modern Art's 'Room with a View', which offers a panoramic view of the Imperial Palace East Garden.

> ✕ **Take a Break**
> Wind down the day with a drink on the terrace at So Tired (p174).

Akihabara Pop Culture

Venture into the belly of the pop culture beast that is Akihabara, the centre of Tokyo's otaku (geek) subculture. But you don't have to obsess about manga or anime to enjoy this quirky neighbourhood: with its neon-bright electronics stores, retro arcades and cosplay (costume play) cafes, it's equal parts sensory overload, cultural mind-bender and just plain fun.

Great For...

ℹ Need to Know

The JR Yamanote and Sōbu lines stop at Akihabara; Electric Town exit is the most convenient.

★ **Top Tip**

Head to Chūō-dōri where anime fans dressed as their favourite characters congregate on Sunday afternoons.

Shopping

Mandarake Complex   Manga, Anime

(まんだらけコンプレックス; Map p254; www.
mandarake.co.jp; 3-11-2 Soto-Kanda, Chiyoda-ku;
◷noon-8pm; ℝJR Yamanote line to Akihabara,
Electric Town exit) When *otaku* (geeks) dream
of heaven, it probably looks a lot like this
giant go-to store for manga and anime.
Eight storeys are piled high with comic
books and DVDs, action figures and cell art
just for starters. The 5th floor, in all its pink
splendour, is devoted to women's comics,
while the 4th floor is for men.

Yodobashi Akiba   Electronics

(ヨドバシカメラ Akiba; Map p254; www.
yodobashi-akiba.com; 1-1 Kanda Hanaoka-chō,
Chiyoda-ku; ◷9.30am-10pm; ℝJR Yamanote
line to Akihabara, Shōwa-tōriguchi exit) This is
the monster branch of Yodobashi Camera

where many locals shop. It has eight floors
of electronics, cameras, toys, appliances,
CDs and DVDs on the 7th-floor branch of
Tower Records; it even has restaurants.
Ask about export models and VAT-free
purchases.

Eating & Drinking

@Home Cafe   Cafe

(@ほぉ〜むカフェ; Map p254; www.cafe-athome.
com; 4th-7th fl, 1-11-4 Soto-Kanda, Chiyoda-ku;
drinks from ¥500; ◷11.30am-10pm Mon-Fri,
10.30am-10pm Sat & Sun; ℝJR Yamanote line
to Akihabara, Electric Town exit) 'Maid cafes'
with *kawaii* (cute) waitresses, dressed as
saucy French or prim Victorian maids, are
a stock in trade of Akiba. @Home is one of
the more 'wholesome' of them. You'll be
welcomed as *go-shujinsama* (master) or
o-jōsama (miss) the minute you enter. The

Arcade in Akihabara

maids serve drinks and dishes, such as curried rice, topped with smiley faces.

N3331 Cafe

(Map p254; ☑03-5295-2788; http://n3331.com; 2nd fl, mAAch ecute, 1-25-4 Kanda-Sudachō, Chiyoda-ku; ⊙11am-10.30pm Mon-Sat, to 8.30pm Sun; 🚇JR Yamamote line to Akihabara, Electric Town exit) Climb the original white-tile-clad stairs to the former platform of Mansei-bashi Station to find this ultimate trainspotters' cafe. Through floor-to-ceiling windows, watch commuter trains stream by while you sip on coffee, craft beer or sake and enjoy snacks.

✗ Take a Break

For a change of pace head to stylish mall mAAch Ecute (p164).

VASSAMON ANANSUKKASEM / SHUTTERSTOCK ©

Sights & Activities

Akiba Kart Scenic Drive

(アキバカート; Map p254; ☑03-6206-4752; http://akibanavi.net; 2-4-6 Soto-kanda, Chiyoda-ku; 1hr from ¥2700; ⊙10am-8pm; 🚇JR Yamanote line to Akihabara, Electric Town exit) Naturally, it was a no-brainer for this *cosplay* plus go-karting operation to set up in Akiba. Reserve in advance and make sure you have an international driver's licence handy if you wish to motor around Tokyo in a go-kart dressed as a character from *Super Mario Brothers*.

Super Potato Retro-kan Arcade

(スーパーポテトレトロ館; Map p254; www.superpotato.com; 1-11-2 Soto-kanda, Chiyoda-ku; ⊙11am-8pm Mon-Fri, from 10am Sat & Sun; 🚇JR Yamanote line to Akihabara, Electric Town exit) Are you a gamer keen to sample retro computer games? On the 5th floor of this store specialising in used video games, there's a retro video arcade where you can get your hands on some old-fashioned consoles at a bargain ¥100 per game.

P.A.R.M.S Live Performance

(Map p254; ☑012-075-9835; www.pasela.co.jp; 7th fl, Pasela Resorts Akihabara-Denkigai, 1-13-2 Soto-kanda, Chiyoda-ku; admission incl 1 drink Mon-Fri ¥1500, Sat & Sun ¥3500; ⊙shows 5.30pm & 8.15pm Mon-Fri, 10.30am Sat & Sun; 🚇JR Yamanote line to Akihabara, Electric Town exit) Shows by the girl group Kamen Joshi – singing and dancing young women wearing cute outfits and hockey masks – are all the rage at this live-music show in the Pasela Resort's karaoke emporium. It's a chance to swing around a light sabre (handed out to audience members) in a thoroughly Akiba night out.

★Top Tip

Picking up an English map at **Akiba Info** (Map p254; ☑080-3413-4800; www.animecenter.jp; 2nd fl, Akihabara UDX Bldg, 4-14-1 Soto-Kanda, Chiyoda-ku; ⊙11am-5.30pm Tue, Wed & Fri-Sun; 🛜) the helpful staff here speak English. For more Akihabara shopping options, see p164, for eating, see p138 and for entertainment, see p194.

PAOLO GIANTI / SHUTTERSTOCK ©

Rikugi-en

Tokyo's most beautiful garden is hidden in the city's north. Built by a feudal lord in 1702, with a large central pond, it was designed to reflect the aesthetic of traditional Waka poetry.

Great For...

☑ **Don't Miss**

The cherry trees in spring and the maples in autumn.

Japanese Pleasure Gardens

Rikugi-en is a classic example of a Japanese *kaiyū* ('varied pleasures') garden. This style features many smaller gardens within the larger one and teahouses surrounding a central pond. It is meant to be explored on foot and offers the visitor a variety of changing scenes, many with literary allusions. The name 'Rikugi-en' refers to the six principles of classical poetry.

Poetic Views

The bridge, **Togetsukyō**, created from two huge stone slabs, references a poem about a crane flying over a moonlit field. Stone markers around the garden make note of other scenic views, many of which reference famous works of Japanese or

❶ Need to Know

六義園; ☎03-3941-2222; http://teien.
tokyo-park.or.jp/en/rikugien; 6-16-3
Hon-Komagome, Bunkyō-ku; adult/child
¥300/free; ⏰9am-5pm; 🚃JR Yamanote line
to Komagome, south exit

✕ Take a Break

The garden has a teahouse and also a
cafe near the entrance.

★ Top Tip

Pair a trip to Rikugien with one to
the Tokyo National Museum in Ueno;
It's just five stops away on the JR
Yamanote line.

Chinese literature. Climb to the top of the
Fujishiro-tōge, a hill named after a real one
in Wakayama Prefecture, for panoramic
views across the garden.

Teahouses

Rikugi-en has two vintage teahouses, where
you can sit and rest, taking in the scenery.
The **Tsutsuji-chaya** dates to the Meiji
period and is perfectly primed for viewing
the maples in autumn. The **Takimi-chaya**
is perched on the edge of the stream where
you can enjoy the view of a mini waterfall
over rocks and giant koi (carp) swimming
in the water.

While it doesn't have the same historic
pedigree as the other two, **Fukiage-chaya**
is attractive all the same and provides a
beautiful view of the central pond as you

sip *matcha* (powered green tea; ¥510)
and enjoy a seasonal *wagashi* (Japanese
sweet), alfresco.

Seasonal Blooms

Something is almost always in bloom
at Rikugi-en, though the garden is most
famous for its maple leaves, which turn
bright red usually around late November
or early December. During this time, the
park stays open until 9pm and the trees are
illuminated after sunset.

In early spring you can catch plum
blossoms, followed by the flowering of the
magnificent weeping cherry tree near the
entrance. Even in winter the gardens are
worth visiting to note interesting features
such as the ropes strung from the pruned
pine trees that protect their branches from
heavy snowfall.

Shibuya Crossing

This is the Tokyo you've dreamed about and seen in movies: the frenetic pace, the mind-boggling crowds, the twinkling neon lights and the giant video screens beaming larger-than-life celebrities over the streets.

Great For...

☑ Don't Miss

The crossing at night, all lit up.

The Scramble

Rumoured to be the busiest intersection in the world, Shibuya Crossing is like a giant beating heart, sending people in all directions with every pulsing light change. Perhaps no other place says 'Welcome to Tokyo' better than this.

Hundreds of people – and at peak times said to be over 1000 people – cross at a time, coming from all directions at once yet still managing to dodge each other with a practised, nonchalant agility. Then, in the time that it takes for the light to go from red to green again, all corners have replenished their stock of people – like a video on loop.

The intersection is most impressive after dark on a Friday or Saturday night, when the crowds pouring out of the station are dressed in their finest and neon-lit by the

Jingū-dōri
Shibuya
Shibuya Crossing
Miyamasu-zaka

Need to Know

渋谷スクランブル交差点; Shibuya Scramble; Map p246; JR Yamanote line to Shibuya, Hachikō exit

Take a Break

Nearby d47 Shokudō (p129) has nice views over the neighbourhood.

★ Top Tip

The Starbucks on the 2nd floor of the Q-front building across the street has views over the crossing.

signs above. (Rainy days have their own visual appeal, with their sea of umbrellas.) The rhythms here are, however, tied to the train station and after the last train pulls out for the night, the intersection becomes eerily quiet.

What's Nearby?

Shibuya Center-gai Area

(渋谷センター街; Shibuya Sentā-gai; Map p246; JR Yamanote line to Shibuya, Hachikō exit) Shibuya's main drag is closed to cars and chock-a-block with fast-food joints and high-street fashion shops. At night, lit bright as day, with a dozen competing soundtracks (coming from who knows where), wares spilling onto the streets, shady touts in sunglasses and strutting teens, it feels like a huge block party.

Hachikō Statue Statue

(ハチ公像; Map p246; Hachikō Plaza; JR Yamanote line to Shibuya, Hachikō exit) Meet Tokyo's most famous dog, Hachikō, an Akita who came to Shibuya Station every day to meet his master, a professor, returning from work. The professor died in 1925, but Hachikō kept coming to the station until his own death 10 years later. The story became legend and a small statue was erected in the dog's memory in front of Shibuya Station.

Myth of Tomorrow Public Art

(明日の神話; Asu no Shinwa; Map p246; JR Yamanote line to Shibuya, Hachikō exit) Okamoto Tarō's mural, *Myth of Tomorrow* (1967), was commissioned by a Mexican luxury hotel, but went missing two years later. It finally turned up in 2003 and, in 2008, the 30m-long work, which depicts the atomic bomb exploding over Hiroshima, was installed inside Shibuya Station. It's on the 2nd floor, on the way to the Inokashira line.

DAJ / GETTY IMAGES ©

Karaoke in Tokyo

Nightlife trends may come and go, but karaoke never goes out of style and even the most jaded Tokyoite can be cajoled into letting loose. Grab a mike and let your inner diva shine.

Karaoke (カラオケ; pronounced kah-rah-oh-kay) isn't just about singing: it's an excuse to let loose, a bonding ritual, a reason to keep the party going past the last train and a way to kill time until the first one starts in the morning. When words fail, it's a way to express yourself: are you the type to sing the latest J-pop hit (dance moves included) or do you go for an Okinawan folk ballad? It doesn't matter if you're not a good singer, so long as you've got heart.

Karaoke Basics

In Japan, karaoke is usually sung in a private room among friends (though some bars have karaoke as well). Admission is usually charged per person per half-hour. Sign up at the counter and staff will direct you to a room. Most offer *nomi-hōdai* (all-you-can-drink) plans, which allow you

Great For...

☑ Don't Miss

Singing the night away, until the first trains start running in the morning.

ℹ Need to Know

Karaoke parlours can be found near any major train station – and especially in nightlife districts such as Shinjuku, Shibuya and Roppongi. They're always brightly lit and easy to spot.

✕ Take a Break

Food and drinks can be ordered by the phone in the room and are brought to the door.

★ Top Tip

Karaoke rates fluctuate by day and time; the cheapest time to go is on a weekday afternoon. For more drinking and karaoke options, see p168.

to sing and drink uninhibited for hours. Rooms generally cost around ¥700 per person per hour.

To choose a song, use the touch-screen device to search by artist or title; most have an English function and plenty of English songs to choose from.

Karaoke Parlours

The big chains are the way to go, as they have the best song lists. These include: Shidax (シダックス), Karaoke-kan (カラオケ館), Pasela (パセラ) Big Echo (ビッグエコー) and Uta Hiroba (歌広場).

Shidax Village   Karaoke

(シダックスビレッジ; Map p246; ☎03-3461-9356; 1-12-13 Jinnan, Shibuya-ku; per person per 30min from ¥400; ◎11am-5am Sun-Thu, to 6am Fri & Sat; ⓡJR Yamanote line to Shibuya, Hachikō exit) Shidax is a step up from the

other karaoke chains, with roomier booths and hundreds of English songs. Note that prices go up by ¥50 to ¥100 on weekends and during holidays; if you stay longer than two hours (which often happens) the 'free time' plan (フリータイム; ¥1950, until 5am) is a good deal; with *nomihōdai* (all-you-can-drink; 飲み放題) it's ¥4950. Nonsmoking rooms available.

Karaoke-kan   Karaoke

(カラオケ館; Map p246; www.karaokekan.jp; 25-6 Udagawa-chō, Shibuya-ku; per 30min Mon-Thu ¥535, Fri-Sun ¥635; ◎11am-6am; ⓐ; ⓡJR Yamanote Line to Shibuya, Hachikō exit) This branch of a generic national karaoke chain was immortalised as a location in the film *Lost in Translation*. Another draw: the rack of costumes in the lobby you can borrow for free. Two-hour all-you-can-drink (*nomihōdai*; 飲み放題) plan: ¥3780. During the week before 7pm rates drop to ¥120 per 30 minutes.

National Museum of Emerging Science & Innovation (Miraikan)

COWARDLION / SHUTTERSTOCK ©

Tokyo Bay

Standing among the skyscrapers of central Tokyo, it's easy to forget that this is a city on the water. Come to Tokyo Bay for the museums, amusement parks, bay cruises and waterfront vistas.

Odaiba

Odaiba is a collection of artificial islands on Tokyo Bay tethered to the mainland by the 798m Rainbow Bridge. Much of the area that forms the touristed district was developed in the 1990s as a family-friendly leisure and entertainment zone.

National Museum of Emerging Science & Innovation (Miraikan)   Museum

(未来館; www.miraikan.jst.go.jp; 2-3-6 Aomi, Kōtō-ku; adult/child ¥620/210; ◎10am-5pm Wed-Mon; ◉Yurikamome line to Telecom Center) *Miraikan* means 'hall of the future', and exhibits here present the science and technology that will (possibly!) shape the years to come. Lots of hands-on displays make this a great place for kids, while a new multilingual smartphone app makes

Great For...

☑ **Don't Miss**

Taking a night cruise to see the lit-up shoreline from the bay.

Shibaura Futō
Tokyo Bay
Rainbow Bridge
Tokyo Joypolis
ChihiraJunco
Kokusai-tenjijō-seimon
Tennōzu-Isle
National Museum of Emerging Science & Innovation (Miraikan)

❶ Need to Know

The JR Rinkai line and the Yurikamome line run to destinations on Tokyo Bay.

✗ Take a Break

All of Odaiba's malls have food courts. The best one is in the Diver City mall.

★ Top Tip

Take the Yurikamome line from Shimbashi; the elevated tracks wend in between skyscrapers before doing a loop to reach Rainbow Bridge.

a game out of visiting. Don't miss the demonstrations of humanoid robot ASIMO and the lifelike android Otonaroid. The Gaia dome theatre/planetarium (adult/child ¥300/100) has an English audio option and is popular; book online one week in advance.

Tokyo Joypolis   Amusement Park

(東京ジョイポリス; http://tokyo-joypolis.com; 3rd-5th fl, DECKS Tokyo Beach, 1-6-1 Daiba, Minato-ku; adult/child ¥800/300, all-rides passport ¥4300/3300, passport after 5pm ¥3300/2300; ☻10am-10pm; ◳Yurikamome line to Odaiba Kaihin-kōen) This indoor amusement park is stacked with virtual-reality attractions and adult thrill rides, such as the video-enhanced Halfpipe Canyon; there are rides for little ones, too. Separate admission and individual ride tickets (¥500 to ¥800) are available, but if you plan to go

on more than half a dozen attractions, the unlimited 'passport' makes sense.

ChihiraJunco   Robot

(地平ジュンこ; 3rd fl, Aqua City, 1-7-1 Daiba, Minato-ku; ☻11am-9pm; ◳Yurikamome line to Odaiba Kaihin-kōen) FREE The future is here. Maybe. ChihiraJunco is a demure lady android created by Toshiba who has her own information counter adjacent to the people-staffed information counter at the Aqua City shopping mall. At the time of research, she was not (yet?) able to answer spoken questions; however, she does answer questions entered into the touch panel – in Japanese, English or Chinese.

Tennōzu Isle

Tennōzu Isle, another of Tokyo Bay's artificial islands, spent the 20th century as a warehouse district. It still is – just now some of those warehouses contain breweries and galleries.

Archi-Depot   Gallery

(建築倉庫; Kenchiku Sōko; ☏03-5769-2133; http://archi-depot.com; Warehouse Terrada,

2-6-10 Higashi-Shinagawa, Shinagawa-ku; adult/child ¥1000/500; ⏱11am-9pm Tue-Sun; 🚆Rinkai line to Tennōzu Isle, exit B) This is brilliant: a facility that lets architects store the miniature models they make to conceptualise buildings (thus preserving them) and the public to see them up close. Many of the big names of Japanese architecture are represented here (Ban Shigeru, Kuma Kengo).

TY Harbor Brewery   American ¥¥

(☎03-5479-4555; www.tyharborbrewing.co.jp; 2-1-3 Higashi-Shinagawa, Shinagawa-ku; lunch set meal ¥1200-1700, dinner mains from ¥1700; ⏱11.30am-2pm & 5.30-10pm; ➡🅿; ⑤Rinkai line to Tennōzu Isle, exit B) In a former warehouse on the waterfront, TY Harbor serves up excellent burgers, steaks and crab cakes and offers views of the canals around Tennōzu Isle. It also brews its own beer on the premises and is a favourite brunch spot for expats. Call ahead to book a seat on the terrace.

Pigment   Arts & Crafts

(☎03-5781-9550; https://pigment.tokyo; Terrada Harbor One Bldg., 2-5-5 Higashi-Shinagawa, Shinagawa-ku; ⏱11am-8pm, closed Mon & Thu; 🚆Rinkai line to Tennōzu Isle, exit B) This is an art-supply store to make you go weak in the knees: the walls are lined with vials of pigments – including the crushed mineral pigments used in traditional Japanese painting – in shades from vermilion to *matcha* (green tea).

Bay Cruises

The low-slung wooden boats, bedecked with lanterns, that you see on Tokyo Bay

View of Tokyo Bay at dusk

are called *yakatabune* and they've been a Tokyo tradition since the days of Edo. They're usually used for private parties, which typically include all-you-can-eat-and-drink banquets and karaoke.

Tsukishima Monja Yakatabune
Cruise

(月島もんじゃ屋形船; ☑03-3533-6699; www.4900yen.com; 2-6-3 Shin-Kiba, Kōtō-ku; per person from ¥5000; ⑤ Yūrakuchō line to Shin-Kiba, main exit) Two-hour (day and night) cruises around Tokyo Bay on a *yakatabune* (traditional pleasure boat), with free-flowing beer and all-you-can eat *monja-yaki* (a savoury, scrambled batter-style dish): this

---

> ### ★ Top Tip
> To keep a night out in Tokyo Bay going till dawn, head to Ageha (p183), one of Asia's largest clubs.

IMAGE PROVIDED BY DUANE WALKER / GETTY IMAGES ©

---

is the cheapest *yakatabune* package around and the only one that regularly lets you book for as few as two people. Reservations essential; you'll need a Japanese speaker to help book.

Jicoo the Floating Bar
Cocktail Bar

(ジークザフローティングバー; ☑0120-049-490; www.jicoofloatingbar.com; cover from ¥2600; ⏰8-10.30pm Thu-Sat; ⓇYurikamome line to Hinode or Odaiba Kaihin-kōen) For a few nights a week, the futuristic cruise-boat *Himiko*, designed by manga and anime artist Leiji Matsumoto, morphs into this floating bar. Board on the hour at Hinode pier and the half-hour at Odaiba Kaihin-koen. The evening-long 'floating pass' usually includes some sort of live music; check the schedule online as events can drive up the price.

What's Nearby?

Tokyo Disney Resort
Amusement Park

(東京ディズニーリゾート; ☑domestic calls 0570-00-8632, from overseas +81-45-330-5211; www.tokyodisneyresort.co.jp; 1-1 Maihama, Urayasu-shi, Chiba-ken; 1-day ticket for 1 park adult/child ¥7400/4800, after 6pm ¥4200; ⏰varies by season; ⓇJR Keiyō line to Maihama) Here you'll find not only Tokyo Disneyland, modelled after the one in California, but also Tokyo DisneySea, an original theme park with seven 'ports' evoking locales real and imagined (the Mediterranean and 'Mermaid Lagoon', for example). Disney-Sea targets a more grown-up crowd, but still has many attractions for kids. Both resorts get extremely crowded, especially on weekends and during summer holidays. Book admission tickets online to save time.

> ### ⓘ Local Knowledge
> Waterfront park **Odaiba Kaihin-kōen** is popular with amateur photographers working to perfect their city-by-night shot.

DINING OUT

Teahouses, conveyor-belt sushi
restaurants and *izakaya*

日進商事

禁煙

Dining Out

Tokyo has a vibrant and cosmopolitan dining scene and a strong culture of eating out – popular restaurants are packed most nights of the week. Best of all, you can get superlative meals on any budget. Tokyo foodies take pride in what they like to think of as their 'boutique' dining scene. Rather than offer long menus of elaborate dishes, many of the best restaurants make just a few things – and sometimes even just one! Sushi shops make sushi, tempura shops make tempura. A restaurant that does too much might be suspect: how can it compare to a speciality shop that has been honing its craft for three generations?

In This Section

Marunouchi & Nihombashi 122

Ginza & Tsukiji 123

Roppongi & Akasaka............................126

Ebisu & Meguro....................................127

Shibuya & Shimo-Kitazawa................129

Harajuku & Aoyama 133

Kōenji, Kichijōji & West Tokyo............ 135

Shinjuku & Ikebukuro 137

Kagurazaka, Kanda & Akihabara 138

Ueno & Yanesen 142

Asakusa & Ryōgoku............................ 143

Price Ranges

The following price ranges represent the cost of a meal for one person.

¥ less than ¥2000

¥¥ ¥2000–¥5000

¥¥¥ more than ¥5000

Tipping

Tipping is not customary, though most high-end restaurants will add a 10% service charge to the bill.

Ueno & Yanesen
Classic Japanese restaurants with heaps of atmosphere (p142)

Asakusa & Ryōgoku
Unpretentious Japanese fare, old-school charm and modest prices (p143)

Shinjuku & Ikebukuro
High-end restaurants, under-the-tracks dives and everything in-between (p137)

Kōenji, Kichijōji & West Tokyo
Nothing fancy, but lots of local faves doing Japanese classics (p135)

Kagurazaka, Kanda & Akihabara
Historic eateries and comfort food (p138)

Harajuku & Aoyama
Fashionable midrange restaurants and excellent lunch spots and cafes (p133)

Marunouchi & Nihombashi
Lunch options galore and classic Japanese cuisine (p122)

Roppongi & Akasaka
Splurge-worthy restaurants and lots of international cuisine (p126)

Ginza & Tsukiji
Upscale restaurants and the best sushi in the city (p123)

Shibuya & Shimo-Kitazawa
Lively, inexpensive *izakaya* and some hidden gems (p129)

Odaiba & Tokyo Bay

Tokyo Bay

Ebisu & Meguro
Cosmopolitan and hip, with excellent options for all budgets (p127)

Best Blogs

Tokyo Food Page (www.bento.com) Listings and review site edited by a *Japan Times* dining columnist.

Food Sake Tokyo (www.foodsaketokyo.com) Blog penned by a local food writer with excellent recommendations.

Ramen Adventures (www.ramen adventures.com) The best English-language ramen blog.

Classic Dishes

Yakitori Nominally grilled chicken skewers, but in practice a huge variety of meat, seafood and veg salted or sauced and set to grill over hot coals.

Tonkatsu Tender pork cutlets battered and deep-fried, served with a side of grated cabbage.

Tempura Seafood and vegetables deep-fried in a fluffy, light batter.

The Best...

Experience Tokyo's best restaurants and cuisines

Yakitori

Bird Land (p124) Upscale *yakitori* from free-range, heirloom birds.

Yūrakuchō Sanchoku Inshokugai (p124) Lantern-lit alleyway brimming with stalls (and diners).

Tetchan (p137) An old market joint restyled by architect Kuma Kengo.

Kōenji Gādo-shita (p137) String of *yakitori* offerings beneath the railway lines.

Izakaya

Shirube (p131) Loud, lively and hip, serving creative fusion dishes.

Donjaca (p38) An *izakaya* straight out of the Shōwa era.

Okajōki (p137) Sit at the counter around the huge hearth and watch the chefs work their magic.

Japanese Cuisine

Innsyoutei (p143) Lovely place to eat *kaiseki*-style in Ueno-kōen.

Kado (p140) Classic home cooking in an old house.

Kozue (p138) Exquisite Japanese dishes and stunning night views over Shinjuku.

Maisen (p133) Delectable *tonkatsu* (deep-fried pork cutlets; pictured above) in a former bathhouse.

Teahouses

Cha Ginza (p123) Stylish contemporary version of a teahouse in the heart of Ginza.

Uni Stand (p137) Sample single-origin teas and carefully crafted *matcha* lattes.

Imasa (p138) Sip tea in a lovely old wooden house and protected cultural property.

Jugetsudo (p123) Stop by in the morning for a tea-tasting experience.

Torindō (p142) Stroll Ueno-kōen, then stop here for *matcha* and sweets.

For Seafood

Yanmo (p135) Extravagant spreads of seafood, raw and grilled.

Numazukō (p138) Tokyo's best conveyor-belt sushi restaurant.

Trattoria Tsukiji Paradiso! (p124) Linguine and clams instead of sushi at Tsukiji Market.

Kaikaya (p132) Surfboards on the wall and seafood on the menu.

For the best sushi in Tokyo, see p54.

For Classic Dishes

Tonki (p127) *Tonkatsu* raised to an art.

Ethiopia (p138) A classic Jimbōchō curry shop.

Daikokuya (p144) Down-home tempura in Asakusa.

Harajuku Gyōza-rō (p133) Addictive *gyōza* (dumplings) served all night.

For Old Tokyo Atmosphere

Hantei (p142) Deep-fried skewers in a century-old heritage house.

Otafuku (p145) Charming 100-year-old *oden* restaurant.

Omoide-yokochō (p137; pictured above) Atmospheric *yakitori* stalls near the train tracks.

★ Lonely Planet's Top Choices

Tofuya-Ukai (p127) Handmade tofu becomes haute cuisine.

Kyūbey (p57) Rarefied Ginza sushi at its finest.

Shinsuke (p143) Century-old *izakaya* adored by sake aficionados.

Kikunoi (p127) Gorgeous *kaiseki* in the classic Kyoto style.

Tensuke (p135) Magical tempura from a master chef (and showman).

⊗ Marunouchi & Nihombashi

Hōnen Manpuku　Japanese ¥

(豊年萬福; Map p250; ☎03-3277-3330; www.
hounenmanpuku.jp; 1-8-16 Nihombashi-Muromachi,
Chūō-ku; mains ¥1280-1850; ⊗11.30am-2.30pm
& 5-11pm Mon-Sat, 5-10pm Sun; 🔘; Ⓢ Ginza line to
Mitsukoshimae, exit A1) Hōnen Manpuku's interior is dominated by giant *washi* (Japanese
handmade paper) lanterns, beneath which
patrons tuck into bargain-priced beef or pork
sukiyaki and other traditional dishes. Ingredients are sourced from gourmet retailers in
Nihombashi. Lunchtime set menus are great
value and there's a riverside terrace in the
warmer months.

Taimeiken　Japanese ¥

(たいめいけん; Map p250; ☎03-3271-2464;
www.taimeiken.co.jp; 1-12-10 Nihombashi, Chūō-
ku; lunch from ¥800, omelette ¥1950; ⊗11am-
8.30pm Mon-Sat, to 8pm Sun; 🔘; Ⓢ Ginza line
to Nihombashi, exit C5) *Yoshoku,* Western
cuisine adapted to Japanese tastes, has
been the draw here since 1931, in particular

its borscht and coleslaw (a bargain ¥50
each). For the food movie *Tampopo* (1985),
directed by Itami Jūzō, it created *Tampopo
omuraisu* (an omelette wrapped around
tomato-flavoured rice) and it's been a
signature dish ever since.

Nihonbashi Dashi Bar　Japanese ¥

(日本橋だし場　はなれ; Map p250; ☎03-
5205-8704; www.ninben.co.jp; 1st fl, Coredo
Muromachi 2-3-1 Nihombashi-Muromachi, Chūō-
ku; mains from ¥840, lunch/dinner set course
from ¥950/1500; ⊗11am-10pm; Ⓢ Ginza line to
Mitsukoshimae, exit A4) A key ingredient of the
stock *dashi* is flakes of *katsuobushi* (dried
bonito), which the Nihombashi-based
Ninben has been making and selling since
the Edo period. In this restaurant the
company showcases its product in myriad
delicious ways, including soups, salads and
rice dishes.

Rose Bakery Marunouchi　Bakery ¥

(ローズベーカリー　丸の内; Map p250; ☎03-
3212-1715; http://rosebakery.jp; Meiji-Yasada
Bldg, 2-1-1 Marunouchi, Chiyoda-ku; cakes &
quiches from ¥410, lunch set ¥1250; ⊗11am-7pm;

Oyakodon at Tamahide (p123)

🏛 📷; S Chiyoda line to Nijūbashimae, exit 3)
Tokyo has taken to Paris' Rose Bakery style
of dining. Branches of this delicious organic
cafe have popped up in this Comme des
Garçons boutique and others. Vegetarians
are well served here, as are those with a
sweet tooth.

100% Chocolate Cafe   Cafe ¥

(Map p250; 📞03-3273-3184; www.meiji.co.jp/
sweets/choco-cafe; 2-4-16 Kyōbashi, Chūō-ku;
🕐8am-8pm Mon-Fri, 11am-7pm Sat & Sun;
S Ginza line to Kyōbashi, exit 5) Meiji is one
of Japan's top confectionery companies
and this cafe, at its Tokyo headquarters,
showcases the brand's range of chocolate.
Fittingly the interior sports a ceiling that
mimics a slab of chocolate. Sample three
types of drinking chocolate for ¥500, then
peruse the scores of different flavoured
bars that you can take away.

Tamahide   Japanese ¥¥¥

(📞03-3668-7651; www.tamahide.co.jp; 1-17-1
Nihombashi-Ningyōchō, Chūō-ku; oyakodon from
¥1500, dinner set-course menu from ¥6800;
🕐11.30am-1pm daily, 5-10pm Mon-Fri, 4-10pm
Sat & Sun; S Hibiya line to Ningyōchō, exit A1)
For generations people have been lining up
outside this restaurant to try its signature
dish *oyakodon* – a sweet-savoury mix of
chicken, soy broth and egg, served over a
bowl of rice. It also has dishes with minced
chicken or duck and they're all delicious
and filling. Pay before you sit down at lunch.

⊗ Ginza & Tsukiji

Cha Ginza   Teahouse ¥

(茶 · 銀座; Map p250; 📞03-3571-1211; www.
uogashi-meicha.co.jp/shop/ginza; 5-5-6 Ginza,
Chūō-ku; 🕐11am-5pm, shop to 6pm Tue-Sun;
S Ginza line to Ginza, exit B3) At this slick
contemporary tea room, it costs ¥800 for
either a cup of perfectly prepared *matcha*
(green tea) and a small cake or two, or for
a choice of *sencha* (premium green tea).
Buy your token for tea at the shop on the
ground floor, which sells top-quality teas
from various growing regions in Japan.

🍴◎ Restaurants: What to Expect

When you enter a restaurant in Japan
the staff will likely all greet you with a
hearty '*Irasshai!*' (Welcome!). In all but
the most casual places, where you seat
yourself, the waiter or waitress will next
ask you '*Nan-mei sama?*' (How many
people?). Indicate the answer with your
fingers, which is what the Japanese
do. You may also be asked if you would
like to sit at a *zashiki* (low table on the
tatami), at a *tēburu* (table) or the *kauntā*
(counter). Once seated you will be given
an *o-shibori* (hot towel), a cup of tea or
water (this is free) and a menu.

   When your food arrives, it's the
custom to say '*Itadakimasu*' (literally 'I
will receive', but closer to 'bon appétit'
in meaning) before digging in. If a bill
hasn't already been placed on your
table, ask for it by catching your server's
eye and making a cross in the air (to
form a kind of 'x') with your index fingers. Payment is usually settled at the
counter. On your way out, it's polite to
say '*Gochisō-sama deshita*' (literally 'it
was a feast'; a respectful way of saying
you enjoyed the meal) to the staff.

Cafe de l'Ambre   Cafe ¥

(カフェ・ド・ランブル; Map p250; 📞03-3571-
1551; www.h6.dion.ne.jp/~lambre; 8-10-15 Ginza,
Chūō-ku; coffee from ¥650; 🕐noon-10pm Mon-
Sat, to 7pm Sun; 📷; R Ginza line to Ginza, exit A4)
The sign over the door here reads 'Coffee
Only' but, oh, what a selection. Sekiguchi
Ichiro started the business in 1948 and –
remarkably at the age of 100 – still runs it
himself, sourcing and roasting aged beans
from all over the world. It's dark, retro and
classic Ginza.

Jugetsudo   Teahouse ¥¥

(寿月堂; Map p250; 📞03-6278-7626; www.
jugetsudo.fr; 5th fl, Kabuki-za Tower, 4-12-15 Ginza,
Chūō-ku; 🕐10am-5.30pm; 📷; S Hibiya line to
Higashi-Ginza, exit 3) This venerable tea seller's

main branch is closer to Tsukiji, but this classy outlet in the Kabuki-za Tower has a Kengo Kuma–designed cafe where you can sample the various Japanese green teas, including *matcha*, along with food. Book for its tea-tasting experience (¥4000), which covers four different types of tea and runs from 10am to noon.

Trattoria Tsukiji Paradiso!
Italian ¥¥

(Map p250; ☏03-3545-5550; www.tsukiji-paradiso.com; 6-27-3 Tsukiji, Chūō-ku; mains ¥1500-3600; ◷11am-2pm & 6-10pm; ⑤Hibiya line to Tsukiji, exit 2) Paradise for food lovers, indeed. This charming, aqua-painted trattoria serves seafood pasta dishes that will make you want to lick the plate clean. Its signature linguine is packed with shellfish in a scrumptious tomato, chilli and garlic sauce. Lunch (from ¥980) is a bargain, but you may well need to wait in line; book for dinner.

Apollo
Greek ¥¥

(Map p250; ☏03-6264-5220; www.theapollo.jp; 11th fl, Tōkyū Plaza Ginza, 5-2-1 Ginza, Chūō-ku; mains ¥1800-5800; ◷11.30am-10pm; ⑤Ginza line to Ginza, exits C2 & C3) Ginza's glittering lights are the dazzling backdrop to this ace import from Sydney with its delicious take on modern Greek cuisine. The Mediterra-

nean flavours come through strongly in dishes such as grilled octopus and fennel salad, taramasalata, or Kefalograviera cheese fried in a saganaki pan with honey, oregano and lemon juice. Portions are large and meant for sharing.

Maru
Japanese ¥¥

(銀座圓; Map p250; ☏03-5537-7420; www.maru-mayfont.jp/ginza; 2nd fl, Ichigo Ginza 612 Bldg, 6-12-15 Ginza, Chūō-ku; lunch/dinner from ¥1100/4800; ◷11.30am-2pm & 5.30-9pm Mon-Sat; ⑥; ⑤Ginza line to Ginza, exit A3) Maru offers a contemporary take on *kaiseki* (Japanese haute cuisine) fine dining. The chefs are young and inventive and the appealing space is dominated by a long, wooden, open kitchen counter across which you can watch them work. Its good-value lunches offer a choice of mainly fish dishes.

Yūrakuchō Sanchoku Inshokugai
Japanese ¥¥

(有楽町産直飲食街; Map p250; www.sanchoku-inshokugai.com/yurakucho; International Arcade, 2-1-1 Yūrakuchō, Chiyoda-ku; cover charge per person ¥400, dishes from ¥500; ◷24hr; ℝJR Yamanote line to Yūrakuchō, Yūrakuchō exit) Stalls dishing up *yakitori* (charcoal-grilled meat or vegetable skewers) have long huddled under the tracks here. This red-lantern-lit alleyway is a modern collective, which sticks to the cheap, cheerful and smoky formula, but uses quality ingredients sourced direct from producers around the country. Sample steak from Hokkaidō and seafood from Shizuoka.

Bird Land
Yakitori ¥¥¥

(バードランド; Map p250; ☏03-5250-1081; http://ginza-birdland.sakura.ne.jp; 4-2-15 Ginza, Chūō-ku; dishes around ¥450, set meals from ¥6300; ◷5-9.30pm Tue-Sat; ⑥; ⑤Ginza line to Ginza, exit C6) This is as suave as it gets for gourmet grilled chicken. Chefs in whites behind a U-shaped counter dispense *yakitori* in all shapes, sizes, colours and organs – don't pass up the dainty serves of liver pâté or the tiny cup of chicken soup. Enter beneath Suit Company. Reservations are recommended.

🍽️ **Izakaya**

Izakaya (居酒屋) translates as 'drinking house' – the Japanese equivalent of a pub. Here food – a mix of raw, grilled, steamed and fried dishes – is ordered for the table a few dishes at a time and washed down with plenty of beer, sake or *shōchū* (a strong distilled alcohol often made from potatoes).

There are orthodox *izakaya*, ones that incorporate pub-style dishes (like chips), and chef-driven ones with creative menus. While the vibe is lively and social, it's perfectly acceptable to go by yourself and sit at the counter.

★ Ordering in Izakaya

If you don't want alcohol, it's fine to order a soft drink instead, but it would be strange to not order a drink. If you're unsure what to order, you can say *'Omakase de onegaishimas[u]'* ('I'll leave it up to you'). It's probably a good idea to set a price cap, like: *'Hitori de san-zen-en'* ('one person for ¥3000'). Depending on how much you drink, a typical bill runs about ¥2500 to ¥5000 per person.

Clockwise from top: Eating in an *izakaya*; Omoide-yokochō (p137); Ramen restaurant in Omoide-yokochō (p137)

Restaurant in Akasaka

🍴 Roppongi & Akasaka

The Garden — Cafe ¥

(Map p252; 📞03-3470-4611; www.i-house.or.jp/
eng/facilities/tealounge; International House of
Japan, 5-11-16 Roppongi, Minato-ku; 🕐7am-
10pm; 🛜📶; 🚇Ōedo line to Azabu-Jūban, exit
7) Stare out from this serene tea lounge
across the beautiful late-16th-century
garden, hidden behind International House
of Japan. There are plenty of tempting
pastries and cakes, as well as more substantial meals should you wish to linger –
and who could blame you!

Lauderdale — International ¥

(Map p252; 📞03-3405-5533; www.lauderdale.
co.jp; 6-15-1 Roppongi, Minato-ku; mains from
¥1400; 🕐7am-midnight Mon-Fri, from 8am Sat &
Sun; 🛜📶; 🚇Hibiya line to Roppongi, exit 1) Just
off chic Keyaki-zaka and sporting a spacious outdoor terrace, this is an on-trend,
all-day dining space that works as well for
breakfast as it does for dinner. Weekend
brunch is very popular here, particularly
the egg dishes.

Sougo — Vegetarian ¥

(宗胡; Map p252; 📞03-5414-1133; www.sougo.
tokyo; 3rd fl, Roppongi Green Bldg, 6-1-8 Roppongi, Minato-ku; mains ¥600-2000, set lunch/
dinner from ¥1500/5000; 🌱📶; 🚇Hibiya line
to Roppongi, exit 3) Sit at the long counter
beside the open kitchen or in booths and
watch the expert chefs prepare delicious
and beautifully presented *shōjin-ryōri*
(vegetarian cuisine as served at Buddhist
temples). Reserve at least one day in advance if you want a vegan meal. Look for it
in the building opposite the APA Hotel.

Honmura-An — Soba ¥

(本むら庵; Map p252; 📞03-5772-6657; www.
honmuraantokyo.com; 7-14-18 Roppongi,
Minato-ku; soba from ¥900, set lunch/dinner
¥1600/7400; 🕐noon-2.30pm & 5.30-10pm
Tue-Sun, closed 1st & 3rd Tue of month; 🚭🛜📶;
🚇Hibiya line to Roppongi, exit 4) This fabled
soba shop, once located in Manhattan, now
serves its handmade buckwheat noodles at
this rustically contemporary noodle shop
on a Roppongi side street. The delicate
flavour of these noodles is best appreciated

when served on a bamboo mat, with tempura or with dainty slices of *kamo* (duck).

Jōmon   Izakaya ¥¥

(ジョウモン; Map p252; ☑03-3405-2585; http://teyandei.com/?page_id=18; 5-9-17 Roppongi, Minato-ku; skewers ¥300-1000; ◷6pm-5am; ✈📱; ⑤Hibiya line to Roppongi, exit 3) This wonderfully cosy kitchen has bar seating, rows of ornate *shōchū* (liquor) jugs lining the wall and hundreds of freshly prepared skewers splayed in front of the patrons – don't miss the heavenly *zabuton* beef stick. It's almost directly across from the Family Mart – look for the name in Japanese on the door.

Kikunoi   Kaiseki ¥¥¥

(菊乃井; Map p252; ☑03-3568-6055; http://kikunoi.jp; 6-13-8 Akasaka, Minato-ku; lunch/dinner set menu from ¥5940/17,820; ◷noon-1pm Tue-Sat, 5-8pm Mon-Sat; ⑤Chiyoda line to Akasaka, exit 7) Exquisitely prepared seasonal dishes are as beautiful as they are delicious at this Michelin–starred Tokyo outpost of a three-generation-old Kyoto-based *kaiseki* (Japanese haute cuisine) restaurant. Kikunoi's chef Murata has written a book translated into English on *kaiseki* that the staff helpfully use to explain the dishes you are served, if you don't speak Japanese. Reservations are necessary.

Tofuya-Ukai   Kaiseki ¥¥¥

(とうふ屋うかい; ☑03-3436-1028; www.ukai.co.jp/english/shiba; 4-4-13 Shiba-kōen, Minato-ku; lunch/dinner set menu from ¥5500/8400; ◷11am-10pm, last order 8pm; ✈📱; ⑤Ōedo line to Akabanebashi, exit 8) One of Tokyo's most gracious restaurants is located in a former sake brewery (moved from northern Japan), with an exquisite traditional garden, in the shadow of Tokyo Tower. Seasonal preparations of tofu and accompanying dishes are served in the refined *kaiseki* style. Make reservations well in advance.

❷ Ebisu & Meguro

Tonki   Tonkatsu ¥

(とんき; 1-2-1 Shimo-Meguro, Meguro-ku; meals ¥1900; ◷4-10.45pm Wed-Mon, closed 3rd Mon of month; ❸📱; ℝJR Yamanote line to Meguro, west exit) Tonki is a Tokyo *tonkatsu* (crumbed pork cutlet) legend; it has been deep-frying pork cutlets, recipe unchanged, for nearly 80 years. The seats at the counter – where you can watch the perfectly choreographed chefs – are the most coveted, though there is usually a queue. There are tables upstairs.

Afuri   Ramen ¥

(あふり; Map p246; 1-1-7 Ebisu, Shibuya-ku; noodles from ¥880; ◷11am-5am; ❸📱; ℝJR Yamanote line to Ebisu, east exit) Hardly your typical, surly *rāmen-ya*, Afuri has upbeat young cooks and a hip industrial interior. The unorthodox menu might draw eye-rolls from purists, but house specialities such as *yuzu-shio* (a light, salty broth flavoured with yuzu, a type of citrus) draw lines at lunchtime. Order from the vending machine.

🍽 Etiquette

First of all, relax. No one expects you to be perfect. Still, a few points to note if you want to make a good impression: avoid sticking your chopsticks upright in a bowl of rice or passing food from one pair of chopsticks to another – both are reminiscent of Japanese funereal rites. When serving yourself from a shared dish, it's polite to use the back end of your chopsticks (ie not the end that goes into your mouth) to place the food on your own small dish.

Lunch is one of Japan's great bargains; however, restaurants can only offer cheap lunch deals because they anticipate high turnover. Spending too long sipping coffee after finishing your meal might earn you dagger eyes from the kitchen. Despite all the tasty takeaway options sold in department stores, the Japanese frown upon eating in public places (on the subway, for example); festivals and parks are two big exceptions.

🍴 Monja-yaki

Monja-yaki (もんじゃ焼き) is a Tokyo speciality similar to the classic dish okonomiyaki (a thick savoury pancake stuffed with meat, seafood and cabbage), but the batter is runnier, making for a thin crêpe that crisps at the edges. Tsukishima, near Ginza, is the birthplace of the dish and has a whole strip of specialists. **Monja Kondō** (もんじゃ近どう; Map p250; ☑️03-3533-4555; 3-12-10 Tsukishima, Chūō-ku; monjayaki from ¥1000; ⏰5-10pm Mon-Fri, 11.30am-10pm Sat & Sun; ⑤Ōedo line to Tsukishima, exit 8), dating back to 1950, is said to be Tsukishima's oldest monja-yaki shop. There are some 90 different toppings you can add to the basic mix; the staff will help you to make the dish at your own table grill.

Monja-yaki in Tsukishima
GARY CONNER / GETTY IMAGES ©

Megutama   Shokudo ¥
(めぐたま; Map p246; http://megutama.com/; 3-2-7 Higashi, Shibuya-ku; lunch/dinner from ¥1000/1500; ⏰11.30am-2pm & 5-11pm Mon-Fri, noon-10pm Sat & Sun; 📶; 🚃JR Yamanote line to Ebisu, east exit) Megutama calls itself a 'photo books diner' – because thousands of photo tomes are shelved on its walls. Diners are free to flip through them (use the coloured card as a placeholder). The food here is good, too: classic home cooking from a trio of very able women. It's a modern wooden building with a red awning.

Ouca   Ice Cream ¥
(櫻花; Map p246; www.ice-ouca.com; 1-6-6 Ebisu, Shibuya-ku; ice cream from ¥400; ⏰11am-11.30pm Mar-Oct, noon-11pm Nov-Feb; 🚃JR Yamanote line to Ebisu, east exit) Green tea isn't the only flavour Japan has contributed to the ice-cream playbook; other delicious innovations available (seasonally) at Ouca include kuro-goma (black sesame), kinako kurosato (roasted soy-bean flour and black sugar) and beni imo (purple sweet potato).

Udon Yamachō   Udon ¥
(うどん山長; Map p246; 1-1-5 Ebisu, Shibuya-ku; udon ¥630-1000; ⏰11.30am-4pm, 5pm-4.30am; 📶; 🚃JR Yamanote line to Ebisu, east exit) Go for bowls of perfectly al dente udon (thick wheat noodles) in this stylish noodle joint alongside the Shibuya-gawa. In the evening you can tack on sides (such as seasonal veg tempura) and flasks of sake. The shop, with white curtains over the door, is next to a park with a slide shaped like an octopus.

Ōtaru   Izakaya ¥
(おおたる; Map p246; ☑️03-3710-7439; 1-5-15 Naka-Meguro, Meguro-ku; dishes ¥330-600; ⏰11.30am-2am) Ōtaru isn't winning any Michelin stars, but we're giving it three stars of our own for atmosphere. In increasingly redeveloped Naka-Meguro, this izakaya (Japanese pub-eatery), in an old wooden building festooned with lanterns, stands out. The food is standard izakaya fare – sashimi, grilled fish, fried chicken – and exceedingly reasonable. Ōtaru is right on the Meguro-gawa, open through the afternoon. Table charge ¥400.

Ippo   Izakaya ¥
(一歩; Map p246; ☑️03-3445-8418; 2nd fl, 1-22-10 Ebisu, Shibuya-ku; dishes ¥500-1500; ⏰6pm-3am; 📶; 🚃JR Yamanote line to Ebisu, east exit) This mellow little izakaya (Japanese pub-eatery) specialises in simple pleasures: fish and sake (there's an English sign out front that says just that). The friendly chefs speak some English and can help you decide what to have grilled, steamed, simmered or fried (or if you can't decide, the ¥2500 set menu is great value). The entrance is up the wooden stairs.

Yakiniku Champion — Barbecue ¥¥

(焼肉チャンピオン; Map p246; ☑03-5768-6922; www.yakiniku-champion.com; 1-2-8 Ebisu, Shibuya-ku; dishes ¥780-3300, course from ¥5250; ⏱5pm-12.30am Mon-Fri, to 1am Sat, 4.30pm-midnight Sun; 🅿; 🚉JR Yamanote line to Ebisu, west exit) Ready for an introduction into the Japanese cult of *yakiniku* (Korean barbecue)? Champion's sprawling menu includes everything from sweetbreads to the choicest cuts of grade-A5 *wagyu* (Japanese beef); the menu even has a diagram of the cuts. You can't go wrong with popular dishes such as *kalbi* (short ribs, ¥980). It's very popular, best to reserve ahead.

Ebisu-yokochō — Street Food ¥¥

(恵比寿横町; Map p246; www.ebisu-yokocho.com; 1-7-4 Ebisu, Shibuya-ku; dishes ¥500-1500; ⏱5pm-late; 🚉JR Yamanote line to Ebisu, east exit) Retro arcade chock-a-block with food stalls dishing up everything from humble *yaki-soba* (fried buckwheat noodles) to decadent *hotate-yaki* (grilled scallops). It's a loud, lively (and smoky) place, especially on a Friday night; go early to get a table.

Higashi-Yama — Japanese ¥¥¥

(ヒガシヤマ; Map p246; ☑03-5720-1300; www.higashiyama-tokyo.jp; 1-21-25 Higashiyama, Meguro-ku; lunch/dinner from ¥1650/4950; ⏱11.30am-2pm Tue-Sat, 6pm-1am Mon-Sat; 🅿; ⑤Hibiya line to Naka-Meguro) Higashi-Yama serves scrumptious modern Japanese cuisine paired with gorgeous crockery. The interior, a rustic take on minimalism, is stunning too. The restaurant is all but hidden, on a side street with little signage; see the website for a map. Tasting courses make ordering easy; the 'chef's recommendation' course (¥9020) is a worthwhile splurge. Best to book ahead.

✖ Shibuya & Shimo-Kitazawa

d47 Shokudō — Japanese ¥

(d47食堂; Map p246; www.hikarie8.com/d47shokudo/about.shtml; 8th fl, Shibuya Hikarie, 2-21-1 Shibuya, Shibuya-ku; meals ¥1200-1780; ⏱11am-2.30pm & 6-10.30pm; 🚫🅿; 🚉JR Yamanote line to Shibuya, east exit) There are 47 prefectures in Japan and d47 serves a changing line-up of *teishoku* (set meals)

Yakiniku (Korean barbecue) in Japan

ANUCHA PONGPATMETH / SHUTTERSTOCK ©

that evoke the specialities of each, from the fermented tofu of Okinawa to the stuffed squid of Hokkaido. A larger menu of small plates is available in the evening. Picture windows offer bird's-eye views over the trains coming and going at Shibuya Station.

Gyūkatsu Motomura   Tonkatsu ¥
(牛かつ もと村; Map p246; 03-3797-3735; basement fl, 3-18-10 Shibuya, Shibuya-ku; set meal ¥1200; ⊙10.30am-10.30pm Mon-Sat, 10.30am-8.30pm Sun; 🚇; 🚉JR Yamanote line to Shibuya, east exit) You know *tonkatsu*, the deep-fried breaded pork cutlet that is a Japanese staple; meet *gyūkatsu*, the deep-fried breaded beef cutlet that is Tokyo's latest food craze. At Motomura, the beef is super-crisp on the outside and still very rare on the inside; diners get a small individual grill to finish the job to their liking. Set meals include cabbage, rice and soup.

Sagatani   Soba ¥
(嵯峨谷; Map p246; 2-25-7 Dōgenzaka, Shibuya-ku; noodles from ¥290; ⊙24hr; 🚇; 🚉JR Yamanote line to Shibuya, Hachikō exit) Proving that Tokyo is only expensive to those who don't know better, this all-night joint serves up bamboo steamers of delicious noodles for just ¥290. You won't regret 'splurging' on the ごまだれそば (*goma-dare soba;* buckwheat noodles with sesame dipping sauce) for ¥390. Look for the stone mill in the window and order from the vending machine.

Camelback   Sandwiches ¥
(キャメルバック; Map p246; www.camelback. tokyo; 42-2 Kamiyama-chō, Shibuya-ku; sandwiches ¥410-900; ⊙10am-7pm Tue-Sun; 🚇; ⑤Chiyoda line to Yoyogi-kōen, exit) As Camelback demonstrates, when a sushi chef switches allegiance from rice to bread the result can be a beautiful thing. The speciality here is the *tamago-yaki* (the kind of rolled omelet that you get at sushi shops) sandwich, served on a fluffy roll with mayonnaise and a hint of hot mustard.

Bear Pond Espresso   Cafe ¥
(✆03-5454-2486; www.bear-pond.com; 2-36-12 Kitazawa, Setagaya-ku; ⊙11am-5.30pm Wed-Mon; 🚇; 🚉Keiō Inokashira line to Shimo-Kitazawa, north exit) Bear Pond is

Tokyo's most haloed espresso stand and its most divisive: the thick syrupy 'angel stain' espresso is considered holy grail by many; others vow never to return because of the often testy service (rules include no photos without permission). Espresso shots are limited, so come in the morning; lattes etc are served all day. Drinks ¥300 to ¥700.

Food Show   Supermarket ¥
(フードショー; Map p246; basement fl, 2-24-1 Shibuya, Shibuya-ku; ⏰10am-9pm; 🍴; 🚉JR Yamanote line to Shibuya, Hachikō exit) This take-away paradise in the basement of Shibuya Station has steamers of dumplings, crisp *karaage* (Japanese-style fried chicken), artfully arranged *bentō* (boxed meals), sushi sets, heaps of salads and cakes almost too pretty to eat. It's also home of the ¥10,000 melons. A green sign pointing downstairs marks the entrance at Hachikō Plaza.

Nagi Shokudō   Vegan ¥
(なぎ食堂; Map p246; http://nagishokudo.com; 15-10 Uguisudani-chō, Shibuya-ku; lunch/dinner set menu ¥1050/1550; ⏰noon-4pm daily, 6-11pm Mon-Sat; 😊🍴📶; 🚉JR Yamanote line to Shibuya,

west exit) A vegan haven in fast-food laced Shibuya, Nagi serves up dishes such as falafel and coconut curry. The most popular thing on the menu is a set meal with three small dishes, miso soup and rice. It's a low-key, homey place with mismatched furniture, cater-corner from a post office (and hidden behind a concrete wall; look for the red sign).

Shirube   Izakaya ¥¥
(汁べゑ; 📞03-3413-3785; 2-18-2 Kitazawa, Setagaya-ku; dishes ¥730-1060; ⏰5.30pm-midnight; 🍴📶; 🚉Keiō Inokashira line to Shimo-Kitazawa, south exit) Shirube is among Tokyo's most beloved *izakaya*. It's a toss up as to which has the most character here: the inventive fusion dishes or the charismatic staff. Don't miss the *aburi saba* (blow-torch grilled mackerel). The 90-minute all-you-can-drink course (¥4000 per person), which includes all the most popular dishes, is a great deal. Reservations a must on weekends.

Ahiru Store   Bistro ¥¥
(アヒルストア; Map p246; 📞03-5454-2146; 1-19-4 Tomigaya, Shibuya-ku; dishes ¥800-1800; ⏰6pm-midnight Mon-Fri, 3-9pm Sat; 😊; Ⓢ Chiyoda line to Yoyogi-kōen, exit 2) This tiny counter

> ★ **Top Five Cafes**
>
> Mugimaru 2 (p138)
>
> Cafe de l'Ambre (p123)
>
> Little Nap Coffee Stand (p133)
>
> Imasa (p138)
>
> A to Z Cafe (p134)

From left: Cafe exterior; *Sampuru* (samples), plastic food models on display; Bakery counter

🍴 Kissaten

Long before Starbucks washed up in Japan and changed the game, there were *kissaten* (喫茶店), independent coffee shops. Today what differentiates a *kissaten* from a cafe or a coffee shop is its vintage vibe. Don't try ordering a latte here; only pour-over coffee, usually a dark roast, is served (you can get cream in tiny single-serve pitchers). And don't expect wi-fi: regular *kissaten* customers are more likely to be reading a newspaper.

Atmosphere aside, the biggest *kissaten* perk is breakfast. Many serve 'morning sets' (モーニングセット; *mōningu setto*) from 8am until around 11am that include thick, buttery toast, a hard-boiled egg and a cup of coffee, for about the same price as a cup of coffee (around ¥500).

Two to try:

Kayaba Coffee (カヤバ珈琲; Map p254; 🎵03-3823-3545; http://kayaba-coffee.com; 6-1-29 Yanaka, Taitō-ku; drinks from ¥450; ⏰8am-11pm Mon-Sat, to 6pm Sun; 📷; 🚇Chiyoda line to Nezu, exit 1) 1930s coffee shop in Yanaka.

Berg (ベルグ; Map p253; www.berg.jp; basement fl, Lumine Est, 3-38-1 Shinjuku, Shinjuku-ku; ⏰7am-11pm, 📷; 🚉JR Yamanote line to Shinjuku, east exit) Popular haunt inside Shinjuku Station.

Vintage-style coffee shop
MICHAEL H / GETTY IMAGES ©

bistro, dishing up homemade sausages, fresh-baked bread and bio wines (¥9-12 per glass), has a huge local following. Reservations are accepted only for the first seating at 6pm; otherwise join the queue (late, or during the middle of the week, is the best time to score a spot).

Kaikaya   Seafood ¥¥

(開花屋; Map p246; 🎵03-3770-0878; www.kaikaya.com; 23-7 Maruyama-chō, Shibuya-ku; lunch from ¥850, dishes ¥850-2300; ⏰11.30am-2pm & 5.30-10.30pm Mon-Fri, 5.30-10.30pm Sat & Sun; 🚇📷; 🚉JR Yamanote line to Shibuya, Hachikō exit) 🍴 Traveller favourite Kaikaya is one chef's attempt to bring the beach to Shibuya. Surfboards hang on the walls and much of what's on the menu is caught in nearby Sagami Bay. Seafood is served both Japanese- and Western-style. One must-try is the *maguro no kama* (tuna collar; ¥1200). Reservations recommended; there's a table charge of ¥400 per person.

Matsukiya   Hotpot ¥¥¥

(松木家; Map p246; 🎵03-3461-2651; 6-8 Maruyama-chō, Shibuya-ku; sukiyaki from ¥5400; ⏰5-11pm Mon-Sat; 📷; 🚉JR Yamanote line to Shibuya, Hachikō exit) Matsukiya has been making *sukiyaki* (thinly sliced beef, simmered and then dipped in raw egg) since 1890 and the chefs really, really know what they're doing. It's worth upgrading to the premium course (¥7500) for even meltier meat. Prices are per person and for a full course that includes veggies and finishes with noodles cooked in the broth.

Narukiyo   Izakaya ¥¥¥

(なるきよ; Map p246; 🎵03-5485-2223; 2-7-14 Shibuya, Shibuya-ku; dishes ¥700-4800; ⏰6pm-12.30am; 🚉JR Yamanote line to Shibuya, east exit) For evenings when you want to eat well and adventurously, head here. The menu, handwritten on a scroll, is undecipherable – which is fine, because you just want to have what the chef recommends anyway. Tell him how much you're willing to spend (say ¥5000 or ¥7000 per person) and say the magic word: *omakase* (I leave it up to you).

⊗ Harajuku & Aoyama

Harajuku Gyōza-ro   Dumplings ¥

(原宿餃子楼; Map p246; 6-4-2 Jingūmae, Shibuya-ku; 6 gyōza ¥290; ⊗11.30am-4.30am; 🖻; 🚊JR Yamanote line to Harajuku, Omote-sandō exit) *Gyōza* (dumplings) are the only thing on the menu here, but you won't hear any complaints from the regulars who queue up to get their fix. Have them *sui* (boiled) or *yaki* (pan-fried), with or without *niniku* (garlic) or *nira* (chives) – they're all delicious. Expect to wait on weekends, but the line moves quickly.

Maisen   Tonkatsu ¥

(まい泉; Map p246; http://mai-sen.com/; 4-8-5 Jingūmae, Shibuya-ku; lunch/dinner from ¥995/1680; ⊗11am-10pm; 🖨🖻; 🇸Ginza line to Omote-sandō, exit A2) You could order something else (maybe fried shrimp), but everyone else will be ordering the famous *tonkatsu* (breaded, deep-fried pork cutlets). There are different grades of pork on the menu, including prized *kurobuta* (black pig), but even the cheapest is melt-in-your-mouth divine. The restaurant is housed in an old public bathhouse. A takeaway window serves delicious *tonkatsu sando* (sandwich).

Little Nap Coffee Stand   Cafe ¥

(リトルナップコーヒースタンド; Map p246; www.littlenap.jp; 5-65-4 Yoyogi, Shibuya-ku; ⊗9am-7pm Tue-Sun; 🖻; 🇸Chiyoda line to Yoyogi-kōen, exit 3) Few people enter Yoyogi-kōen from the entrance near the subway stop of the same name, except those who live nearby. Odds are, on their way, they've stopped by Little Nap for a well-crafted latte (¥400). On Sundays, there's always a crowd loitering out front.

Commune 246   Market ¥

(Map p246; http://commune246.com/; 3-13 Minami-Aoyama, Minato-ku; ⊗11am-10pm; 🖨🖉🖻; 🇸Ginza line to Omote-sandō, exit A4) Commune 246 is one of the rare alfresco dining spots in Tokyo. It's really more like a semi-permanent food-truck gathering (no one knows how long it will last; the land is incredibly valuable). There are a dozen or so vendors offering inexpensive curries, hotdogs, beer and the like. You can put

Sukiyaki (sauteed beef dipped in raw egg)

> ★ **Top Five Vegetarian**
>
> Sougo (p126)
>
> Nagi Shokudō (p131)
>
> Mominoki House (p135)
>
> Komaki Shokudō (p139)
>
> Rose Bakery Marunouchi (p122)

together a meal for around ¥1000, then grab a bench.

A to Z Cafe
Cafe ¥

(エートゥーゼットカフェ; Map p246; 5th fl, 5-8-3 Minami-Aoyama, Minato-ku; ⊗11.30am-11.30pm; 🖥; ⑤Ginza line to Omote-sandō, exit B3) Artist Yoshitomo Nara (known for his portraits of punkish tots) teamed up with design firm Graf to create this spacious and only slightly off-kilter cafe. Along with wooden schoolhouse chairs, whitewashed walls and a small cottage, you can find a few scattered examples of Nara's work. Drinks from ¥600.

Sakura-tei
Okonomiyaki ¥

(さくら亭; Map p246; ☑03-3479-0039; www.sakuratei.co.jp; 3-20-1 Jingūmae, Shibuya-ku; okonomiyaki ¥950-1500; ⊗11am-midnight; ⊜🛜🖊🖥; ℝJR Yamanote line to Harajuku, Takeshita exit) Grill your own *okonomiyaki* (savoury pancakes) at this funky place inside the gallery Design Festa. In addition to classic options (with pork, squid and cabbage), there are some wacky innovations (like taco or carbonara *okonomiyaki*). There's also a great-value 90-minute all-you-can-eat plan (lunch/dinner ¥1250/2100).

Higashiya Man
Sweets ¥

(ひがしや まん; Map p246; ☑03-5414-3881; www.higashiya.com/shop/man/; 3-17-14 Minami-Aoyama, Minato-ku; sweets ¥300; ⊗11am-7pm; 🖊; ⑤Ginza line to Omote-sandō, exit A4) *Manjū* (まんじゅう) – that's where the shop's name comes from; it's not just for men! – are hot buns stuffed with sweetened red-bean paste. They're steamed fresh at this take-away counter, a popular pit stop for Aoyama shoppers. Inside the tiny shop, there's a greater selection of traditional Japanese sweets, many packaged beautifully for gifts.

🍽️ Vegetarian Tokyo

Tokyo has a few vegetarian restaurants and many can accommodate the request *'Bejitarian dekimasu ka'* ('Can you do vegetarian?'). One note of caution: often dishes that look vegetarian are not (miso soup, for example) because they are prepared with *dashi* (fish stock).

Pariya International ¥

(パリヤ; Map p246; 3-12-14 Kita-Aoyama, Minato-ku; meals from ¥1130; ⏱11.30am-11pm; ♿🍴; SGinza line to Omote-sandō, exit B2) Pariya is the local cafeteria for the fashionable set. It's not cheap slop though; typical dishes include shrimp croquettes and curried potato salad. Grab a tray and choose one main, one salad and one side dish (or two salads and a side for veggies). There are colourful cupcakes and gelati for dessert.

Mominoki House Japanese ¥¥

(もみの木ハウス; Map p246; www.mominoki-house.net; 2-18-5 Jingūmae, Shibuya-ku; lunch/dinner set menu from ¥980/2500; ⏱11am-3pm & 5-11pm; ♿🍴; ℝJR Yamanote line to Harajuku, Takeshita exit) 🌱 Boho Tokyoites have been coming here for tasty macrobiotic fare since 1976. The casual dining room, which looks like a grown-up (indoor) tree fort and features several cosy, semi-private booths, has seen some famous visitors too, such as Paul McCartney. Chef Yamada's menu is heavily vegan, but also includes free-range chicken and *Ezo shika* (Hokkaidō venison, ¥4800).

Yanmo Seafood ¥¥¥

(やんも; Map p246; ℐ03-5466-0636; www.yanmo.co.jp/aoyama/index.html; basement fl, T Place bldg, 5-5-25 Minami-Aoyama, Minato-ku; lunch/dinner set menu from ¥1100/7560; ⏱11.30am-2pm & 6-10.30pm Mon-Sat; ♿; SGinza line to Omote-sandō, exit A5) Freshly caught seafood from the nearby Izu Peninsula is the speciality at this upscale, yet unpretentious restaurant. If you're looking to splash out on a seafood dinner, this is a great place to do so. The reasonably priced set menus include sashimi and steamed and grilled fish. Reservations are essential for dinner. Lunch is a bargain, but you might have to queue.

⊗ Kōenji, Kichijōji & West Tokyo

Tensuke Tempura ¥

(天すけ; ℐ03-3223-8505; 3-22-7 Kōenji-kita, Suginami-ku; lunch/dinner from ¥1100/1600; ⏱noon-2.15pm & 6-10pm Tue-Fri, 11.30am-3pm & 6-10pm Sat & Sun; ♿; ℝJR Sōbu line to Kōenji, north exit) An entirely legitimate candidate for eighth wonder of the modern world

Tokyo in a Bowl

artful arrangement of toppings

made to order; always hot and never soggy

tender *chāshū* (sliced roast pork)

aromatic broth, the result of hours on the stove

katame (literally 'hard' but more like al dente) noodles

SASAKEN / SHUTTERSTOCK ©

Classic Ramen

Ramen Essentials

Ramen (egg noodles in broth) is a staple for lunch or dinner, or as a late-night snack. Most *ramen-ya* (ramen shops) are small, counter joints with a signature taste. The broth may be made from pork or chicken bones or dried seafood – usually it's a top-secret combination – seasoned with *shio* (salt), *shōyu* (soy sauce) or hearty miso. Ramen should be eaten at whip speed, before the noodles get soggy, which is why you'll hear diners slurping, sucking in air to cool their mouths.

Preparing ramen
ANGELO DESANTIS / GETTY IMAGES ©

★ Top Three Ramen Shops

Kagari (篝; Map p250; 4-4-1 Ginza; small/large ramen ¥950/1050; ⊙11am-3.30pm & 5.30-10.30pm; ⓢ Ginza line to Ginza, exit A10 or B1) **The shop of the hour, made with a luscious, flavoursome chicken broth.**

Harukiya (春木屋; www.haruki-ya.co.jp; 1-4-6 Kami-Ogi, Suginami-ku; ramen from ¥850; ⊙11am-9pm; ⊜ 🅿; 🅡 JR Sōbu-Chūō line to Ogikubo, north exit) **Classic Tokyo-style ramen: a light chicken and fish stock seasoned with soy sauce.**

Gogyō (五行; Map p252; ☎03-5775-5566; www.ramendining-gogyo.com; 1-4-36 Nish-Azabu, Minato-ku; ramen from ¥1290; ⊙11.30am-4pm & 5pm-3am, to midnight Sun; ⓢ Hibiya line to Roppongi, exit 2) **Dark, intense (and a little funky) *kogashi* (burnt) ramen.**

is Tensuke's *tamago* (egg) tempura. We don't know how the chef (who is quite a showman) does it, but the egg comes out batter-crisp on the outside and runny in the middle. It's served on rice with seafood and vegetable tempura as part of the *tamago tempura teishoku* (玉子天ぷら定食).

Tetchan Yakitori ¥

(てっちゃん; 1-1-2 Kichijōji-Honchō, Musashino-shi; skewers from ¥110; ⊘4-11pm; 闵JR Sōbu-Chūō line to Kichijōji, north exit) Located inside the labyrinthine covered market Harmonica-yokochō, Tetchan has been drawing locals for years. It's now become something of a tourist destination too, thanks to its new interior of acrylic 'ice' by architect Kuma Kengo (known for his more establishment works). There's no English menu, but safe bets include *tsukune* (chicken meatballs), *buta bara* (pork belly) and *motsu-ni* (stewed offal).

Uni Stand Teahouse ¥

(ユニスタンド; http://unistand.jp/; 1-16-1 Shimorenjaku, Mitaka-shi; drinks ¥480-560; ⊘10am-7pm Wed-Mon; 闵JR Sōbu-Chūō line to Mitaka, south exit) Taking a cue from the third-wave coffee movement, Uni Stand sells single origin teas and carefully crafted *matcha* lattes (with high-grade powdered green tea from Uji). A little pretentious, sure, but also a welcome addition – a good cup of tea is surprisingly hard to find on the go in Tokyo.

Kōenji Gādo-shita Street Food ¥

(高円寺ガード下; Kōenji, Suginami-ku; ⊘5pm-late; 闵JR Sōbu line to Kōenji, north exit) A collection of shabby (and cheap!) *yakitori* joints and spruced-up wine bars underneath the overhead JR tracks in Kōenji. Some (indicated by a small sticker) have English menus.

Okajōki Izakaya ¥¥

(陸奥気; ☎03-3228-1230; www.nakano-okajoki.com; 5-59-3 Nakano, Nakano-ku; lunch/dinner set menu ¥900/3980; ⊘11.30am-3pm & 4-10pm Mon-Fri, 4-10pm Sat & Sun; 闵JR Sōbu-Chūō line to Nakano, north exit) The *yaki-zakana* (焼き魚; grilled fish) lunch here is legendary. The fish are roasted around a large central hearth and are served as a set with rice, miso

soup and pickles. There's no English menu, but some common fish are *shake* (しゃけ; salmon), *nishin* (にしん; Pacific herring) and *saba* (さば; mackerel). Order at the kiosk at the entrance and expect a line.

Steak House Satou Steak ¥¥

(ステーキハウス さとう; ☎0422-21-6464; www.shop-satou.com; 1-1-8 Kichijōji Honchō, Mitaka-shi; lunch set ¥1200-4000; dinner set ¥2600-10,000; ⊘11am-2.30pm & 5-8.30pm Mon-Fri, 11am-8.30pm Sat & Sun; ⊗🗐; 闵JR Sōbu-Chūō line to Kichijōji, north exit) This is a classic Japanese-style steak house, where the meat is cooked at the counter on a *teppanyaki* (iron hot plate), diced before serving and paired with rice, miso soup and pickles. It's also excellent value, considering the quality of the beef; even a 'splurge' on the chef's choice (lunch/dinner ¥4000/7000) is reasonable.

⊗ Shinjuku & Ikebukuro

Nakajima Kaiseki ¥

(中嶋; Map p253; ☎03-3356-4534; www.shinjyuku-nakajima.com; basement fl, 3-32-5 Shinjuku, Shinjuku-ku; lunch/dinner from ¥800/8640; ⊘11.30am-2pm & 5.30-10pm Mon-Sat; ⊗🗐; ⑤Marunouchi line to Shinjuku-sanchōme, exit A1) In the evening, this Michelin-starred restaurant serves exquisite *kaiseki* (Japanese haute cuisine) dinners. On weekdays, it also serves a set lunch of humble *iwashi* (sardines) for one-tenth the price; in the hands of Nakajima's chefs they're divine. The line for lunch starts to form shortly before the restaurant opens at 11.30am. Look for the white sign at the top of the stairs.

Omoide-yokochō Yakitori ¥

(思い出横丁; Map p253; Nishi-Shinjuku 1-chōme, Shinjuku-ku; skewers from ¥150; ⊘noon-midnight, vary by shop, 🗐; 闵JR Yamanote line to Shinjuku, west exit) Since the postwar days, smoke has been billowing night and day from the rickety, wooden *yakitori* stalls that line this alley by the train tracks, literally translated as 'Memory Lane' (and less politely known as Shonben-yokochō, or 'Piss Alley'). Several stalls have English menus.

🍽️ Department Store Food Halls

The below-ground floors of Tokyo's department stores hold fantastic food halls called *depachika* (literally 'department store basement'). Dozens of vendors offer a staggering array of foodstuffs of the highest order; most are branches of famous restaurants, producers and confectioners. You can find prepared food, such as sushi and salads, as well as sweets, *sembei* (rice crackers), tea and sake gorgeously packaged for presentation as gifts. Two *depachika* to try are Isetan (p161) in Shinjuku and Mitsukoshi (p155) in Ginza.

See if you can't spot the one that has appeared on the cover of Lonely Planet's Tokyo guide.

Numazukō   Sushi ¥
(沼津港; Map p253; 3-34-16 Shinjuku, Shinjuku-ku; plates ¥100-550; ⏰11am-10.30pm; 🍴🚇📶; 🚉JR Yamanote line to Shinjuku, east exit) Shinjuku's best *kaiten-sushi* (conveyor-belt sushi) restaurant is pricier than many, but the quality is worth it. Its popularity means that few plates make it around the long, snaking belt without getting snatched up (you can also order off the menu, if you don't see what you want). This is a good choice if you don't want a full meal.

Tsunahachi   Tempura ¥¥
(つな八; Map p253; 📞03-3352-1012; www.tsunahachi.co.jp; 3-31-8 Shinjuku, Shinjuku-ku; lunch/dinner from ¥1512/2484; ⏰11am-10.30pm; 🍴📶; 🚉JR Yamanote line to Shinjuku, east exit) Tsunahachi has been expertly frying prawns and vegies for more than 90 years and is an excellent place to get initiated in the art of tempura (foreign tourists get a handy cheat sheet on the different condiments). Set menus (except for the cheaper ones at lunch) are served piece by piece, so everything comes hot and crisp. Indigo *noren* (curtains) mark the entrance.

Kozue   Japanese ¥¥¥
(梢; Map p253; 📞03-5323-3460; http://tokyo.park.hyatt.jp/en/hotel/dining/Kozue.html; 40th fl, Park Hyatt, 3-7-1-2 Nishi-Shinjuku, Shinjuku-ku; lunch set menu ¥2850-12,400, dinner set menu ¥12,400-27,300; ⏰11.30am-2.30pm & 5.30-9.30pm; 🍴📶; 🚇Ōedo line to Tochōmae, exit A4) It's hard to beat Kozue's combination of well-executed, seasonal Japanese cuisine, artisan crockery and soaring views over Shinjuku from the floor-to-ceiling windows. As the (kimono-clad) staff speak English and the restaurant caters well to allergies and personal preferences, this is a good splurge spot for diners who don't want to give up complete control. Reservations are essential.

✖️ Kagurazaka, Kanda & Akihabara

Imasa   Cafe ¥
(井政; Map p254; 📞03-3255-3565; www.kanda-imasa.co.jp; 2-16 Soto-Kanda, Chiyoda-ku; drinks ¥600; ⏰11am-4pm Mon-Fri; 🚉JR Chūō or Sōbu lines to Ochanomizu, Hijiri-bashi exit) It's not every day that you get to sip your coffee or tea in a cultural property. Imasa is the real deal, an old timber merchant's shophouse dating from 1927, but with Edo-era design and detail, and a few pieces of contemporary furniture. Very few houses like this exist in Tokyo or are open to the public.

Ethiopia   Japanese ¥
(エチオピア; Map p254; 📞03-3295-4310; 3-10-6 Kanda-ogawamachi, Chiyoda-ku; curry from ¥900; ⏰11am-10pm Mon-Fri, to 8.30pm Sat & Sun; 📶; 🚇Hanzōmon line to Jimbōchō, exit A5) In studenty Jimbōchō, Japanese curry cafes are 10 a penny and fiercely competitive. Ethiopia is a seasoned champ, offering jumbo serves and curries packed with meat and vegetables. The spice level goes from zero to a nuclear-thermal 70! Pay at the machine as you enter the wonderfully retro shop.

Mugimaru 2   Cafe ¥
(ムギマル 2; 📞03-5228-6393; www.mugimaru2.com; 5-20 Kagurazaka, Shinjuku-ku; coffee

¥550; ⏲noon-8pm Thu-Tue; 🛗; Ⓢ Tozai line to Kagurazaka, exit 1) This old house, completely covered in ivy, is a charmer with a welcoming owner and a couple of cats. Seating is on floor cushions; warm, squishy *manjū* (steamed buns) are the house speciality.

Kikanbō   Ramen ¥

(鬼金棒; Map p250; http://karashibi.com; 2-10-8 Kaji-chō, Chiyoda-ku; ramen from ¥800; ⏲11am-9.30pm Mon-Sat, to 4pm Sun; 🚉JR Yamanote line to Kanda, north exit) The *karashibi* (カラシビ) spicy miso ramen here has a cult following. Choose your level of *kara* (spice) and *shibi* (a strange mouth-numbing sensation created by Japanese sanshō pepper). We recommend *futsu-futsu* (regular for both) for first-timers; *oni* (devil) level costs an extra ¥100. Look for the red door curtains and buy an order ticket from the vending machine.

Kanda Yabu Soba   Soba ¥

(神田やぶそば; Map p254; 🕿03-3251-0287; www.yabusoba.net; 2-10 Kanda-Awajichō, Chiyoda-ku; noodles ¥670-1910; ⏲11.30am-8.30pm; 🛗; Ⓢ Marunouchi line to Awajichō, exit A3)

Totally rebuilt following a fire in 2013, this is one of Tokyo's most venerable buckwheat noodle shops, in business since 1880. Come here for classic handmade noodles and accompaniments such as shrimp tempura *(ten-seiro soba)* or slices of duck *(kamo-nanban soba)*.

Komaki Shokudō   Vegan ¥

(こまきしょくどう; Map p254; 🕿03-5577-5358; http://konnichiha.net/fushikian; Chabara, 8-2 Kanda Neribei-chō, Chiyoda-ku; set meals from ¥980; ⏲11am-7.30pm; 🛗; 🚉JR Yamanote line to Akihabara, Electric Town exit) A Kamakura cooking school specialising in *shōjin-ryōri* (Buddhist-style vegan cuisine) runs this cafe within the Chabara (p165) food market. Its nonmeat dishes are very tasty and it sells some of the ingredients used. Round off your meal with excellent coffee from Yanaka Coffee opposite.

Amanoya   Desserts ¥

(天野屋; Map p254; www.amanoya.jp; 2-8-15 Soto-Kanda, Chiyoda-ku; desserts from ¥500; ⏲10am-6pm Mon-Sat, to 5pm Sun; 🛗; 🚉JR Chūo or Sōbu lines to Ochanomizu, Hijiri-bashi exit) The

Soba noodles

owner of this charming dessert cafe is a bit of a collector, as you'll discover from the eclectic bits and bobs on display ranging from model trains to carved masks. Motherly women dole out sweet treats, such as *mochi* rice cakes, as well *amazake,* a mildly alcoholic milky sake beverage that's long been a house speciality.

Kado   Japanese ¥¥

(カド; ☎03-3268-2410; http://kagurazaka-kado. com; 1-32 Akagi-Motomachi, Shinjuku-ku; lunch/ dinner set menus from ¥800/3150; ⊗11.30am-2.30pm & 5-11pm; ➡ 🅱; 🚇Tōzai line to Kagurazaka, exit 1) Set in an old wooden house with a white lantern out front, Kado specialises in *katei-ryōri* (home-cooking). Dinner is a set course of seasonal dishes (such as grilled quail or crab soup). At lunch there's no English menu, so your best bet is the カド定食 *(kado teishoku),* the daily house special. Bookings are required for dinner.

Isegen   Japanese ¥¥

(いせ源; Map p254; ☎03-3251-1229; www. isegen.com; 1-11-1 Kanda-Sudachō, Chiyoda-ku; dishes from ¥1000; ⊗11.30am-2pm & 5-9pm Mon-Sat, closed Sat Jun-Aug; 🅱; 🅂Marunouchi line to Awajichō, exit A3) This illustrious fish restaurant, in business since the 1830s, operates out of a handsomely crafted 1930 wooden building. The speciality is *ankō-nabe* (monkfish stew; ¥3400 per person, minimum order for two), served in a splendid communal tatami room. The menu offers lots of other fish dishes, including *unagi* (eel).

Botan   Hotpot ¥¥¥

(ぼたん; Map p254; ☎03-3251-0577; http://r. gnavi.co.jp/g198900; 1-15 Kanda-Sudachō, Chiyoda-ku; set meals from ¥7300; ⊗11.30am-9pm Mon-Sat; 🅱; 🅂Marunouchi line to Awajichō, exit A3) Botan has been making a single, perfect dish in the same traditional wooden house since the 1890s. Sit cross-legged on rattan mats as chicken *nabe* (meat cooked in broth with vegetables) simmers over a charcoal brazier next to you, allowing you to take in the scent of prewar Tokyo. Try to get a seat in the handsome upstairs dining room.

★ Food Alleys

Food alleys – often called *yokochō* – are a popular post-work gathering spot for Tokyoites. These narrow strips are lined with teeny-tiny bars and restaurants; some offer seating outside on overturned beer carts.

居酒屋 どん

魚○本店

Clockwise from top: Omoide-yokochō (p137); Hoppy-dōri (p144); Yūrakuchō Sanchoku Inshokugai (p124)

⊗ Ueno & Yanesen

Kamachiku — Udon ¥
(釜竹; Map p254; ☎03-5815-4675; http://ka machiku.com/top_en; 2-14-18 Nezu, Bunkyō-ku; noodles from ¥850, small dishes ¥350-850; ⏱11.30am-2pm Tue-Sun, 5.30-9pm Tue-Sat; 🗓; ⑤Chiyoda line to Nezu, exit 1) Udon (thick wheat noodles) made fresh daily is the speciality at this popular restaurant, in a beautifully restored brick warehouse from 1910 with a view onto a garden. In addition to noodles, the menu includes lots of *izakaya*-style small dishes (such as grilled fish and vegies). Expect to queue on weekends.

Torindō — Teahouse ¥
(桃林堂; Map p254; 1-5-7 Ueno-Sakuragi, Taitō-ku; tea ¥450; ⏱9am-5pm Tue-Sun; ⑤Chiyoda line to Nezu, exit 1) Sample a cup of paint-thick *matcha* (powdered green tea) at this tiny teahouse on the edge of Ueno-kōen (p59). Tradition dictates that the bitter tea be paired with something sweet, so choose from the artful desserts in the glass coun-

ter, then pull up a stool at the communal table. It's a white building on a corner.

Nezu no Taiyaki — Sweets ¥
(根津のたいやき; Map p254; 1-23-9-104 Nezu, Bunkyō-ku; taiyaki ¥170; ⏱10.30am until sold out, closed irregularly; 🗓; ⑤Chiyoda line to Nezu, exit 1) This street stall, beloved of locals for half a century, sells just one thing: *taiyaki* – hot, sweet, bean-jam buns shaped like *tai* (sea bream), a fish considered to be lucky. Come early before they sell out (always by 2pm and sometimes by noon).

Hantei — Japanese ¥¥
(はん亭; Map p254; ☎03-3828-1440; http://hantei.co.jp; 2-12-15 Nezu, Bunkyō-ku; meals from ¥3000; ⏱noon-3pm & 5-10pm Tue-Sun; 🗓; ⑤Chiyoda line to Nezu, exit 2) Housed in a beautifully maintained, century-old traditional wooden building, Hantei is a local landmark. Delectable skewers of seasonal *kushiage* (fried meat, fish and vegetables) are served with small, refreshing side dishes. Lunch includes eight or 12 sticks and dinner starts with six, after which you'll

Udon (thick wheat noodles)

HENRI / GETTY IMAGES ©

continue to receive additional rounds (¥210 per skewer) until you say stop.

Innsyoutei   Japanese ¥

(韻松亭; Map p254; ☑03-3821-8126; www.inn syoutei.jp; 4-59 Ueno-kōen, Taitō-ku; lunch/dinner from ¥1680/5500; ⓒrestaurant 11am-3pm & 5-9.30pm, tearoom 11am-5pm; 回; 回JR lines to Ueno, Ueno-kōen exit) In a gorgeous wooden building dating back to 1875, Innsyoutei (pronounced 'inshotei' and meaning 'rhyme of the pine cottage') has long been a favourite spot for fancy *kaiseki*-style meals for visitors to Ueno-kōen. Without a booking (essential for dinner) you'll have a long wait but it's worth it. Lunchtime *bentō* (boxed meals) offer beautifully presented morsels and are great value.

Shinsuke   Izakaya ¥¥

(シンスケ; Map p254; ☑03-3832-0469; 3-31-5 Yushima, Bunkyō-ku; ⓒ5-9.30pm Mon-Fri, to 9pm Sat; ⊜回; ⑤Chiyoda line to Yushima, exit 3) In business since 1925, Shinsuke has honed the concept of an ideal *izakaya* to perfection. long cedar counter, 'master' in *happi* (traditional short coat) and *hachimaki* (traditional headband), and smooth-as-silk *dai-ginjo* (premium-grade sake). The food – contemporary updates of classics – is fantastic. Don't miss the *kitsune raclette* – deep-fried tofu stuffed with raclette cheese.

Sasa-no-Yuki   Tofu ¥¥

(笹乃雪; Map p254; ☑03-3873-1145; 2-15-10 Negishi, Taitō-ku; dishes ¥400-700, lunch/dinner course from ¥2200/5000; ⓒ11.30am-8.30pm Tue-Sun; ⚑回; 回JR Yamanote line to Uguisudani, north exit) ⚑ Sasa-no-Yuki opened its doors in the Edo period and continues to serve its signature dishes with tofu made fresh every morning using water from the shop's own well. Some treats to expect: *ankake-dofu* (tofu in a thick, sweet sauce) and *goma-dofu* (sesame tofu). The best seats overlook a tiny garden with a koi (carp) pond.

Kingyozaka   Japanese ¥¥

(金魚坂; Map p254; ☑03-3815-7088; www.kingyozaka.com; 5-3-15 Hongo, Bunkyō-ku; set lunch from ¥1400, dinner mains from ¥1800; ⓒ11.30am-9.30pm Tue-Fri, to 8pm Sat & Sun;

🍴◯ Shokudō

Dining trends may come and go but *shokudō* (食堂; inexpensive, all-round eateries) remain. The city's workers take a significant number of their meals at these casual joints; you'll find them around every train station and in tourist areas. Meals typically cost ¥800 to ¥1500 per person.

Most serve *teishoku* (定食; set-course meals), which include a main dish of meat or fish, a bowl of rice, miso soup, a small salad and some *tsukemono* (pickles). Usually on the menu are various *donburi* (どんぶり or 丼; meat or seafood on a bowl of rice) and comfort food dishes, such as *tonkatsu* (deep-fried pork cutlets) and *ebi-katsu* (breaded and fried prawns).

⑤Oedo line to Hongō-sanchōme, exit 3) They've been selling ornamental fish from this spot for some 350 years, so it's only fitting that the attached restaurant and cafe takes a goldfish theme (*kingyo* means goldfish). It's a charming place in a timber-framed building. The star dish is a Japanese-style beef curry with a thick sauce and sizeable chunks of meat. It also serves tea, cakes and *kaiseki*-style meals.

⊗ Asakusa & Ryōgoku

Onigiri Yadoroku   Japanese ¥

(おにぎり 浅草 宿六; Map p254; ☑03-3874-1615; http://onigiriyadoroku.com; 3-9-10 Asakusa, Taitō-ku; set lunch ¥660 & ¥900, onigiri ¥200-600; ⓒ11.30am-5pm Mon-Sat, 6pm-2am Thu-Tue; 回; 回Tsukuba Express to Asakusa, exit 1) *Onigiri* (rice-ball snacks) usually wrapped in crispy sheets of *nori* (seaweed) are a great Japanese culinary invention and this humbly decorated and friendly place specialises in them. The set lunches, including a choice of two or three *onigiri*, are a great deal. At night there's a large range of flavours to choose from along with alcohol.

★ Top Five for Sweets

Nezu no Taiyaki (p142)

Higashiya Man (p134)

Amanoya (p139)

Rose Bakery Marunouchi (p122)

100% Chocolate Cafe (p123)

From left: *Taiyaki* (hot, sweet, bean-jam buns shaped like sea bream); Japanese confectionary; Brownie and iced coffee in a Tokyo cafe

Daikokuya   Tempura ¥

(大黒家; Map p254; ☎03-3844-1111; www.tempura.co.jp/english/index.html; 1-38-10 Asakusa, Taitō-ku; meals ¥1550-2100; ⏰11am-8.30pm Sun-Fri, to 9pm Sat; 🅿; Ⓢ Ginza line to Asakusa, exit 1) Near Nakamise-dōri, this is the place to get old-fashioned tempura fried in pure sesame oil, an Asakusa speciality. It's in a white building with a tile roof. If there's a queue (and there often is), you can try your luck at the annexe one block over, where they also serve set-course meals.

Komagata Dozeu   Japanese ¥

(駒形どぜう; Map p254; ☎03-3842-4001; www.dozeu.com/en; 1-7-12 Komagata, Taitō-ku; mains from ¥1550; ⏰11am-9pm; 🚭🅿; Ⓢ Ginza line to Asakusa, exits A2 & A4) Since 1801, Komagata Dozeu has been simmering and stewing *dojō* (Japanese loach, which looks something like a miniature eel). *Dojō-nabe* (loach hotpot), served here on individual *hibachi* (charcoal stoves), was a common dish in the days of Edo, but few restaurants serve it today. The open seating around wide, wooden planks heightens the traditional flavour. There are lanterns out front.

Rokurinsha   Ramen ¥

(六厘舎; Map p254; www.rokurinsha.com; 6th fl, Solamachi, 1-1-2 Oshiage, Sumida-ku; ramen from ¥850; ⏰10.30am-11pm; 🚭🅿; Ⓢ Hanzōmon line to Oshiage, exit B3) Rokurinsha's speciality is *tsukemen* – ramen noodles served on the side with a bowl of concentrated soup for dipping. The noodles here are perfectly al dente and the soup has a rich pork-bone base. It's an addictive combination that draws lines to this outpost in Tokyo Sky Tree Town.

Sometarō   Okonomiyaki ¥

(染太郎; Map p254; ☎03-3844-9502; 2-2-2 Nishi-Asakusa, Taitō-ku; mains from ¥650; ⏰noon-10pm; 🅿; Ⓢ Ginza line to Tawaramachi, exit 3) Sometarō is a fun and funky place to try *okonomiyaki*. This historic, vine-covered house is a friendly spot where the menu includes a how-to guide for novice cooks.

Hoppy-dōri   Yakitori ¥

(ホッピー通り; Map p254; 2-5 Asakusa, Taitō-ku; skewers from ¥120; 🚃Tsukuba Express to Asakusa, exit 4) Asakusa strip (nicknamed after 'hoppy', a cheap malt beverage) with outdoor tables and *yakitori* (skewers of grilled meat or vegetables) from noon until late.

WATARU SEMBA / EYEEM / GETTY IMAGES ©

Otafuku Japanese ¥¥

(大多福; Map p254; ☑03-3871-2521; www.otafu
ku.ne.jp; 1-6-2 Senzoku, Taitō-ku; oden ¥110-550;
☺5-11pm Tue-Sat, to 10pm Sun; 🗗; 🚇Tsukuba
Express to Asakusa, exit 1) Over a century old,
Otafuku specialises in *oden* (a classic Japanese stew). It's simmered at the counter
and diners pick what they want from the
pot. You can dine cheaply on radishes and
kelp, or splash out on scallops and tuna or
a full-course menu for ¥5400 – whichever
way you go, you get to soak up Otafuku's
convivial, old-time atmosphere.

Kappō Yoshiba Japanese ¥¥

(割烹吉葉; Map p254; ☑03 3623 4480; www.
kapou-yoshiba.jp/english/index.html; 2-14-
5 Yokoami, Sumida-ku; dishes ¥600-6600;
☺11.30am-2pm & 5-10pm Mon-Sat; 🗗; 🚇Ōedo
line to Ryōgoku Station, exit 1) The former
Miyagino sumo stable is the location for
this one-of-a-kind restaurant that has
preserved the *dōyo* (practice ring) as its
centrepiece. Playing up to its sumo roots,
you can order the protein-packed stew
chanko-nabe (for two people from ¥4600),
but Yoshiba's real strength is its sushi,
which is freshly prepared in jumbo portions.

Asakusa
Unagi Sansho Japanese ¥¥

(浅草 うなぎ さんしょ; Map p254; ☑03-
3843-0344; 2-25-7 Nishi-Asakusa, Taitō-ku; eel
¥2700-4300; ☺11.30am-2pm & 4-8pm Fri-Wed;
🗗; 🚇Tsukuba Express to Asakusa, exit 4) At
this super-friendly and simple *unagi* (eel)
restaurant the grilled eel is served in three
different sizes: only go for large if you're
really hungry. On the walls hangs detailed
traditional embroidery done by the mum,
while the dad cooks the eels to perfection.

Asakusa
Imahan Japanese ¥¥¥

(浅草今半; Map p254; ☑03-3841-1114; www.
asakusaimahan.co.jp; 3-1-12 Nishi-Asakusa, Taitō-
ku; lunch/dinner set menu from ¥3800/10,000;
☺11.30am-9.30pm; ❄🗗; 🚇Tsukuba Express
to Asakusa, exit 4) For a meal to remember,
owing by this famous beef restaurant, in
business since 1895. Choose between
courses of *sukiyaki* (sauteed beef dipped in
raw egg) and *shabu-shabu* (beef blanched
in broth); prices rise according to the grade
of meat. For diners on a budget, Imahan
sells a limited number of cheaper lunch
sets (from ¥1500).

TREASURE HUNT

Begin your shopping adventure

Treasure Hunt

Since the Edo era, when courtesans set the day's trends in towering geta (traditional wooden sandals), Tokyoites have lusted after both the novel and the outstanding. The city remains the trendsetter for the rest of Japan and its residents shop – economy be damned – with an infectious enthusiasm. Shopping highlights include the grand department stores of Ginza and Nihombashi; the fashionable boutiques in Harajuku, Ebisu and Daikanyama; the traditional craft shops in Kuramae and Asakusa; and the flea markets (good for used kimono) that pop up around the city.

In This Section

Marunouchi & Nihombashi	152
Ginza & Tsukiji	153
Roppongi & Akasaka	155
Ebisu & Meguro	157
Shibuya & Shimo-Kitazawa	159
Harajuku & Aoyama	159
Kōenji, Kichijōji & West Tokyo	160
Shinjuku & Ikebukuro	161
Kagurazaka, Kanda & Akihabara	164
Ueno & Yanesen	166
Asakusa & Ryōgoku	167

Duty-Free Shopping

Major department stores and electronics stores offer duty-free shopping; increasingly, so do smaller-scale shops. Look for stickers in windows that say 'tax-free shop'. To qualify, you must show your passport and spend over ¥5000 in any one shop. For details, see http://enjoy.taxfree.jp. Otherwise, sales tax is 8%.

Ueno & Yanesen
Old-time open shopping arcades (p166)

Shinjuku & Ikebukuro
Major shopping hubs with something for everyone (p161)

Asakusa & Ryōgoku
Traditional crafts and artisan workshops (p167)

Kōenji, Kichijōji & West Tokyo
Vintage clothing and artsy homewares (p160)

Kagurazaka, Kanda & Akihabara
Electronics, manga, homewares and more (p164)

Harajuku & Aoyama
Quirky street fashion and designer labels (p159)

Marunouchi & Nihombashi
Classic department stores and fashionable malls (p152)

Roppongi & Akasaka
Designer wares and ultramodern malls (p155)

Shibuya & Shimo-Kitazawa
Trendy youthful clothes and second-hand shops (p159)

Ginza & Tsukiji
High-end department stores, boutiques and gourmet goods (p153)

Ebisu & Meguro
One-of-a-kind boutiques for clothes and more (p157)

Tokyo Bay

Opening Hours

Department stores open from 10am to 8pm, while major electronic stores open from 10am to 10pm. Boutiques get a late start, opening at 11am or noon and closing around 8pm. Most shops are open on Sundays, but may close an hour earlier; boutiques close one or two days a week, often during the middle of the week.

Sales

Clothing sales happen, sadly, just twice a year in Japan: at the beginning of January (after the New Year's holiday) and again at the beginning of July. Markdowns start at 30% and gradually increase towards the end of the month.

The Best...

Experience Tokyo's best shopping

Fashion & Design

Laforet (p48) Harajuku department store stocked with quirky and cutting-edge brands.
Fake Tokyo (p159) A hotbed of up-and-coming Japanese fashion designers.
Kapital (p157) Denim woven on vintage looms and lush, hand-dyed textiles.
Sou-Sou (p160) Traditional Japanese clothing with contemporary panache.
Kita-Kore Building (p161) Over-the-top, only-in-Tokyo designs.
Isetan (p161) Tokyo's most fashion-forward department store.

Character Goods

Kiddyland (p49) Toy emporium stocked to the rafters.
Sanrioworld Ginza (p155) For all your Hello Kitty needs.
Pokemon Center Mega Tokyo (p162) The gang's all here.
Tokyo Character Street (p153) Official plush toys and all things *kawaii*.

Arts & Crafts

Takumi (p153) One-stop shop for earthy traditional crafts from all over Japan.
Japan Traditional Crafts Aoyama Square (p155) Collection of high-end Japanese artisan work.
Kurodaya (p167) One-hundred-and-fifty-year-old *washi* (Japanese paper) specialist.

Food & Kitchen

Marugoto Nippon (p167) Showcase of food products from around Japan.
Mitsukoshi (p155) Classic department store basement food hall.
Kappabashi-dōri (p166) Tokyo's kitchenware shopping strip (pictured above), favoured by pros.

Books

Daikanyama T-Site (p157) Designer digs for art and travel tomes.

Kinokuniya (p162) The city's best selection of books on Japan in English.

Shibuya Publishing Booksellers (p159) Hip hangout with some good titles on Tokyo in English.

Homewares

Yanaka Matsunoya (p166) Handmade household staples, such as brooms and baskets.

Muji (p152) Minimalist, utilitarian and utterly indispensable homewares at reasonable prices (pictured above).

Starnet (p153) Beautiful pottery and wooden bowls.

Antiques & Vintage

Ōedo Antique Market (p153) Quality vendors twice a month at Tokyo International Forum.

Tokyo Hotarudo (p167) Treasure trove of early-20th-century accessories and homewares.

Dog (p48) Outré vintage clothes favoured by club kids.

★ Lonely Planet's Top Choices

Tokyu Hands (p162) Fascinating emporium of miscellaneous oddities.

2k540 Aki-Oka Artisan (p164) Modern artisan bazaar under the train tracks.

Akomeya (p154) Beautifully packaged, traditional gourmet foodstuffs.

Itōya (p153) Ginza institution for stationery and art supplies.

Okura (p157) Indigo-hue fashion against a whitewashed backdrop.

Dover Street Market (p154) Ginza Comme des Garçons and other avant-garde labels.

🅐 Marunouchi & Nihombashi

Coredo Muromachi   Mall

(コレド室町; Map p250; http://31urban.jp/lng/eng/muromachi.html; 2-2-1 Nihonbashi-Muromachi, Chūō-ku; ⊙most shops 11am-7pm; Ⓢ Ginza line to Mitsukoshimae, exit A4) Spread over three buildings, this stylish development hits its stride at Coredo Muromachi 3. This section houses several well-curated floors of top-class, Japanese-crafted goods including cosmetics, fashion, homewares, eyeglasses and speciality food.

Muji   Homewares

(無印良品; Map p250; ☎03-5208-8241; www.muji.com; 3-8-3 Marunouchi, Chiyoda-ku; ⊙10am-9pm; Ⓡ JR Yamanote line to Yūrakuchō, Kyōbashi exit) The flagship store of the famously understated brand sells elegant, simple clothing, accessories and homewares. There are scores of other outlets across Tokyo, including a good one in Tokyo Midtown, but the Yūrakuchō store is the largest with the biggest range. It also offers tax-free shopping, bicycle rental (¥1080 a day from 10am to 8pm) and a great cafeteria.

KITTE   Mall

(Map p250; https://jptower-kitte.jp/en; 2-7-2 Marunouchi, Chiyoda-ku; ⊙11am-9pm Mon-Sat, to 8pm Sun; Ⓡ JR lines to Tokyo, Marunouchi south exit) This well-designed shopping mall at the foot of JP Tower incorporates the restored facade of the former Tokyo Central Post Office. It is notable for its atrium, around which is arrayed a quality selection of craft-orientated Japanese brand shops selling homewares, fashion, accessories and lifestyle goods.

Takashimaya   Department Store

(高島屋; Map p250; www.takashimaya.co.jp/tokyo/store_information; 2-4-1 Nihombashi, Chūō-ku; ⊙10am-8pm; Ⓢ Ginza line to Nihombashi, Takashimaya exit) The design of Takashimaya's flagship store (1933) tips its pillbox hat to New York's Gilded Age with marble columns, chandeliers and uniformed female elevator operators announcing each floor in high-pitched sing-song voices.

KITTE

Bic Camera — Electronics

(ビックカメラ; Map p250; ☑03-5221-1111; www.
biccamera.co.jp; 1-11-1Yūrakuchō, Chiyoda-ku;
⏱10am-10pm; 🚉JR Yamanote line to Yūrakuchō,
Kokusai Center exit) Cameras are just the
start of the electronic items and much
more (toys, sake, medicine and cosmetics)
sold in this mammoth discount store occu-
pying a block. Shopping here is like being
inside a very noisy computer game, but it's
worth enduring for the discounts and the
tax-free deals available to tourists.

Tokyo Character Street — Toys

(東京キャラクターストリート; Map p250;
www.tokyoeki-1bangai.co.jp; B1 First Avenue
Tokyo Station, 1-9-1 Marunouchi, Chiyoda-ku;
⏱10am-8.30pm; 🚉JR lines to Tokyo Station, Yaesu exit) From Doraemon to Hello Kitty and
Ultraman, Japan knows *kawaii* (cute) and
how to merchandise it. In the basement
on the Yaesu side of Tokyo Station (p101),
some 15 Japanese TV networks and toy
manufacturers operate stalls selling official
plush toys, sweets, accessories and the
all-important miniature character to dangle
from your mobile phone.

Starnet — Arts & Crafts

(Map p250; ☑03-5809-3336; www.starnet-bkds.
com; 1-3-9 Higashi-Kanda, Chiyoda-ku; ⏱11am-
7pm Tue-Sun; 🚉JR Sobu line to Bakurochō, exit 2)
Stocking artisan crafts mainly from Mashiko,
a famous pottery town in Tochigi Prefecture,
appealing Starnet is an earthy boutique that
looks like it's straight out of a hip design
magazine. Come to browse beautiful pieces
of pottery, wooden bowls and hand-dyed
clothing. Also sells organic food products.

🔘 Ginza & Tsukiji

Itōya — Arts & Crafts

(伊東屋; Map p250; www.ito-ya.co.jp; 2-7-15
Ginza, Chūō-ku; ⏱10.30am-8pm Mon-Sat, to 7pm
Sun; 🚇Ginza line to Ginza, exit A13) Nine floors
(plus several more in the nearby annexe) of
stationery-shop love await visual-art pro-
fessionals and seekers of office accessories
with both everyday and luxury items such

Flea Markets

Flea markets pop up regularly around
Tokyo; odds are there will be at least one
on when you visit. Many take place on
the grounds of Shintō shrines. Though
bargaining is permitted, remember that
it is considered bad form to drive too
hard a bargain. Note that sometimes
shrine events (or weather) interfere with
markets.

Hipster flea market **Raw Tokyo** (Map
p246; www.rawtokyo.jp; 5-53-7 Jingūmae,
Shibuya-ku; ⏱11am-6pm, 1st Sat & Sun of
the month; 🚇Ginza line to Omote-sandō, exit
B2) is held on the first weekend of the
month. Quality vendors gather twice a
month at Tokyo International Forum for
the excellent **Ōedo Antique Market**
(大江戸骨董市; Map p250; ☑03-6407-6011;
www.antique-market.jp; 3-5-1 Marunouchi,
Chiyoda-ku; ⏱9am-4pm 1st & 3rd Sun of
month; 🚉JR Yamanote line to Yūrakuchō,
Kokusai Forum exit).

For an updated schedule of all the
city's flea markets, see www.frma.jp (in
Japanese).

Flea market in Harajuku
ADOLDEJ / SHUTTERSTOCK©

as fountain pens and Italian leather agen-
das. You'll also find *washi* (fine Japanese
handmade paper), *tenugui* (beautifully
hand-dyed thin cotton towels) and *furoshiki*
(wrapping cloths).

Takumi — Arts & Crafts

(たくみ; Map p250; ☑03-3571-2017; www.gin-
za-takumi.co.jp; 8-4-2 Ginza, Chūō-ku; ⏱11am-7pm
Mon-Sat; 🚇Ginza line to Shimbashi, exit 5) You're

★ **Top Five Malls**
mAAch ecute (p164)
Coredo Muromachi (p152)
Ginza Six
KITTE (p152)
Solamachi (p167)

From left: KITTE (p152); Solamachi (p167); Ginza Six

unlikely to find a more elegant selection of traditional folk crafts, including toys, textiles and ceramics from around Japan. Ever thoughtful, this shop also encloses information detailing the origin and background of the pieces if you make a purchase.

Akomeya   Food
(Map p250; ☑03-6758-0271; www.akomeya.jp; 2-2-6 Ginza, Chūō-ku; ⊘shop 11am-9pm, restaurant 11.30am-10pm; ⑤Yūrakuchō line to Ginza-itchōme, exit 4) Rice is at the core of Japanese cuisine and drink. This stylish store sells not only many types of the grain but also products made from it (such as sake), a vast range of quality cooking ingredients and a choice collection of kitchen, home and bath items.

Dover Street Market Ginza   Fashion & Accessories
(DSM; Map p250; ☑03-6228-5080; http://ginza.doverstreetmarket.com; 6-9-5 Ginza, Chūō-ku; ⊘11am-8pm; ⑤Ginza line to Ginza, exit A2) A department store as envisioned by Kawakubo Rei (of Comme des Garçons), DSM has seven floors of avant-garde brands, including several Japanese labels

and everything in the Comme des Garçons line-up. The quirky art installations alone make it worth the visit.

Tsukiji Hitachiya   Homewares
(つきじ常陸屋; Map p250; 4-14-18 Tsukiji, Chūō-ku; ⊘8am-3pm Mon-Sat, 10am-2pm Sun; ⑤Hibiya line to Tsukiji, exit 1) Tokyo chefs and cooks seek out Hitachiya for hand-forged knives, sturdy bamboo baskets and other great kitchen and cooking tools.

Ginza Six   Mall
(Map p250; http://ginza6.tokyo; 6-10 Ginza, Chūō-ku; ⊘10am-10pm; ⑤Ginza line to Ginza, exit A2) This high-end mall, opened in 2017, includes international and local top-brand shops, restaurants, a superior food hall, a 4000-sq-metre rooftop garden and art in the public areas.

Uniqlo   Fashion & Accessories
(ユニクロ; Map p250; www.uniqlo.com; 5-7-7 Ginza, Chūō-ku; ⊘11am-9pm; ⑤Ginza line to Ginza, exit A2) This now-global brand has made its name by sticking to the basics and tweaking them with style. Offering inexpensive, quality clothing, this is the Tokyo flagship

NED SNOWMAN / SHUTTERSTOCK ©

store with 11 floors and items you won't find elsewhere.

Mitsukoshi
Department Store

(三越, Map p250; www.mitsukoshi.co.jp; 4-6-16 Ginza, Chūō-ku; ⊗10am-8pm; ⑤Ginza line to Ginza, exits A7 & A11) One of Ginza's grande dames, Mitsukoshi embodies the essence of the Tokyo department store. Don't miss the basement food hall.

Natsuno
Homewares

(夏野; Map p250; ☑03-3569-0952; www.e-ohashi.com; 6-7-4 Ginza, Chūō-ku; ⊗10am-8pm Mon-Sat, to 7pm Sun; ⑤Ginza line to Ginza, exit B3) Shelf after ashelf of *o-hashi* (chopsticks) in wood, lacquer and even gold leaf line the walls of this intimate shop, alongside plenty of *hashi-oki* (chopstick rests) to match. Prices run from a few hundred yen to ¥10,000. On the 6th floor, its sister shop Konatsu sells adorable tableware for kids.

Sanrioworld Ginza
Fashion & Accessories

(サンリオワールド ギンザ; Map p250; ☑03-3566-4060; www.sanrio.co.jp/english/store/sh1703100; Nishi Ginza Department Store 4-1

Saki, Ginza, Chuo-ku; ⊗11am-8.30pm Mon, Tue & Sat, to 9pm Wed-Fri, to 8pm Sun; ⑤Ginza line to Ginza, exit C5) Sanrio's flagship store is piled high with all the Hello Kitty merchandise your heart could desire, including some pretty blinged-up items of the famous feline fashion icon.

Antique Mall Ginza
Antiques

(アンティークモール銀座; Map p250; ☑03-3535-2115; www.antiques-jp.com; 1-13-1 Ginza, Chūō-ku; ⊗11am-7pm Thu-Tue; ⑤Yūrakuchō line to Ginza-itchōme, exit A10) At this subterranean market of antique and retro goods, you can pick up anything from old lacquerware and pottery to beautifully embroidered *obi* (the broad belt of a kimono) and jewellery. There are also some European pieces.

⊕ Roppongi & Akasaka

Japan Traditional Crafts Aoyama Square
Arts & Crafts

(伝統工芸 青山スクエア; ☑03-5785-1301; http://kougeihin.jp/home.shtml; 8-1-22 Akasaka, Minato-ku; ⊗11am-7pm; ⑤Ginza line to Aoyama-itchōme, exit 4) Supported by the Japanese

Shopping for Kimono

New kimonos are prohibitively expensive – a full set can easily cost a million yen; used kimono, on the other hand, can be found for as little as ¥1000 – though one in good shape will cost more like ¥10,000. It takes a lot of practice to get down the art of tying an *obi* (sash) properly, so it's a good idea to get shop staff to help you (though there's no reason you can't just wear one like a dressing gown and forgo the sash entirely). Another option is a *yukata*, a lightweight, cotton kimono that's easier to wear. Used kimono and *yukata* can also be found year-round for bargain prices at flea markets. Also try the following:

Gallery Kawano (ギャラリー川野; Map p246; www.gallery-kawano.com; 4-4-9 Jingūmae, Shibuya-ku; ◎11am-6pm; 🚇Ginza line to Omote-sandō, exit A2) Vintage kimonos in good condition.

Tsukikageya (月影屋; Map p246; www.tsukikageya.com; 1-9-19 Tomigaya, Shibuya-ku; ◎noon-8pm Thu-Sun; 🚇Chiyoda line to Yoyogi-kōen, exit 2) Yukata in punk-rock prints.

Chicago (シカゴ; Map p246; 6-31-21 Jingūmae, Shibuya-ku; ◎10am-8pm; 🚇JR Yamanote line to Harajuku, Omote-sandō exit) Bargain bins of secondhand kimonos and yukata.

Kimonos for sale on Nakamise-dōri (p78)
SIMONLONG / GETTY IMAGES ©

cut glass, paper, textiles and earthy pottery. The emphasis is on high-end pieces, but you can find beautiful things in all price ranges here.

Souvenir from Tokyo
Gifts & Souvenirs

(スーベニアフロムトーキョー; Map p252; 📞03-6812 9933; www.souvenirfromtokyo.jp; basement fl, National Art Center Tokyo, 7-22-2 Roppongi, Minato-ku; ◎10am-6pm Sat-Mon, Wed & Thu, to 8pm Fri; 🚇Chiyoda line to Nogizaka, exit 6) This shop, in the basement of the National Art Center Tokyo, sells an expert selection of home-grown design bits and bobs that make for perfect, unique souvenirs: a mobile by Tempo, a bag made from fabric dyed using the *shibori* technique or a fun face pack with a kabuki design.

Axis Design
Design

(アクシスビル; Map p252; www.axisinc.co.jp; 5-17-1 Roppongi, Minato-ku; ◎11am-7pm; 🚇Hibiya line to Roppongi, exit 3) Salivate over some of Japan's most innovative interior design at this high-end design complex of galleries and shops selling art books, cutting-edge furniture and other objets d'art.

Blue & White
Arts & Crafts

(ブルー アンド ホワイト; http://blueandwhitetokyo.com; 2-9-2 Azabu-Jūban, Minato-ku; ◎11am-6pm; 🚇Namboku or Ōedo line to Azabu-Jūban, exit 4) Expat American Amy Katoh sells traditional and contemporary items such as *tenugui* (hand-dyed towels), indigo-dyed *yukata* (light cotton kimonos), bolts of nubby cloth and painted chopsticks. Pick through dishes of ceramic beads or collect bundled-up swatches of fabric for your own creations.

Tolman Collection
Arts & Crafts

(トールマンコレクション; 📞03-3434-1300; www.tolmantokyo.com; 2-2-18 Shiba-Daimon, Minato-ku; ◎11am-7pm Wed-Mon; 🚇Ōedo line to Daimon, exit A3) Based in a traditional wooden building, this reputable gallery represents nearly 50 leading Japanese artists of printing, lithography, etching, woodblock and more. Quality prints start at around ¥10,000 and rise steeply from there. From

Ministry of Economy, Trade and Industry, this is as much a showroom as a shop exhibiting a broad range of traditional crafts, including lacquerwork boxes, woodwork,

Daimon Station, walk west towards Zōjō-ji. Turn left at the shop Create. You'll soon see the gallery on your left.

🔒 Ebisu & Meguro

Okura
Fashion & Accessories

(オクラ; Map p246; www.hrm.co.jp/okura; 20-11 Sarugaku-chō, Shibuya-ku; ⊗11.30am-8pm Mon-Fri, 11am-8.30pm Sat & Sun; 🚇Tōkyū Tōyoko line to Daikanyama) Almost everything in this enchanting shop is dyed a deep indigo blue – from contemporary tees and sweatshirts to classic work shirts. There are some beautiful, original items (though unfortunately most aren't cheap). The shop itself looks like a rural house, with worn, wooden floorboards and whitewashed walls. Note: there's no sign out the front, but the building stands out.

Kapital
Fashion & Accessories

(キャピタル; Map p246; 📞03-5725-3923; http://kapital.jp; 2-20-2 Ebisu, Shibuya-ku; ⊗11am-8pm; 🚇JR Yamanote line to Ebisu, west exit) Cult brand Kapital is hard to pin down, but perhaps a de-constructed mash-up of the American West and the centuries-old Japanese aesthetic of *boro* (tatty) chic comes close. Almost no two items are alike; most are unisex. The shop itself is like an art installation. The staff, not snobby at all, can point you towards the other two shops nearby.

Daikanyama T-Site
Books

(代官山T-SITE; Map p246; http://tsite.jp/daikanyama; 17-5 Sarugaku-chō, Shibuya-ku; ⊗7am-2am; 🚇Tōkyū Tōyoko line to Daikanyama) Locals love this stylish shrine to the printed word, which has a fantastic collection of books on travel, art, design and food (and some of them in English). The best part is that you can sit at the in-house Starbucks and read all afternoon – if you can get a seat that is.

Vase
Fashion & Accessories

(Map p246; vasenakameguro.com; 1-7-7 Kami-Meguro, Meguro-ku; ⊗noon-8pm; 🚇Hibiya line to Naka-Meguro) A perfect example of one of

It takes a lot of practice to get down the art of tying an obi (sash) properly

Nakamise-dōri (p78)

Top Five Tokyo Souvenirs

Japanese Design

Bring back some wearable Tokyo style from ahead-of-the-curve boutiques or department stores, such as Fake Tokyo (p159) or Isetan (p161).

Kitchenware

You saw that sushi chef work magic with that knife. Get one for yourself (and other useful kitchen tools) at Tsukiji Hitachiya (p154).

Furoshiki

These colourful patterned cloths, found in myriad designs, can be knotted into totes and reusable wrappings. Try Musubi (p48) and Itōya (p153).

Gourmet Goods

Pick up green tea, jars of seasoned miso paste, *wagashi* (pictured above) and *matcha*-flavoured sweets at gourmet shops such as Akomeya (p154).

Cute Characters

Shop for mascots of Japanese pop culture (such as Hello Kitty and Pikachu) at Kiddyland (p49).

Naka-Meguro's tiny, impeccably curated boutiques, Vase stocks avant-garde designers and vintage pieces (for men and women), also hosting the occasional trunk show. It's in a little white house set back from the Meguro-gawa (with the name on the post box).

Ⓐ Shibuya & Shimo-Kitazawa

Fake Tokyo   Fashion & Accessories
(Map p246; ☑03-5456-9892; www.faketokyo.com; 18-4 Udagawa-chō, Shibuya-ku; ◷noon-10pm; ◪JR Yamanote line to Shibuya, Hachikō exit) This is one of the best places in the city to discover hot underground Japanese designers. It's actually two shops in one. downstairs is Candy, full of brash, unisex streetwear; upstairs is Sister, which specialises in more ladylike items, both new and vintage. Look for the 'Fake Tokyo' banners out front.

Shibuya 109   Fashion & Accessories
(渋谷109; Ichimarukyū; Map p246; www.shibuya109.jp/en/top; 2-29-1 Dōgenzaka, Shibuya-ku; ◷10am-9pm; ◪JR Yamanote line to Shibuya, Hachikō exit) See all those dolled-up teens walking around Shibuya? This is where they shop. Nicknamed *marukyū*, this cylindrical tower houses dozens of small boutiques, each with its own carefully styled look (and competing soundtrack). Even if you don't intend to buy anything, you can't understand Shibuya without making a stop here.

Otonomad   Music
(オトノマド; www.otonomad.com; 3-26-4 Kitazawa, Setagaya-ku; ◷1-8pm Mon-Wed, Fri & Sat, noon-7pm Sun; ◪Keiō Inokashira line to Shimo-Kitazawa, north exit) Otonomad is one of Shimo-Kitazawa's hole-in-the-wall record shops, a tiny cubbyhole with an impeccably curated selection of CDs and records (new and used; classic and current) from around the globe. If you're hunting for eclectic and avant-garde Japanese music, you'll find some here.

Haight & Ashbury   Vintage
(http://haightandashbury.com; 2nd fl, 2-37-2 Kitazawa, Setagaya-ku; ◷noon-9pm; ◪Keiō Inokashira line to Shimo-Kitazawa, north exit) Shimo-Kitazawa's best vintage shop, H&A – not H&M – provides all the props and costumes you'd need to re-enact almost any theatrical number, from the goatherd scene in *The Sound of Music* to the opening act of *Cabaret*.

Shibuya Publishing Booksellers   Books
(SPBS; Map p246; www.shibuyabooks.co.jp; 17-3 Kamiyamachō, Shibuya-ku; ◷noon-midnight Mon-Sat, noon-10pm Sun; ◪JR Yamanote line to Shibuya, Hachikō exit) Leading the wave of hipster bookshops, SPBS is a high-brow alternative to the bars along Shibuya's Kamiyamachō *shōtengai* (market street). There's a decent offering of English-language books and a fine collection of artsy, photo-heavy Japanese magazines.

Tower Records   Music
(タワーレコード; Map p246; ☑03-3496-3661; http://tower.jp/store/Shibuya; 1-22-14 Jinnan, Shibuya-ku; ◷10am-11pm; ◪JR Yamanote line to Shibuya, Hachikō exit) Yes, Tower lives – in Japan at least! This eight-storey temple of music has a deep collection of Japanese and world music. Even if you're not into buying, it can be a great place to browse and discover local artists.

Shibuya Hikarie   Mall
(渋谷ヒカリエ; Map p246; www.hikarie.jp; 2-21-1 Shibuya, Shibuya-ku; ◷10am-9pm; ◪JR Yamanote line to Shibuya, east exit) The first five floors of this glass skyscraper are filled with the latest trendy boutiques. In the basement levels are dozens of gourmet take-away counters.

Ⓑ Harajuku & Aoyama

See p46 for more shopping options in Harajuku.

Sou-Sou   Fashion & Accessories
(そうそう; Map p246; ☑03-3407-7877; http://sousounetshop.jp; 5-3-10 Minami-Aoyama,

Minato-ku; ⊗11am-8pm; [S]Ginza line to Omotesandō, exit A5) Kyoto brand Sou-Sou gives traditional Japanese clothing items – such as split-toed *tabi* socks and *haori* (coats with kimono-like sleeves) – a contemporary spin. It is best known for producing the steel-toed, rubber-soled *tabi* shoes worn by Japanese construction workers in fun, playful designs, but it also carries bags, tees and super-adorable children's clothing.

Arts & Science
Fashion & Accessories

(Map p246; http://arts-science.com/; 101, 103, 105 & 109 Palace Aoyama, 6-1-6 Minami-Aoyama, Minato-ku; ⊗noon-8pm; [S]Ginza line to Omotesandō, exit A5) Strung along the 1st floor of a mid-century apartment (across from the Nezu Museum) is a collection of small boutiques from celebrity stylist Sonya Park. Park's signature style is a vintage-inspired minimalism in luxurious, natural fabrics. Homewares, too.

Comme des Garçons
Fashion & Accessories

(コム・デ・ギャルソン; Map p246; www. comme-des-garcons.com; 5-2-1 Minami-Aoyama,

Minato-ku; ⊗11am-8pm; [S]Ginza line to Omotesandō, exit A5) Designer Kawakubo Rei threw a wrench in the fashion machine in the early '80s with her dark, asymmetrical designs. That her work doesn't appear as shocking today as it once did speaks volumes for her far-reaching success. This eccentric, vaguely disorienting architectural creation is her brand's flagship store.

⑥ Kōenji, Kichijōji & West Tokyo

PukuPuku
Antiques

(ぷくぷく; http://pukupukukichi.blogspot. jp/; 2-26-2 Kichijōji Honchō, Musashino-shi; ⊗11.30am-7.30pm; [R]JR Sōbu-Chūō line to Kichijōji, north exit) This cluttered little antiques shop stocks ceramics from the early Shōwa (昭和; 1926–1989) period, through Taishō (大正; 1912–1926) and Meiji (明治; 1868–1912) and all the way back to old Edo (江戸; 1603–1868). Flip the dishes over for a sticker that indicates the period. Hundred-year-old saucers can be had for as little as ¥1000.

Shibuya 109 (p159)

Outbound   Homewares

(アウトバウンド; http://outbound.to/; 2-7-4-101 Kichijōji Honchō, Musashino-shi; ☺11am-7pm Wed-Mon; 🚉JR Sōbu-Chūō line to Kichijōji, north exit) Outbound stocks beautiful homewares and objets d'art for your bohemian dream house. Works are earthy, made by contemporary artisans and displayed in gallery-like exhibitions.

🅖 Shinjuku & Ikebukuro

Isetan   Department Store

(伊勢丹; Map p253; www.isetan.co.jp; 3-14-1 Shinjuku, Shinjuku-ku; ☺10am-8pm; Ⓢ Marunouchi line to Shinjuku-sanchōme, exits B3, B4 & B5) Most department stores play to conservative tastes, but this one doesn't. For an always-changing line-up of up-and-coming Japanese womenswear designers, check out the Tokyo Closet (2nd floor) and Re-Style (3rd floor) boutiques. Men get a whole building of their own (connected by a passageway). Don't miss the basement food hall, featuring famous purveyors of sweet and savoury goodies.

Beams   Fashion & Accessories

(ビームス; Map p253; www.beams.co.jp; 3-32-6 Shinjuku, Shinjuku-ku; ☺11am-8pm; 🚉JR Yamanote line to Shinjuku, east exit) Beams, a national chain of boutiques, is a cultural force in Japan. This multistorey Shinjuku shop is particularly good for the latest Japanese streetwear labels and work from designers giving traditional looks a modern twist (including men, women and unisex fashions). Also sometimes available: crafts, housewares and original artwork (the line-up is always changing).

Bingoya   Arts & Crafts

(備後屋; www.quasar.nu/bingoya; 10-6 Wakamatsu-chō Shinjuku-ku; ☺10am-7pm Tue-Sun, closed 3rd Sat & Sun of the month; Ⓢ Toei Ōedo line to Wakamatsu-Kawada) Bingoya has five floors of quality, unpretentious crafts sourced from all over Japan. There's a particularly good selection of folksy pottery and textiles. Since it's a little out of the way, it's

🛍 **Creative Kōenji**

Kōenji, a neighbourhood on the west side of Tokyo, west of Shinjuku, is a draw for shoppers who prefer vintage duds and artistic one-offs to brand-name labels. Among the dozens of secondhand shops, **Sokkyō** (即興; www.sokkyou.net; 102 Nakanishi Apt Bldg, 3-59-14 Kōenji-minami, Suginami-ku; ☺1-9pm, holidays irregular; 🚉JR Sōbu line to Kōenji, south exit) stands out. The stock is impeccably edited down to a look that is both dreamy and modern. (That said, we may have sent you on an impossible mission: the shop is unmarked in an ordinary house down a tiny alley. When it's open, however, an article of clothing will be hanging outside).

Another must-see in Kōenji, the **Kita-Kore Building** (キタコレビル; 3-4-11 Kōenji-kita, Suginami-ku; ☺1-8pm; 🚉JR Sōbu line to Kōenji, north exit) is a dilapidated shack of a structure housing a handful of seriously outré shops. Really, it's more art installation than shopping destination, though we do know of at least one person who's actually bought stuff here – Lady Gaga.

better for buyers than browsers; the store can help arrange shipping overseas. It's just in front of Wakamatsu-Kawada Station; look across the main street, to the right.

Don Quijote   Gifts & Souvenirs

(ドン・キホーテ; Map p253; ☎03-5291-9211; www.donki.com; 1-16-5 Kabukichō, Shinjuku-ku;

 Variety Stores

Zakka-ten (literally 'miscellaneous stores') carry an offbeat selection of beauty goods, clever kitchen gadgets and other quirky sundries in attractive packaging – all intended to add a little colour, ease or joy to daily life. They're excellent for souvenir hunting.

Hands-down the best is Tokyu Hands, which has multiple floors of everything you didn't know you needed, such as reflexology slippers, bee-venom face masks and cartoon-character-shaped rice-ball moulds. There are branches in **Shibuya** (東急ハンズ; Map p246; http:// shibuya.tokyu-hands.co.jp; 12-18 Udagawa-chō, Shibuya-ku; ☺10am-8.30pm; 🚊JR Yamanote line to Shibuya, Hachikō exit) and **Shinjuku** (東急ハンズ; Map p253; Takashimaya Times Sq, 5-24-2 Sendagaya, Shibuya-ku; ☺10am-8.30pm; 🚊JR Yamanote line to Shinjuku, new south exit). Warning: you could lose hours in here.
Loft (ロフト; Map p246; ☎03-3462-3807; www.loft.co.jp; 18-2 Udagawa-chō, Shibuya-ku; ☺10am-9pm; 🚊JR Yamanote line to Shibuya, Hachikō exit) in Shibuya is another good bet.

Loft
USJ / SHUTTERSTOCK ©

☺24hr; 🚊JR Yamanote line to Shinjuku, east exit) This fluorescent-lit bargain castle is filled to the brink with weird loot. Chaotic piles of electronics and designer goods sit alongside sex toys, fetish costumes and packaged foods. Though it's now a national chain, it started as a rare (at the time) 24-hour store for the city's night workers.

Pokemon Center
Mega Tokyo   Toys
(ポケモンセンターメガトウキョー; ☎03-5927-9290; www.pokemon.co.jp/gp/pokecen/english/megatokyo_access.html; Sunshine City, 3-1-2 Higashi-Ikebukuro, Toshima-ku; ☺10am-10pm; 🅂Yūrakuchō line to Higashi-Ikebukuro, exit 2) Japan's largest Pokémon centre sells every piece of the series' merchandise. You can also pose with several large statues around the store, including the store's mascot: Pikachu riding on the back of a Mega Charizard Y.

Disk Union   Music
(ディスクユニオン; Map p253; 3-31-4 Shinjuku, Shinjuku-ku; ☺11am-9pm; 🚊JR Yamanote line to Shinjuku, east exit) Scruffy Disk Union is known by local audiophiles as Tokyo's best used-CD and vinyl store. Eight storeys carry a variety of musical styles; if you still can't find what you're looking for there are several other branches in Shinjuku that stock more obscure genres (pick up a map here).

Kinokuniya   Books
(紀伊國屋書店; Map p253; www.kinokuniya.co.jp; Takashimaya Times Sq, 5-24-2 Sendagaya, Shibuya-ku; ☺10am-8pm; 🚊JR Yamanote line to Shinjuku, south exit) The 6th floor here has a broad selection of foreign-language books and magazines, including many titles on Japan and English-teaching texts.

Acos   Fashion & Accessories
(www.acos.me; 3-2-1 Higashi Ikebukuro, Toshima-ku; ☺11am-8pm; 🚊JR Yamanote line to Ikebukuro, east exit) Acos is *otaku* superstore Animate's cosplay speciality shop, but you don't need to be a fan to appreciate the mesmerising selection of reasonably good quality wigs (literally hundreds of styles in all the colours of the rainbow), pancake make-up, coloured contact lenses and accessories (like stick-on tear drops). It's on Otome Rd.

Lumine Est   Mall
(ルミネエスト; Map p253; www.lumine.ne.jp/est; 3-38-1 Shinjuku, Shinjuku-ku; ☺11am-10pm; 🚊JR Yamanote line to Shinjuku, east exit) Connected to Shinjuku Station (enter from the

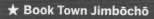

★ Book Town Jimbōchō

This fascinating neighbourhood of more than 170 new and secondhand booksellers is proof that the printed word is alive and well in Tokyo. Amid tottering stacks of volumes you'll find everything from antique guidebooks of the Yoshiwara pleasure district to obscure sheet music from your favourite symphony.

2k540 Aki-Oka Artisan

east exit), this Lumine (there are several) stocks trendy and youthful Japanese labels.

NEWoMan
Mall

(Map p253; www.newoman.jp; 4-1-6 Shinjuku, Shinjuku-ku; ⊙11am-10pm, food hall 8am-10pm; 🚃JR Yamanote line to Shinjuku, new south exit) Awkward name and unlikely location (within the Shinjuku Bus Terminal complex) aside, this new mall is one of Tokyo's swankiest places to shop. There's a branch of the excellent food-and-kitchen-stuffs shop Akomeya (p154) in the basement and a line-up of posh takeaway vendors on the 2nd-floor terrace.

🔘 Kagurazaka, Kanda & Akihabara

2k540
Aki-Oka Artisan
Arts & Crafts

(アキオカアルチザン; Map p254; www.jrtk. jp/2k540; 5-9-23 Ueno, Taitō-ku; ⊙11am-7pm Thu-Tue; 🚃Ginza line to Suehirochō, exit 2) This ace arcade under the JR tracks (its name refers to the distance from Tokyo Station)

offers an eclectic range of stores selling Japanese-made goods – everything from pottery and leatherwork to cute aliens, a nod to Akihabara from a mall that is more akin to Kyoto than Electric Town. The best for colourful crafts is **Nippon Hyakkuten** (日本百貨店; http://nippon-dept.jp).

mAAch ecute
Mall

(Map p254; 📞03-3257-8910; www.maach-ecute.jp; 1-25-4 Kanda-Sudachō, Chiyoda-ku; ⊙11am-9pm Mon-Sat, to 8pm Sun; 🚃Chūō or Sōbu lines to Akihabara, Electric Town exit) JR has another shopping and dining hit on its hands with this complex crafted from the old station and red-brick railway arches at Mansei-bashi. Crafts, homewares, fashions and food from across Japan are sold here; look out for craft beers from **Hitachino Brewing Lab** and freshly roasted beans from **Obscura Coffee Roasters**.

Chabara
Food

(ちゃばら; Map p254; www.jrtk.jp/chabara; 8-2 Kanda Neribei-chō, Chiyoda-ku; ⊙11am-8pm; 🚃JR Yamanote line to Akihabara, Electric Town exit) This under-the-train-tracks shopping mall focuses on artisan food and drinks from across Japan, including premium sake, soy sauce, sweets, teas and crackers – all great souvenirs and presents.

Ohya Shobō   Books

(大屋書房; Map p254; ✆03-3291-0062; www. ohya-shobo.com; 1-1 Kanda-Jimbōchō, Chiyoda-ku; ⏰10am-6pm Mon-Sat; ☒Hanzōmon line to Jimbōchō, exit A7) This splendid, musty old bookshop specialises in *ukiyo-e* (wood-block prints), both old and newly printed (from ¥2000). There are antique books and maps, too. The staff are friendly and can help you with whatever you're looking for. All purchases are tagged with a small origami crane.

Baikatei   Food

(梅花亭; ✆03-5228-0727; www.baikatei.co.jp; 6-15 Kagurazaka, Shinjuku-ku; ⏰10am-8pm, to 7.30pm Sun; ☒Tōzai line to Kagurazaka, exit 1) See (and sample) humble beans and rice whipped into pastel flowers at this award-winning traditional sweets shop, in business since 1935. There are blue door curtains out front.

Kukuli   Arts & Crafts

(くくり; ✆03-6280-8462; www.kukuli.co.jp; 1-10 Tsukudo-chō, Shinjuku-ku; ⏰11am-7pm; ☒JR Yamanote line to Iidabashi, west exit) One of several shops in Kagurazaka specialising in traditional craftwork. Here it's hand-dyed textiles (such as scarves and tea towels) with a modern touch.

La Ronde D'Argile   Homewares

(ラ・ロンダジル; ✆03-3260-6801; http:// la-ronde.com; 11 Wakamiya-chō, Shinjuku-ku; ⏰11.30am-6pm Tue-Sat; ☒Ōedo line to Ushigome-Kagurazaka, exit A2) A changing selection of homewares made by local artisans fills two floors of this old house turned shop. It has a picture window out front, with a small stained-glass sign above it.

Komiyama Shoten   Books

(小宮山書店; Map p254; ✆03-3291-0495; www.book-komiyama.co.jp; 1-7 Kanda-Jimbōchō, Chiyoda-ku; ⏰11am-6.30pm Mon-Sat, to 5.30pm Sun; ☒Hanzōmon line to Jimbōchō, exit A7) Here

 Crafty Kuramae

A short walk south of Asakusa and beside the Sumida-gawa is Tokyo's old rice-granary district of Kuramae (蔵前). The low rents and ingrained culture of craftsmanship here have inspired a new generation of entrepreneurs to make traditional crafts, but with a contemporary twist. As it eschews the flash of other Tokyo shopping districts, an amble around the small boutiques and ateliers here is a pleasure.

Start with **Koncent** (Map p254; ✆03-3862-6018; www.koncent.net; 2-4-5 Kuramae, Taitō-ku; ⏰11am-7pm; ☒Asakusa line to Kuramae, exit A3), a trendy homewares and gift boutique on Edo-dōri, stocking mainly Japanese design products. It serves coffee and produces a detailed, free map (in Japanese) that covers many of the area's interesting businesses. Move on to Kokusai-dōri to shop for customised notebooks and other stationery at **Kakimori** (カキモリ; Map p254; ✆03-3864-3898; www.kakimori. com; 4-20-12 Kuramae, Taitō-ku; ☒Asakusa line to Kuramae, exit 3); naturally dyed clothing and accessories at **Maito** (マイ ト; Map p254; ✆03-3863-1128; www.maito. info; 4-14-2 Kuramae, Taitō-ku; ☒Asakusa line to Kuramae, exit A3); and lovely leather goods at **Camera** (Map p254; ✆03-5825-4170; http://camera1010.tokyo; 4-21-8 Kuramae, Taitō-ku; ⏰11am-6pm Tue-Sun; 📷; ☒Asakusa line to Kuramae, exit A3).

you'll find an incredible selection of art and photography books, posters and prints with

Kappabashi Kitchenware Town

Kappabashi-dōri (合羽橋通り; Map p254; S Ginza line to Tawaramachi, exit 3) is the country's largest wholesale restaurant-supply and kitchenware district. Gourmet accessories include bamboo steamer baskets, lacquer trays, neon signs and *chōchin* (paper lanterns). It's also where restaurants get their freakishly realistic plastic food models.

Ganso Shokuhin Sample-ya (元祖食品サンプル屋; Map p254; ☎0120-17-1839; www.ganso-sample.com; 3-7-6 Nishi-Asakusa, Taitō-ku; ☉10am-5.30pm; S Ginza line to Tawaramachi, exit 3) has a showroom of tongue-in-cheek food models, plus key chains and kits to make your own.

Kitchenware in Kappabashi-dōri
GREG ELMS / GETTY IMAGES ©

some very famous Japanese and international artists represented.

La Kagū　　　Fashion & Accessories
(☎03-5227-6977; www.lakagu.com; 67 Yarai-chō, Shinjuku-ku; ☉11am-8.30pm; S Tōzai line to Kagurazaka, exit 2) Starchitect Kengo Kuma designed this slick revamp of an old book warehouse, turning it into a lifestyle boutique stocking a keenly edited range of fashion and home goods.

🔒 Ueno & Yanesen

Yanaka Matsunoya　　　Homewares
(谷中松野屋; Map p254; www.yanakamatsunoya. jp; 3-14-14 Nishi-Nippori, Arakawa-ku; ☉11am-7pm Mon & Wed-Fri, 10am-7pm Sat & Sun; R JR Yamanote line to Nippori, west exit) At the top of Yanaka Ginza (p63), Matsunoya sells household goods – baskets, brooms and canvas totes, for example – simple in beauty and form, and handmade by local artisans.

Edokoro Allan West　　　Art
(繪処アランウエスト; Map p254; ☎03-3827-1907; www.allanwest.jp; 1-6-17 Yanaka, Taitō-ku; ☉1-5pm, from 3pm Sun, closed irregularly; S Chiyoda line to Nezu, exit 1) **FREE** In this masterfully converted garage, long-time Yanaka resident Allan West paints gorgeous screens and scrolls in the traditional Japanese style, making his paints from scratch just as local artists have done for centuries. Smaller votive-shaped paintings start at ¥5000; the screens clock in at a cool ¥6 million.

Ameyoko Rizumu　　　Music
(アメ横 リズム; Map p254; ☎03-3831-5135; http://open2.sesames.jp/ameyoko_rhythm/html/ameyoko_rhythm; 6-4-12 Ueno, Taitō-ku; ☉11am-7pm Tue-Sun; R JR lines to Okachimachi, north exit) For nearly half a century this tiny stall in Ameya-yokochō (p62) has been selling recordings of popular Japanese music to the faithful. Its forte is *enka*, best described as Japanese folk ballads, which, at its best, is symphonic and emotionally dramatic. The friendly owner Kobayashi-san is happy to make recommendations.

Isetatsu　　　Arts & Crafts
(いせ辰; Map p254; ☎03-3823-1453; 2-18-9 Yanaka, Taitō-ku; ☉10am-6pm; S Chiyoda line to Sendagi, exit 1) Dating back to 1864, this venerable stationery shop specialises in *chiyogami* – gorgeous, colourful paper made using woodblocks – as well as papier-mâché figures and masks.

Shokichi　　　Arts & Crafts
(Map p254; ☎03-3821-1837; http://shokichi. main.jp; 3-2-6 Yanaka, Bunkyō-ku; ☉10am-6pm Wed-Sun; S Chiyoda line to Sendagi, exit 1) Mitsuaki Tsuyuki makes and sells his incredible hand puppets here – look out for lifelike renditions of Japanese celebs and, natch, Elvis. He can hand-make a portrait puppet from a photograph (¥40,000). Far more affordable are the quick portraits he draws via one of his hand puppets (¥1000).

🔒 Asakusa & Ryōgoku

Marugoto Nippon Food & Drinks
(まるごとにっぽん; Map p254; ☎03-3845-0510; www.marugotonippon.com; 2-6-7 Asakusa, Taitō-ku; ⊙10am-8pm; ⑤Ginza line to Tawaramachi, exit 3) Think of this as a modern mini department store, showcasing the best of Japan's best in terms of speciality food and drink (ground floor) and arts and crafts (2nd floor). There are also plenty of tasting samples, as well as cafes and restaurants on the 3rd and 4th floors should you want something more substantial.

Tokyo Hotarudo Vintage
(東京蛍堂; Map p254; ☎03-3845-7563; http://tokyohotarudo.com; 1-41-8 Asakusa, Taitō-ku; ⊙11am-8pm Wed-Sun; ℝTsukuba Express to Asakusa, exit 5) This curio shop is run by an eccentric young man who prefers to dress as if the 20th century hasn't come and gone already. If you think that sounds marvellous, then you'll want to check out his collection of vintage dresses and bags, antique lamps, watches and decorative *objet*.

Kurodaya Stationery
(黒田屋; Map p254; ☎03-3844-7511; 1-2-5 Asakusa, Taitō-ku; ⊙10am-6pm; ⑤Ginza line to Asakusa, exit 3) Since 1856, Kurodaya has been specialising in *washi* (traditional Japanese paper) and products made from paper such as cards, kites and papier-mâché folk-art figures. It sells its own designs and many others from across Japan.

Bengara Arts & Crafts
(べんがら; Map p254; ☎03-3841-6613; www.bengara.com; 1-35-6 Asakusa, Taitō-ku; ⊙10am-6pm Mon-Fri, to 7pm Sat & Sun, closed 3rd Thu of month; ⑤Ginza line to Asakusa, exit 1) *Noren* are the curtains that hang in front of shop doors. This store sells beautiful ones, made of linen and coloured with natural dyes (like indigo or persimmon) or decorated with ink-brush paintings. There are smaller items too, such as pouches and book covers, made of traditional textiles.

Fujiya Arts & Crafts
(ふじ屋; Map p254; ☎03-3841-2283; www.asakusa-noren.ne.jp/tenugui-fujiya/sp.html; 2-2-15 Asakusa, Taitō-ku; ⊙10am-6pm Wed-Mon; ⑤Ginza line to Asakusa, exit 1) Fujiya specialises in *tenugui*: dyed cloths of thin cotton that can be used as tea towels, handkerchiefs, gift wrapping (the list goes on – they're surprisingly versatile). Here they come in traditional designs and humorous modern ones.

Yonoya Kushiho Fashion & Accessories
(よのや櫛舗; Map p254; 1-37-10 Asakusa, Taitō-ku; ⊙10.30am-6pm Thu-Tue; ⑤Ginza line to Asakusa, exit 1) Even in a neighbourhood where old is not out of place, Yonoya Kushiho stands out: this little shop has been selling handmade boxwood combs since 1717. Yonoya also sells old-fashioned hair ornaments (worn with the elaborate up-dos of courtesans in the past) and modern trinkets.

Sumida City Point Arts & Crafts
(Map p254; ☎03-6796-6341; http://machidokoro.com; 5F Tokyo Skytree Town Solamachi, 1-1-2 Oshiage, Sumida-ku; ⊙10am-9pm; ⑤Hanzōmon line to Oshiage, exit B3) Promoting the many artisans and craft businesses of the Sumida ward area, this showroom sells locally made items, from cosmetics and fashion to soy sauce. There's a cafe where you can sample food specialities, watch craftspeople providing demonstrations and ask the experts on hand to guide you to specific shops outside of the gravitational pull of the Sky Tree (p94).

Solamachi Mall
(ソラマチ; Map p254; www.tokyo-solamachi.jp; 1-1-2 Oshiage, Sumida-ku; ⊙10am-9pm; ⑤Hanzōmon line to Oshiage, exit B3) It's not all cheesy Sky Tree (p94) swag here at this mall under the tower (though you can get 634m-long rolls of Sky Tree toilet paper). Shops on the 4th floor offer a better-than-usual selection of Japanese-y souvenirs, including pretty trinkets made from kimono fabric and quirky fashion items.

BAR OPEN

International DJs, craft beer, sake and Japanese whisky

Bar Open

Make like Lady Gaga in a karaoke box; sip sake with an increasingly rosy salaryman in a tiny postwar bar; or dance under the rays of the rising sun at an enormous bayside club: that's nightlife, Tokyo-style. Shinjuku, Shibuya and Roppongi are the biggest nightlife districts, but there are bars everywhere – such is the importance of that time-honoured social lubricant, alcohol, in this work-hard, play-hard city. Tokyo also holds its own with London and New York when it comes to dance parties; top international DJs and domestic artists do regular sets at venues with body-shaking sound systems.

In This Section

Marunouchi & Nihombashi 174

Ginza & Tsukiji 174

Roppongi & Akasaka 175

Ebisu & Meguro 176

Shibuya & Shimo-Kitazawa 176

Harajuku & Aoyama 181

Kōenji, Kichijōji & West Tokyo 182

Ueno & Yanesen 182

Asakusa & Ryōgoku 182

Odaiba & Tokyo Bay 183

Opening Hours

Tokyo's nightspots stay open from 5pm until well into the wee hours – there's no mandated closing time. Many bars are open all week, though some will close on Sundays. Clubs really get going on Fridays and Saturdays after midnight (be sure to bring picture ID for entry).

Ueno & Yanesen
Largely quiet but with some
local gems (p182)

Asakusa & Ryōgoku
Some fun hang-outs in
this historic area (p182)

Shinjuku & Ikebukuro
Lots of *izakaya*, bars, karaoke
parlours and more (p175)

Kōenji, Kichijōji &
West Tokyo
Counter culture
gathering spots
(p182)

Marunouchi &
Nihombashi
After work hang-outs (p174)

Harajuku & Aoyama
Wine bars and cafes (p181)

Roppongi & Akasaka
One big all night
party (p175)

Ginza & Tsukiji
Chic bars and
cafes (p174)

Shibuya &
Shimo-Kitazawa
Nightclubs and bohemian
haunts (p176)

Odaiba & Tokyo Bay
Dance until dawn with
international DJs
(p183)

*Tokyo
Bay*

Ebisu & Meguro
Cocktail bars and
hidden lounges (p176)

Costs & Tipping

To avoid a nasty shock when the bill
comes, check prices and cover charges
before sitting down. If you are served a
small snack (*o-tsumami*) with your first
round, this implies a cover charge of a
few hundred yen or more. Consider this
in lieu of a tip (which is unnecessary
in Tokyo). Most bars are reasonably
priced; avoid ones that pressure you to
purchase a bottle.

Best Blogs

Beer in Japan (www.beerinjapan.com/
bij) The microbrewery scene.

Tokyo Beer Drinker (www.tokyobeer
drinker.blogspot.co.uk) Reviews of craft-
beer bars across the city.

Nonjatta (www.nonjatta.com) Compre-
hensive coverage of Japanese whisky.

Sake-world.com (www.sake-world.
com) Site of leading non-Japanese sake
authority John Gauntner.

The Best...

Experience Tokyo's best nightlife hotspots

Only in Tokyo

Samurai (p39) Classic jazz *kissa* stacked with 2500 *maneki-neko* (praying cats).

Nakame Takkyū Lounge (p176) Hang with ping-pong-playing hipsters in Naka-meguro.

Ren (p37) Wear sunglasses, as the decor will dazzle.

N3331 (p105) Ultimate trainspotters' cafe on a former train platform.

Clubs

Womb (p178) Four levels of lasers and strobes at this Shibuya club fixture.

Contact (p179) Sign up online to get into Tokyo's coolest members-only club.

Ageha (p183) One of Asia's largest clubs, set on Tokyo Bay.

Arty Farty (p175) Rub shoulders (and other body parts) on this bar's packed dance floor.

Cocktails

BenFiddich (p39) Original cocktails made using freshly ground spices and herbs.

Bar Trench (p176) Ebisu-based pioneer in Tokyo's new cocktail scene.

Fuglen Tokyo (p179) Original, seasonal cocktails in a hip Scandi-modern setting.

Craft Beer

Good Beer Faucets (p176) Huge choice of ales at a good price in Shibuya.

Harajuku Taproom (p181) Serves the beers of local star Baird Brewing.

Yanaka Beer Hall (p182) Microbrew ales in a charming complex of old wooden buildings.

For Music Lovers

Beat Cafe (p181) Haunt of musicians and their devotees.

Bar Martha (p176) Moodily lit bar with top whisky list and record collection.

Rhythm Cafe (p179) Buzzing hang-out with fun events; run by a record label.

For the best karaoke bars, see p110.

After Hours

Oath (p181) DJs spin past dawn at this cult-fave after-party spot.

Manpuku Shokudō (p174) Lively izakaya open 24/7.

Enjoy House (p176) Lose track of time at this cosy dive.

These (p175) A secret room with sofas to sink into.

Bars with a View

New York Bar (p95) Make like Bill Murray in the Park Hyatt's starry jazz bar.

Asahi Sky Room Bar (p95) Stunning sunset views of the Sumida river.

Peter: the Bar Cocktail Bar (p95) Views across the Imperial Palace and Ginza.

★ Lonely Planet's Top Choices

Golden Gai (p37) Travel back in time and wander this postwar maze of intimate bars.

Popeye (p183) Get very merry working your way through most of Tokyo's beers on tap.

SuperDeluxe (p175) Tokyo's most interesting club with an eclectic line-up of events.

Cocktail Shobō (p182) Second-hand books and liquid libations.

⊖ Marunouchi & Nihombashi

Manpuku Shokudō   Pub
(まんぷく食堂; Map p250; ☏03-3211-6001; www.manpukushokudo.com; 2-4-1 Yūrakuchō, Chiyoda-ku; cover charge ¥300; ☺24hr; 📶; 🚆JR Yamanote line to Yūrakuchō, central exit) Down your beer or sake as trains rattle overhead on the tracks that span Harumi-dōri at Yūrakuchō. This convivial *izakaya* (Japanese pub-eatery), plastered with old movie posters, is open round the clock and has bags of atmosphere.

So Tired   Bar
(ソータイアード; Map p250; ☏03-5220-1358; www.heads-west.com/shop/so-tired.html; 7th fl, Shin-Marunouchi Bldg, 1-5-1 Marunouchi, Chiyoda-ku; ☺11am-4am Mon-Sat, to 11pm Sun; 📶; 🚆JR lines to Tokyo, Marunouchi north exit) The best thing about this bar on the lively 7th floor of the Shin-Maru Building is that you can buy a drink at the counter and take it out to the terrace. The views aren't sky-high; instead you feel curiously suspended among the office towers, hovering over Tokyo Station below.

⊖ Ginza & Tsukiji

Bistro Marx   Cafe
(Map p250; ☏03-6280-6234; www.thierrymarx. jp; 7th fl, Ginza Place, 5-8-1 Ginza, Chūō-ku; ☺11am-11pm, bar to 2am; 📶📶; 🚇Ginza line to Ginza, exit A2) French chef Thierry Marx has a restaurant here, as well as a casual bistro-bar with an outdoor terrace that has a dress-circle view across to Ginza's iconic Wako department store. It's a fancy spot for an afternoon coffee and dessert above the throng, or a romantic setting for a drink later at night when it morphs into a bar.

Kagaya   Pub
(加賀屋; Map p250; ☏03-3591-2347; http://ka gayayy.sakura.ne.jp; B1 fl, Hanasada Bldg, 2-15-12 Shimbashi, Minato-ku; ☺7pm-midnight Mon-Sat; 📶; 🚆JR Yamanote line to Shimbashi, Shimbashi exit) It is safe to say that there is no other bar owner in Tokyo who can match Mark Kagaya for brilliant lunacy. His side-splitting antics

Bar in Ikebukuro

are this humble *izakaya*'s star attraction, although his mum's nourishing home cooking also hits the spot. Bookings are essential.

Bamboo Cafe
Bar

(バンブーカフェ; Map p250; ☑03-3573-2455; http://bamboocafe.net; 2nd fl, 6-3-5 Ginza, Chūō-ku; ⊙11am-11pm; ⑤Ginza line to Ginza, exit C3) It's Japanese-only at this friendly, cigarette-smoke-filled standing bar in the midst of Ginza's drinking district. There's no cover charge, draught beers are a bargain ¥250 and there's a good range of snacks, including chunks of fresh *maguro* (tuna) sold by the 50g (¥150).

Aux Amis Des Vins
Wine Bar

(オザミデヴァン; Map p250; ☑03-3567-4120; https://auxamis.com/desvins; 2-5-6 Ginza, Chūō-ku; ⊙11.20am-2pm & 5.30pm-midnight Mon-Fri, 11.30am-3pm & 5-11pm Sat; ⑤Yūrakuchō line to Ginza-itchōme, exits 5 & 8) Even when it rains, the plastic tarp comes down and good wine is drunk alleyside. The enclosed upstairs seating area is warm and informal and you can order snacks to go with your wine or full *prix-fixe* dinners. A solid selection of wine comes by the glass (¥800) or by the bottle.

☯ Roppongi & Akasaka

SuperDeluxe
Club

(スーパー・デラックス; Map p252; ☑03-5412-0515; www.super-deluxe.com; B1 fl, 3-1-25 Nishi-Azabu, Minato-ku; admission varies; ⑩; ⑤Hibiya line to Roppongi, exit 1B) This groovy basement performance space (and a cocktail lounge and club of sorts) stages everything from electronic music to literary evenings and creative presentations in the 20 × 20 PechaKucha (20 slides × 20 seconds) format. Check the website for event details. It's in a brown-brick building by a shoe-repair shop.

These
Lounge

(テーゼ; Map p252; ☑03-5466-7331; www.these-jp.com; 2-15-12 Nishi-Azabu, Minato-ku; cover charge ¥500; ⊙7pm-4am, to 2am Sun; ⑤Hibiya line to Roppongi, exit 3) Pronounced *teh*-zeh, this delightfully quirky, nook-ridden 'library

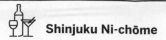

Shinjuku Ni-chōme

Shinjuku-nichōme (nicknamed 'Ni-chōme') is the city's gay and lesbian enclave, where hundreds of establishments are crammed into a space of a few blocks, including bars, dance clubs, saunas and love hotels.

Aiiro Cafe (アイイロ　カフェ; Map p253; http://aliving.net/aiirocafe/; 2-18-1 Shinjuku, Shinjuku-ku; ⊙6pm-2am Mon-Thu, 6pm-5am Fri & Sat, 6pm-midnight Sun; ⑩; ⑤Marunouchi line to Shinjuku-sanchōme, exit C8) is the best place to start any night out in the neighbourhood (thanks to the all-you-can-drink beer for ¥1000 happy-hour special). Aiiro is a welcoming place and staff speak excellent English. This is a good place to meet people and find out about events.

A fixture on Tokyo's gay scene for many a moon, **Arty Farty** (アーティファーティ; Map p253; www.arty-farty.net; 2nd fl, 2-11-7 Shinjuku, Shinjuku-ku; ⊙6pm-1am; ⑤Marunouchi line to Shinjuku-sanchōme, exit C8) welcomes all in the community to come shake a tail feather on the dance floor. It usually gets going later in the evening.

For more Shinjuku nightlife, see p36.

lounge' overflows with armchairs, sofas, and books on the shelves and on the bar. Imbibe champagne by the glass, whiskies or seasonal-fruit cocktails. Bites include escargot garlic toast, which goes down very nicely with a drink in the secret room on the 2nd floor. Look for the flaming torches outside.

Brewdog
Craft Beer

(Map p252; ☑03-6447-4160; www.brewdog.com/bars/worldwide/roppongi; 5-3-2 Roppongi, Minato-ku; ⊙5pm-midnight Mon-Fri, 3pm-midnight Sat & Sun; ⑨⑩; ⑤Hibiya line to Roppongi, exit 3) This Scottish craft brewery's Tokyo outpost is nestled off the main drag. Apart from its own brews, there's a great selection of other beers, including Japanese ones on tap, mostly served in small, regular or large (full-pint) portions. Tasty food and computer and board games to while away the evening round out a class operation.

Agave   Bar
(アガヴェ; Map p252; ☎03-3497-0229; www. agave.jp; B1 fl, 7-15-10 Roppongi, Minato-ku; ⊗6.30pm-2am Mon-Thu, to 4am Fri & Sat; 🗊; Ⓢ Hibiya or Ōedo line to Roppongi, exit 2) Rawhide chairs, *cruzas de rosas* (crosses decorated with roses) and tequila shots for the willing make Agave a good place for a long night in search of the sacred worm. Luckily, this gem in the jungle that is Roppongi is more about savouring the subtleties of its 400-plus varieties of tequila than tossing back shots of Cuervo.

❷ Ebisu & Meguro

Nakame Takkyū Lounge   Lounge
(中目卓球ラウンジ; Map p246; 2nd fl, Lion House Naka-Meguro, 1-3-13 Kami-Meguro, Meguro-ku; cover before/after 10pm ¥500/800; ⊗6pm-2am Mon-Sat; Ⓢ Hibiya line to Naka-Meguro) *Takkyū* means table tennis and it's a serious sport in Japan. This hilarious bar looks like a university table-tennis clubhouse – right down to the tatty furniture and posters of star players on the wall. It's in an apartment building next to a parking garage (go all the way down the corridor past the bikes); ring the doorbell for entry.

Bar Trench   Cocktail Bar
(バートレンチ; Map p246; ☎03-3780-5291; http://small-axe.net/bar-trench/; 1-5-8 Ebisu-Nishi, Shibuya-ku; cover ¥500; ⊗7pm-2am Mon-Sat, 6pm-1am Sun; 🗊; 🚊 JR Yamanote line to Ebisu, west exit) One of the pioneers in Tokyo's new cocktail scene, Trench (named for the trench-like alley in which it is nestled) is a tiny place with the air of old-world bohemianism. It has a short but sweet menu of original tipples. Highlights include the 'Shady Samurai' (green-tea-infused gin with elderflower liquor, egg white and lime; ¥1620). Cover charge ¥500.

Bar Martha   Bar
(バー ・ マーサ; Map p246; www.martha-records.com; 1-22-23 Ebisu, Shibuya-ku; cover incl bar snacks ¥800; ⊗7pm-5am; 🚊 JR Yamanote line to Ebisu, east exit) It's hard to say which is more impressive at this dim, moody bar: the whiskey list or the collection of records. The latter are played on spot-lit turntables, amplified by a 1m-tall vintage Tannoy speaker. The cocktails, especially the *nama shōga mosuko myūru* (生生姜モスコミュール; fresh ginger moscow mule) are excellent, too. Drinks from ¥800.

Enjoy House   Bar
(Map p246; http://enjoyhouse.jugem.jp; 2nd fl, 2-9-9 Ebisu-nishi, Shibuya-ku; ⊗6pm-2am Tue-Thu, 6pm-5am Fri & Sat, 3pm-midnight Sun; 🗊; 🚊 JR Yamanote line to Ebisu, west exit) Decked out with velveteen booths, fairy lights and foliage, Enjoy House is a deeply funky place to spend the evening. DJs spin regularly, but there's no cover charge (drinks from ¥650). Look for the name painted in red letters in English on the 2nd-floor window.

❷ Shibuya & Shimo-Kitazawa

Good Beer Faucets   Craft Beer
(グッドビアフォウセッツ; Map p246; http:// shibuya.goodbeerfaucets.jp; 2nd fl, 1-29-1 Shōtō, Shibuya-ku; pints from ¥800; ⊗5pm-midnight Mon-Thu & Sat, to 3am Fri, 4-11pm Sun; 🚭🛜🗊; 🚊 JR Yamanote line to Shibuya, Hachikō exit) With 40 shiny taps, Good Beer Faucets has one of the city's best selections of Japanese craft brews and regularly draws a full house of locals and expats. The interior is chrome and concrete (and not at all grungy). Come for happy hour (5pm to 8pm Monday to Thursday, 1pm to 7pm Sunday) and get ¥200 off any pint.

Ghetto   Bar
(月灯; 1-45-16 Daizawa, Setagaya-ku; ⊗8.30pm-late; 🚊 Keiō Inokashira line to Shimo-Kitazawa, south exit) What are the odds that the characters for 'moon' and 'light' could be pronounced together as 'ghetto'? It's not

★ Shimo-Kitazawa

The narrow streets of 'Shimokita' have been a favourite haunt of generations of students, musicians and artists. If hippies – not bureaucrats – ran Tokyo, the city would look a lot more like Shimo-Kitazawa. Spend an evening here and raise your glass to (and with) the characters committed to keeping Shimokita weird. Some favourite bars include Mother (p178), Never Never Land (p178), Trouble Peach (p181) and Ghetto (p176).

Whisky

Japan produces some of the finest whiskies in the world and Tokyo now has a growing number of dedicated whisky and scotch bars where travellers can sample the best of the major makers Suntory and Nikka, as well as products from several other active single-malt distilleries in Japan and abroad. Zoetrope (p39), in Shinjuku, has the best selection.

unlike the uncommon synergy that comes together nightly as musicians, travellers and well-intentioned salarymen (and others) descend on this little bar in the rambling Suzunari theatre complex. By open until late we mean very, very late. No cover charge; drinks from ¥600.

Womb   Club
(ウーム; Map p246; ☎03-5459-0039; www. womb.co.jp; 2-16 Maruyama-chō, Shibuya-ku; cover ¥1500-4000; ⏰11pm-late Fri & Sat, 4-10pm Sun; 🚃 JR Yamanote line to Shibuya, Hachikō exit)

A long-time (in club years, at least) club-scene fixture, Womb gets a lot of big-name international DJs playing mostly house and techno on Friday and Saturday nights. Frenetic lasers and strobes splash across the heaving crowds, which usually jam all four floors. Weekdays are quieter, with local DJs playing EDM mix and ladies getting free entry (with flyer).

Mother   Bar
(マザー; ☎03-3421-9519; www.rock-mother. com; 5-36-14 Daizawa, Setagaya-ku; ⏰5pm-2am Sun-Thu, 5pm-5am Fri & Sat; 📶; 🚃Keiō Inokashira line to Shimo-Kitazawa, south exit) Mother is classic Shimo-Kitazawa, a work of art itself. The space, with undulating, mosaic walls, is definitely womb-like (the better to incubate future rock-n-rollers); the soundtrack is '60s and '70s. There's a good line-up of *shōchū* drinks and cocktails (from ¥600) on the menu. Don't miss the made-in-house 'mori' liquor, served from a glass skull.

Never Never Land   Bar
(ネヴァーネヴァーランド; 2nd fl, 3-19-3 Kitazawa, Setagaya-ku; cover ¥200 per person;

⏱6pm-2am; 📱; 🚃Keiō Inokashira line to Shimo-Kitazawa, north exit) Smoky, loud and filled with bohemian characters, Never Never Land is a Shimokita staple, running for more than 30 years. It's a good place to wind up when you're in need of food – the bar snacks are tasty Okinawan dishes. Food and drink from ¥500. Look for the twinkling lights in the window.

Tight   Bar

(タイト; Map p246; 2nd fl, 1-25-10 Shibuya, Shibuya-ku; ⏱6pm-2am Mon-Sat, to midnight Sun; 🚃JR Yamanote line to Shibuya, Hachikō exit) This teeny-tiny bar is wedged among the wooden shanties of Nonbei-yokochō, a narrow nightlife strip along the elevated JR tracks. Like the name suggests, it's a tight fit, but the lack of seats doesn't keep regulars away: on a busy night, they line the stairs. Look for the big picture window. No cover charge; drinks around ¥700.

Rhythm Cafe   Bar

(リズムカフェ; Map p246; 📞03-3770-0244; http://rhythmcafe.jp; 11-1 Udagawa-chō, Shibuya-ku; ⏱6pm-2am; 🚃JR Yamanote line to Shibuya, Hachikō exit) Run by a record label, fun and funky Rhythm Cafe often draws more customers than it can fit, meaning the party spills into the street. It's known for having off-beat event nights (such as the retro Japanese pop night on the fourth Thursday of the month). Drinks start at ¥700; when DJs spin, the cover is around ¥1000.

Fuglen Tokyo   Bar

(Map p246; www.fuglen.com; 1-16-11 Tomigaya, Shibuya-ku; coffee from ¥360; ⏱8am-10pm Mon & Tue, to 1am Wed-Sun; 🍴📶📱; 🚇Chiyoda line to Yoyogi-kōen, exit 2) This Tokyo outpost of a long-running Oslo coffee shop serves Aeropress coffee by day and some of the city's most creative cocktails (from ¥1000) by night. It's Tomigaya's principal gathering spot.

Contact   Club

(コンタクト; Map p246; 📞03-6427-8107; www.contacttokyo.com; basement, 2-10-12 Dōgenzaka, Shibuya-ku; ¥2000-3500; 🍴; 🚃JR Yamanote line to Shibuya, Hachikō exit) This is Tokyo's newest hot spot, a stylish underground club that's keen on keeping up with the times (even if that means it's a little heavy on rules): the dance floor is no smoking and no

⭐ Best Pubs

Popeye (p183)

Harajuku Taproom (p181)

Kagaya (p174)

Manpuku Shokudō (p174)

From left: Bar in Roppongi; Fuglen Tokyo; Japanese whisky

Tokyo in a Glass

Sake is always brewed during the winter

Premium sake is called *dai-ginjō*

Fresh, young sake is ready by late autumn

Sake can be sweet (ama-kuchi) or dry (kara-kuchi)

On average the alcohol content of sake is around 15%

AVIMAGES / GETTY IMAGES ©

Delicious Sake

Get to Know Sake

Sake, aka *nihonshū* (酒 or 日本酒) is made from rice and comes in a wide variety of grades and flavours. According to personal preference, sake can be served hot (*atsu-kan*), but premium ones are normally served well chilled (*reishu*) in a small jug (*tokkuri*) and poured into tiny cups known as *o-choko*.

Sake cups and pots
GREG ELMS / GETTY IMAGES ©

★ Top Spots for Sake

Sake Plaza (日本酒造会館; Map p250; www.japansake.or.jp; 1-6-15 Nishi-Shimbashi, Minato-ku; ◷10am-6pm Mon-Fri; ⑤Ginza line to Toranomon, exit 9) **Tasting showroom where you can get to know the different varieties.**

Buri (ぶり; Map p246; ☏03-3496-7744; 1-14-1 Ebisu-nishi, Shibuya-ku; ◷5pm-3am; 🗐; 🚊JR Yamanote line to Ebisu, west exit) **Popular hang-out where sake is served semi-frozen, like a slushie.**

Nihombashi Toyama (日本橋とやま館; Map p250; ☏03-6262-2723; http://toyamakan.jp; 1-2-6 Nihombashi-muromachi, Chūō-ku; ◷11am-9pm; 🗐; ⑤Ginza line to Mitsukoshimae, exit B5) **Sample the sake from cold, remote Toyama prefecture.**

photos (so you can dance with abandon). Weekends see big international names and a young, fashionable crowd. Under-23s get in for ¥2000. ID required.

Beat Cafe   Bar
(Map p246; www.facebook.com/beatcafe; basement fl, 2-13-5 Dōgenzaka, Shibuya-ku; ⏱7pm-5am; 🚃JR Yamanote line to Shibuya, Hachikō exit) Join an eclectic mix of local and international regulars at this comfortably shabby bar among the nightclubs and love hotels of Dōgenzaka. It's a known hang-out for musicians and music fans; check the website for info on parties (and after-parties). Look for Gateway Studio on the corner; the bar is in the basement. Drinks from ¥600.

Trouble Peach   Bar
(トラブル・ピーチ; ☎03-3460-1468; 2nd fl, 2-9-18 Kitazawa, Setagaya-ku; cover ¥400; ⏱7pm-7am; 🈸; 🚃Keiō Inokashira line to Shimo-Kitazawa, south exit) Pretty much everything here is chipped, frayed or torn – and none of it is artifice. This is a well-worn and well-loved bar, open for some 40-odd years and still playing vinyl. It looks primed for demolition but has somehow managed to survive. Drinks from ¥500. Look for the neon sign by the tracks.

⊖ Harajuku & Aoyama

Two Rooms   Bar
(トゥールームス; Map p246; ☎03-3498-0002; www.tworooms.jp; 5th fl, AO bldg, 3-11-7 Kita-Aoyama, Minato-ku; ⏱11.30am-2am Mon-Sat, to 10pm Sun; 🈸; 🚇Ginza line to Omote-sandō, exit B2) Expect a crowd dressed like they don't care that wine by the glass starts at ¥1600. You can eat here too, but the real scene is at night by the bar. Call ahead (staff speak English) on Friday or Saturday night to reserve a table on the terrace, which has sweeping views towards the Shinjuku skyline.

Oath   Bar
(Map p246; http://bar-oath.com; 4-5-9 Shibuya, Shibuya-ku; ⏱9pm-5am Mon-Thu, to 8am Fri &

🍶 **Shōchū**

Shōchū (焼酎) is a distilled liquor made from a variety of raw materials including potato and barley. Because of its potency (alcohol content of around 30%) it is usually served diluted with hot water (*oyu-wari*) or in a *chūhai* cocktail with soft drinks or tea. At *izakaya*, a popular cocktail to order is *nama remon sawā* (生レモンサワー; fresh lemon sour), a mix of *shōchū*, soda water and lemon juice, which you squeeze yourself at the table.

Sat, 5-11pm Sun; 🚇Ginza line to Omote-sandō, exit B1) A tiny space along a somewhat forlorn strip of highway, Oath is a favourite after-hours destination for clubbers – helped no doubt by the ¥500 drinks and lack of cover charge. Underground DJs spin here sometimes, too.

Montoak   Bar
(モントーク; Map p246; 6-1-9 Jingūmae, Shibuya-ku; ⏱11am-3am; 🈸🈸; 🚃JR Yamanote line to Harajuku, Omote-sandō exit) This stylish, tinted-glass cube is a calm, dimly lit retreat from the busy streets. It's perfect for holing up with a pot of tea or carafe of wine and watching the crowds go by. Or, if the weather is nice, score a seat on the terrace. Drinks from ¥700.

Harajuku Taproom   Pub
(原宿タップルーム; Map p246; http://bairdbeer.com/en/taproom; 2nd fl, 1-20-13 Jingūmae, Shibuya-ku; ⏱5pm-midnight Mon-Fri, noon-midnight Sat & Sun; 🈸🈸; 🚃JR Yamanote line to Harajuku, Takeshita exit) Baird's Brewery is one of Japan's most successful and consistently good craft breweries. This is one of its two Tokyo outposts, where you can sample more than a dozen of its beers on tap; try the top-selling Rising Sun Pale Ale (pints ¥1000). Japanese pub-style food is served as well.

⊘ Kōenji, Kichijōji & West Tokyo

Cocktail Shobō   Bar
(コクテイル書房; 3-8-13 Kōenji-kita, Suginami-ku; ⊘11.30am-3pm Wed-Sun, 5pm-midnight Mon-Sun; 🖂; 🚊JR Sōbu line to Kōenji, north exit) At this bar-bookstore mash-up, the wooden counter doubles as a bookshelf and the local crowd comes as much to sip cocktails (from ¥450) as it does to flip through the selection of worn paperbacks. It's a cosy place and, like most bars in Kōenji, a labour of love. During lunch hours, curry and coffee are served.

Nantoka Bar   Bar
(なんとかバー; http://trio4.nobody.jp/keita/shop/16_nantoka.html; 3-4-12 Kōenji-kita, Suginami-ku; drinks from ¥400; ⊘7pm-late; 🚊JR Sōbu line to Kōenji, north exit) Part of the collective of spaces run by the Kōenji-based

Summer Beer Gardens

Summer beer gardens are a Tokyo tradition (typically running from late May to early September). Two of the city's best are within Meiji-jingū Gaien (the 'Outer Garden' of Meiji-jingū).

Mori-no Beer Garden (森のビアガーデン; www.rkfs.co.jp/brand/beer_garden_detail.html; 1-7-5 Kita-Aoyama, Minato-ku; ⊘5-10pm Mon-Fri, 3-10pm Sat & Sun; 🚊JR Sōbu line to Shinanomachi) hosts up to 1000 revellers for all-you-can-eat-and-drink spreads of beer and barbecue under a century-old tree.

At the more patrician **Sekirei** (鶺鴒; ☎03-3746-7723; www.meijikinenkan.gr.jp/restaurant/company/sekirei; Meiji Kinenkan, 2-2-23 Moto-Akasaka, Minato-ku; cover charge ¥500; ⊘5-10.30pm; 🖂; 🚊JR Sōbu line to Shinanomachi), you can quaff beer on the neatly clipped lawn of the stately Meiji Kinenkan (a hall used for weddings); traditional Japanese dance is performed nightly around 8pm.

activist group Shirōto no Ran (Amateur Revolt), Nantoka Bar is about as uncommercial as a place selling drinks can get: there's no cover charge, drinks are generous and cheap and it's run on any given day by whoever feels like running it (which is sometimes no one at all).

⊘ Ueno & Yanesen

Yanaka Beer Hall   Craft Beer
(Map p254; ☎03-5834-2381; www.facebook.com/yanakabeerhall; 2-15-6 Ueno-sakuragi, Taitō-ku; ⊘noon-8.30pm Tue-Fri, 11am-8.30pm Sat & Sun; 🛜🖂; 🚇Chiyoda line to Nezu, exit 1) Exploring Yanesen can be thirsty work so thank heavens for this craft-beer bar, a cosy place with some outdoor seating. It's part of a charming complex of old wooden buildings that also house a bakery-cafe, bistro and events space. It has several brews on tap, including a Yanaka lager that's only available here.

Bousingot   Bar
(ブーザンゴ; Map p254; ☎03-3823-5501; www.bousingot.com; 2-33-2 Sendagi, Bunkyō-ku; drinks from ¥450; ⊘6-11pm Wed-Mon; 🖂; 🚇Chiyoda line to Sendagi, exit 1) It's fitting that Yanaka, which refuses to trash the past, would have a bar that doubles as a used bookstore. Sure, the books are in Japanese but you can still enjoy soaking up the atmosphere with some resident book lovers.

⊘ Asakusa & Ryōgoku

Café Otonova   Bar
(カフェ・オトノヴァ; Map p254; ☎03-5830-7663; www.cafeotonova.net/#3eme; 3-10-4 Nishi-Asakusa; ⊘noon-11pm, to 9pm Sun; 🚇) Tucked away on an alley running parallel to Kappabashi-dōri (p166), this charming cafe occupies an old house. Exposed beams are whitewashed and an atrium has been created, with cosy booths upstairs and a big communal table downstairs in front of the DJ booth. It's a stylish cafe by day and a romantic bolthole for drinks at night, with no table charge.

Craft beer in Tokyo

Popeye   Pub

(ポパイ; Map p254; ☑03-3633 2120; www.
40beersontap.com; 2-18-7 Ryōgoku, Sumida-ku;
⊙11.30am-4pm & 5-11pm Mon-Sat; ☻⬚;
⬚JR Sōbu line to Ryōgoku, west exit) Popeye
boasts an astounding 70 beers on tap,
including the world's largest selection of
Japanese beers – from Echigo Weizen
to Hitachino Nest Espresso Stout. The
happy-hour deal (5pm to 8pm) offers
select brews with free plates of pizza,
sausages and other munchables. It's extremely popular and fills up fast; get here
early to grab a seat.

Kamiya Bar   Bar

(神谷バー; Map p254; ☑03-3841-5400;
www.kamiya-bar.com; 1-1-1 Asakusa, Taitō-ku;
⊙11.30am-10pm Wed-Mon; ⬚; ⬚Ginza line
to Asakusa, exit 3) One of Tokyo's oldest
Western-style bars, Kamiya opened in
1880 and is still hugely popular – though
probably more so today for its enormous,
cheap draught beer (¥1050 for a litre).
Its real speciality, however, is Denki Bran
(¥270), a herbal liquor that's been produced in-house for over a century. Order

at the counter, then give your tickets to
the server.

'Cuzn Homeground   Bar

(Map p254; www.homeground.jpn.com; 2-17-9
Asakusa, Taitō-ku; beer ¥800; ⊙11am-6am;
⬚⬚; ⬚Ginza line to Tawaramachi, exit 3) Run
by a wild gang of local hippies, 'Cuzn is the
kind of bar where anything can happen: a
barbecue, a jam session or all-night karaoke, for example.

🅦 Odaiba & Tokyo Bay

Ageha   Club

(アゲハ; www.ageha.com; 2-2-10 Shin-Kiba,
Kōtō-ku; cover ¥2500-4000; ⊙11pm-5am Fri &
Sat; ⬚Yūrakuchō line to Shin-Kiba, main exit)
This gigantic waterside club, the largest in
Tokyo, rivals any you'd find in LA or Ibiza.
Top international and Japanese DJs appear
here. Free buses run between the club
and a bus stop on the east side of Shibuya
Station (on Roppongi-dōri) all night. Events
vary widely; check the website for details
and bring photo ID.

TAKETAN / GETTY IMAGES ©

SHOWTIME

Kabuki, international acts, jazz clubs and traditional dance theatre

Showtime

Evening entertainment in Tokyo could be an austere performance of traditional nō (a centuries-old form of dance-drama) or an in-your-face noise performance in a smoky basement club. There's dramatic, visually arresting kabuki, Japan's signature performing art, and also much to please connoisseurs of jazz and classical music. Big international acts often appear at major venues; smaller clubs are the place to discover local talent. The contemporary theatre scene can be difficult to access with the language barrier; however, theatres staging traditional performing arts often offer earphones or subtitles with an English translation of the plots and dialogue.

In This Section

Marunouchi & Nihombashi 188

Ginza & Tsukiji 188

Roppongi & Akasaka..........................189

Ebisu & Meguro...................................189

Shibuya & Shimo-Kitazawa...............190

Harajuku & Aoyama 191

Kōenji, Kichijōji & West Tokyo............192

Shinjuku & Ikebukuro 194

Kagurazaka, Kanda & Akihabara 194

Ueno & Yanesen 195

Asakusa & Ryōgoku 195

Tickets

The easiest way to get tickets for many live shows and events is at one of the **Ticket Pia** (チケットぴあ; ☎0570-02-9111; http://t.pia.jp; ⊙10am-8pm) kiosks scattered across Tokyo. Its online booking site is in Japanese only. The website www.tokyogigguide.com/en/tickets also has information about buying various types of entertainment tickets.

Websites

See Tokyo Time Out (www.timeout.com/tokyo) for event listings and Tokyo Dross (www.tokyodross.blogspot.co.uk) for live gig info.

Kabukiza Theatre (p88)

The Best...

Jazz Clubs

Shinjuku Pit Inn (p39) Tokyo jazz-scene institution for serious devotees.

Blue Note Tokyo (p191) See world-class performers at this sophisticated venue.

Cotton Club (p188) Centrally located venue for high-pedigree performers.

Theatre

National Theatre (p189) Top-notch *nō*, bunraku and other drama in a grand setting.

Kabukiza Theatre (p88) A visual and dramatic feast of traditional theatre awaits inside and out.

Setagaya Public Theatre (p191) Renowned for contemporary drama and dance.

✪ Marunouchi & Nihombashi

Cotton Club　　Jazz
(コットンクラブ; Map p250; ☎03-3215-1555; www.cottonclubjapan.co.jp; 2F Tokia, Tokyo Building, 2-7-3 Marunouchi, Chiyoda-ku; ⊙shows 7pm & 9.30pm Mon-Sat, 5pm & 8pm Sun; 🚃JR lines to Tokyo Station, Marunouchi south exit) You're more likely to hear contemporary international jazz stars here than musicians harking back to the 1920s New York club it honours. Also on the roster is a medley of interesting Japanese artists such as saxophonist Itō Takeshi. Check the website for schedules.

Nippon Budōkan　　Live Music
(日本武道館; Map p250; ☎03-3216-5100; www.nipponbudokan.or.jp; 2-3 Kitanomaru-kōen, Chiyoda-ku; 🚇Hanzōmon line to Kudanshita, exit 2) The 14,000-plus-seat Budōkan, a legendary concert hall for big acts from the Beatles to Beck, was originally built for the martial-arts championships (judo, karate, kendō, aikidō) of the 1964 Olympics (*budō*

means 'martial arts') and will be pressed into service again for the 2020 event.

Meiji-za　　Theatre
(明治座; ☎03-3666-6666; www.meijiza.co.jp; 2-31-1 Nihonbashi-Hamachō, Chūō-ku; 🚇Shinjuku line to Hamachō, exit A2) There's been a kabuki theatre here since the late 19th century. Concerts are also held here, along with the dance, music and animation show *Sakura – Japan in the Box* (http://sakura-meijiza.com/en).

✪ Ginza & Tsukiji

Tokyo Takarazuka Theatre　　Theatre
(宝塚劇場; Map p250; ☎03-5251-2001; http://kageki.hankyu.co.jp/english/index.html; 1-1-3 Yūrakuchō, Chiyoda-ku; tickets ¥3500-12,000; 🚇Hibiya line to Hibiya, exits A5 & A13) If you love camp, this is for you. The all-female Takarazuka revue, going back to 1914, stages highly stylised musicals in Japanese (English synopses are available) where a mostly female audience swoons over actresses, some of whom are in drag.

❂ Roppongi & Akasaka

National Theatre — Theatre
(国立劇場, Kokuritsu Gekijō; ☎03-3265-7411; www.ntj.jac.go.jp/english; 4-1 Hayabusa-chō, Chiyoda-ku; tickets from ¥1500; **S**Hanzōmon line to Hanzōmon, exit 1) This is the capital's premier venue for traditional performing arts with a 1600-seat and a 590-seat auditorium. Performances include kabuki, *gagaku* (music of the imperial court) and bunraku (classic puppet theatre). Earphones with English translation are available for hire (¥650 plus ¥1000 deposit). Check the website for performance schedules.

Billboard Live — Live Music
(ビルボードライブ東京; Map p252; ☎03-3405-1133; www.billboard-live.com; 4th fl, Tokyo Midtown, 9-7-4 Akasaka, Minato-ku; ◷5.30-9.30pm Mon-Fri, 5-9pm Sat & Sun; **S**Hibiya or Ōedo line to Roppongi, exit 8) This glitzy amphitheatre-like space plays host to major foreign talent as well as Japanese jazz, soul and rock groups who all come in to shake the rafters. The service is excellent and the drinks are reasonably priced.

Suntory Hall — Classical Music
(Map p252; ☎03-3505-1001; www.suntory.com/culture-sports/suntoryhall; Ark Hills, 1-13-1 Akasaka, Minato-ku; **S**Ginza line to Tameike-sannō, exit 13) This is one of Tokyo's best venues for classical concerts with a busy schedule including accomplished musicians. Its 2000-seat main hall has one of the largest organs in the world.

❂ Ebisu & Meguro

Unit — Live Music
(ユニット; Map p246; ☎03-5459-8630; www.unit-tokyo.com; 1-34-17 Ebisu-nishi, Shibuya-ku; ¥2500-5000; **R**Tōkyū Tōyoko line to Daikanyama) On weekends, this subterranean club has two shows: live music in the evening and a DJ-hosted event that gets started around midnight. The solid line-up includes Japanese indie bands, veterans playing to a smaller crowd and overseas artists making their Japan debut. Unit is less grungy than other Tokyo live houses and, with high ceilings, doesn't get as smoky.

NATHAN SHANAHAN / STRINGER / GETTY IMAGES ©

★ Top Five for Live Music
Unit
Liquid Room (p190)
Club Quattro (p190)
WWW (p190)
Ni Man Den Atsu (p192)

From left: Bar Anywhere in WWW (p190); Polysics concert at Club Quattro (p190); Concert crowd

PETRI ARTTURI ASIKAINEN / GETTY IMAGES ©

Nō

Nō, a kind of dance-drama, is a centuries-old dramatisation of the aesthetic quality *yūgen* (subtle, elusive beauty). Rather than a drama in the usual sense, *nō* seeks to express a poetic moment by symbolic and almost abstract means: glorious movements, grand and exaggerated costumes and hairstyles, sonorous chorus and music, and subtle expression. Actors frequently wear masks while they perform before a spare, unchanging set, which features a painting of a large pine tree.

Most plays centre around two principal characters: the *shi-te*, who is sometimes a living person but more often a demon or a ghost whose soul cannot rest; and the *waki*, who leads the main character towards the play's climactic moment. The elegant language used is that of the court of the 14th century.

Tokyo has its own public theatre dedicated to *nō*, the National Nō Theatre (p191).

Nō performance
JACK VARTOOGIAN / CONTRIBUTOR / GETTY IMAGES ©

Liquid Room — Live Music

(リキッドルーム; Map p246; ☑03-5464-0800; www.liquidroom.net; 3-16-6 Higashi, Shibuya-ku; ☒JR Yamanote line to Ebisu, west exit) When this storied concert hall moved to Ebisu from seedy Kabukichō, it cleaned up its act. Liquid Room is still a great place to catch big-name acts in an intimate setting. Both Japanese and international bands play here and every once in a while there's an all-night gig. Tickets sell out fast.

☆ Shibuya & Shimo-Kitazawa

WWW — Live Music

(Map p246; www-shibuya.jp/index.html; 13-17 Udagawa-chō, Shibuya-ku; tickets ¥2000-5000; ☒JR Yamanote line to Shibuya, Hachikō exit) In a former arthouse cinema (with the tell-tale tiered floor still intact), this is one of those rare venues where you could turn up just about any night and hear something good. The line-up varies from indie pop to punk to electronica. Upstairs is the new WWW X, with more space.

Club Quattro — Live Music

(クラブクアトロ; Map p246; ☑03-3477-8750; www.club-quattro.com; 32-13-4 Udagawa-chō, Shibuya-ku; tickets ¥3000-4000; ☒JR Yamanote line to Shibuya, Hachikō exit) This small, intimate venue has the feel of a slick nightclub and attracts a more grown-up, artsy crowd than the club's location, near Center-gai, might lead you to expect. Though there's no explicit musical focus, emphasis is on rock and world music, with many an indie darling passing through.

Uplink — Cinema

(アップリンク; Map p246; www.uplink.co.jp; 37-18 Udagawa-chō, Shibuya-ku; adult/student ¥1800/1500; ☒JR Yamanote line to Shibuya, Hachikō exit) Watching indies at Uplink feels a bit like hanging out in a friend's basement; with just 40 (comfy, mismatched) seats, it's officially Tokyo's smallest theatre. Artsy domestic and foreign films (subtitled in Japanese), including documentaries, are screened here. Uplink is also one of the few Tokyo cinemas that screens films with a political bent. On weekdays students pay just ¥1100.

Shelter — Live Music

(シェルター; www.loft-prj.co.jp/SHELTER; 2-6-10 Kitazawa, Setagaya-ku; tickets ¥2000-3500; ☒Keiō Inokashira line to Shimo-Kitazawa, south exit) Of all the venues on the Shimo-Kitazawa circuit, this small basement club, going strong for more than 25 years now, has the most consistently solid line-up. It can be an

The Lou Donaldson Quartet playing at Blue Note Tokyo

excellent place to catch (and even meet) up-and-coming artists, usually of the rock persuasion.

Setagaya
Public Theatre
Performing Arts

(世田谷パブリックシアター; ☎03-5432-1526; www.setagaya-pt.jp; 4-1-1 Taishidō, Setagaya-ku; tickets ¥3500-7500; 🚃Tōkyū Den-en-toshi line to Sangenjaya, Carrot Tower exit) The best of Tokyo's public theatres, Setagaya Public Theatre puts on contemporary dramas as well as modern *nō* (a stylised Japanese dance-drama, performed on a bare stage) and sometimes *butoh* (an avant-garde form of dance). The smaller **Theatre Tram** shows more experimental works. Both are located inside the Carrot Tower building connected to Sangenjaya Station, a five-minute train ride from Shibuya.

⊙ Harajuku & Aoyama

National Nō Theatre
Theatre

(国立能楽堂; Kokuritsu Nō-gakudō; ☎03-3230-3000; www.ntj.jac.go.jp/english; 4-18-1

> Nō *seeks to express a poetic moment by symbolic and almost abstract means*

Sendagaya, Shibuya-ku; adult ¥2600-4900, student ¥1900-2200; 🚃JR Sōbu line to Sendagaya) The traditional music, poetry and dances that *nō* is famous for unfold here on an elegant cypress stage. Each seat has a small screen displaying an English translation of the dialogue. Shows take place only a few times a month and can sell out fast; purchase tickets one month in advance through the Japan Arts Council website.

The theatre is 400m from Sendagaya Station; from the exit, walk right along the main road and turn left at the traffic light.

Blue Note Tokyo
Jazz

(ブルーノート東京; Map p246; www.bluenote. co.jp; 6-3-16 Minami-Aoyama, Minato-ku; ⊙5.30pm-1am Mon-Sat, 5pm-12.30am Sun; 🚇Ginza line to Omote-sandō, exit B3) The serious cognoscenti roll up to Tokyo's prime jazz spot to take in the likes of Maceo

Parker, Herbie Hancock and Doctor John. Just like its sister acts in New York and Milan, the digs here are classily decorated with dark wood and deep velvet. Tickets typically run ¥7000 to ¥9800, plus a drink or food order.

Crocodile   Live Music, Comedy
(クロコダイル; Map p246; www.crocodile-live.jp; basement fl, 6-18-8 Jingūmae, Shibuya-ku; ◷6pm-1am; ⑤Chiyoda line to Meiji-jingūmae, exit 1) Decked out in neon, mirrors and chrome, Crocodile is a classic dive. Live music of all sorts plays here nightly, but the most popular event is the English comedy night put on by Tokyo Comedy Store on the last Friday of the month (admission ¥1500, plus drink order). Advanced bookings are recommended; see www.tokyocomedy.com/improvazilla_main_stage_show.

✪ Kōenji, Kichijōji & West Tokyo

Star Pine's Cafe   Live Music
(スターパインズカフェ; ☎0422-23-2251; www.mandala.gr.jp/spc.html; basement fl, 1-20-16 Kichijōji Honchō, Musashino-shi; tickets ¥2500-4000; ℝJR Sōbu-Chūō line to Kichijōji, north exit) This is an attractive, intimate venue, sunk deep so the ceiling feels refreshingly high. The line-up is jazz, but that's a wide net, encompassing everything from standards to the quirky, avant-garde and experimental. The audience will likely be multigenerational and attentive. One drink minimum order (but the drinks are actually decent).

Ni Man Den Atsu   Live Music
(二万電圧; www.den-atsu.com; basement fl, 1-7-23 Kōenji-Minami, Suginami-ku; tickets ¥1800-4000; ⑤Marunouchi line to Higashi-Kōenji, exit 3) Kōenji's notorious punk venue has something loud going on most nights. This is a good place to start digging into the city's underground

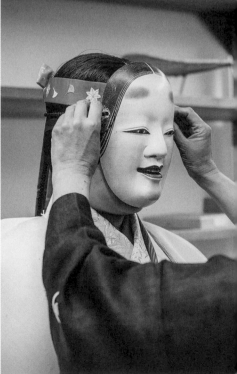

★ Nō

Some visitors find *nō* rapturous and captivating; others (including most Japanese today) find its subtlety all too subtle. The intermissions of *nō* performances are punctuated by *kyōgen* (short, lively, comic farces) – these have a more universal appeal.

Clockwise from top: Folk masks in Asakusa; Traditional *nō* performance; *Nō* actors before the show

scene. Oddly enough, it's in the basement of a large, nondescript apartment complex. One drink (¥500) minimum order.

✪ Shinjuku & Ikebukuro

Tokyo Opera City Concert Hall   Classical Music
(東京オペラシティコンサートホール; ☎03-5353-9999; www.operacity.jp; 3rd fl, Tokyo Opera City, 3-20-2 Nishi-Shinjuku, Shinjuku-ku; ¥3000-5000; 🚃Keiō New line to Hatsudai) This beautiful, oak-panelled, A-frame concert hall, with legendary acoustics, hosts the Tokyo Philharmonic Orchestra among other well-regarded ensembles, including the occasional *bugaku* (classical Japanese music) group. Free lunchtime organ performances take place monthly, usually on Fridays. Information and tickets can be acquired at

> *Props help translate comic takes on universal human experiences*

Asakusa Engei Hall (p195)

the box office next to the entrance to the Tokyo Opera City Art Gallery.

Loft   Live Music
(ロフト; Map p253; www.loft-prj.co.jp; B2 fl, 1-12-9 Kabukichō, Shinjuku-ku; 🚃JR Yamanote line to Shinjuku, east exit) The chequerboard stage here, which celebrated its 40th anniversary in 2016, has hosted the feedback and reverb of countless Tokyo indie and punk bands over the decades. The music is loud and usually good. The venue is small, with capacity for just 500, and is a good place to dig into Tokyo's live-music scene.

✪ Kagurazaka, Kanda & Akihabara

Club Goodman   Live Music
(Map p254; ☎03-3862-9010; http://clubgood man.com; B1 fl, AS Bldg, 55 Kanda-Sakumagashi, Chiyoda-ku; cover from ¥1500; 🚃JR Yamanote line to Akihabara, Electric Town exit) In the basement of a building with a guitar shop and recording studios, it's no surprise that

this live house is a favourite with Tokyo's indie-scene bands and their fans.

⊛ Ueno & Yanesen

Tokyo Bunka Kaikan   Classical Music
(東京文化会館; Map p254; www.t-bunka.jp/en; 5-45 Ueno-kōen, Taitō-ku; ⊕library 1-8pm Tue-Sat, to 5pm Sun; ℝJR lines to Ueno, Ueno-kōen exit) The Tokyo Metropolitan Symphony Orchestra and the Tokyo Ballet both make regular appearances at this concrete bunker of a building designed by Maekawa Kunio, an apprentice of Le Corbusier. Prices vary wildly; look out for monthly morning classical-music performances that cost only ¥500. The gorgeously decorated auditorium has superb acoustics.

⊛ Asakusa & Ryōgoku

Oiwake   Traditional Music
(追分; Map p254; ☑03-3844 6283; www.olwake. info; 3-28-11 Nishi-Asakusa, Taitō-ku; admission ¥2000 plus 1 food item & 1 drink; ⊕5.30pm-midnight; ℝTsukuba Express to Asakusa, exit 1) Oiwake is one of Tokyo's few *minyō izakaya*, pubs where traditional folk music is performed. It's a homey place, where the waitstaff and the musicians – who play *tsugaru-jamisen* (a banjo-like instrument), hand drums and bamboo flute – are one and the same. Sets start at 7pm and 9pm; children are welcome for the early show. Seating is on tatami.

Asakusa Engei Hall   Comedy
(浅草演芸ホール; Map p254; ☑03-3841-6545; www.asakusaengei.com; 1-43-12 Asakusa, Taitō-ku; adult/student ¥2800/2300; ⊕shows 11.40am-4.30pm & 4.40-9pm; ⑤Ginza line to Tawaramachi, exit 3) Asakusa was once full of theatres like this one, where traditional *rakugo* (comedic monologues) and other forms of comedy are performed. There are also jugglers, magicians and the like. It's all in Japanese, but the linguistic confusion is mitigated by lively facial expressions and

🎟 Butō

Butō is Japan's unique and fascinating contribution to contemporary dance. It was born out of a rejection of the excessive formalisation that characterises traditional forms of Japanese dance and of an intention to return to more ancient roots. Hijikata Tatsumi (1928–86) is credited with giving the first *butō* performance in 1959; for more on Hijikata's life and work, see *Hijikata Tatsumi and Butoh* (Bruce Baird; 2012). Ōno Kazuo (1906–2010) was also a key figure.

During a performance, one or more dancers use their naked or seminaked bodies to express the most elemental and intense human emotions. Nothing is forbidden in *butō* and performances often deal with taboo topics such as sexuality and death. For this reason, critics often describe *butō* as scandalous and *butō* dancers delight in pushing the boundaries of what can be considered beautiful in artistic performance. It's also entirely visual, meaning both Japanese and non-Japanese spectators are on level footing.

Dairakudakan (www.dairakudakan.com), which operates out of a small theatre in Kichijōji, west of Shinjuku, is one of the more active troupes today. You can also sometimes catch *butō* at the Setagaya Public Theatre (p191).

Dairakudakan perform in Tokyo
TOSHIFUMI KITAMURA / STAFF / GETTY IMAGES ©

props, which help translate comic takes on universal human experiences.

ACTIVE TOKYO

Baseball, amusement parks, cooking
courses and traditional crafts

Active Tokyo

Tokyo has more English-language courses and tours than ever before. Activities to seek out include traditional crafts workshops and cooking. Not only do these offer a chance to engage with Japanese culture, they also get you talking to and getting to know the savvy locals who run the courses and tours. Spectator sports include fan favourites sumo and baseball; martial arts have a following among both spectators and participants. Sports in general are seeing a boost in popularity as the whole city gears up for the 2020 Summer Olympics.

In This Section

Spectator Sports 200

Amusement Parks 200

Courses 201

Tours 202

What to Watch When

Sumo Tournaments take place in Tokyo in January, May and September.

Baseball The season runs March to October.

Martial Arts Tournaments and demonstrations take place sporadically throughout the year.

MICHAEL H / GETTY IMAGES ©

The art of ikebana

The Best...

Spectator Sports

Ryōgoku Kokugikan (p68) Location of the three annual Tokyo sumo *bashō* (tournaments).

Tokyo Dome (p200) Home to the Yomiuri Giants, Japan's top baseball team.

Jingū Baseball Stadium (p200) The base of Tokyo underdogs Yakult Swallows.

Courses

Wanariya (p201) Indigo-dyeing and hand-loom weaving workshops.

Tokyo Cooking Studio (p202) Soba-making lessons from a seasoned pro.

Mokuhankan (p201) Make your own woodblock prints.

Ohara School of Ikebana (p202) Learn the Japanese art of flower arranging.

🌐 Spectator Sports

Tokyo Dome   Baseball
(東京ドーム; www.tokyo-dome.co.jp/e; 1-3 Kōraku, Bunkyō-ku; tickets ¥2200-6100; ℝ JR Chūō line to Suidōbashi, west exit) Tokyo Dome (aka 'Big Egg') is home to the Yomiuri Giants. Love 'em or hate 'em, they're the most consistently successful team in Japanese baseball. Tickets sell out in advance; get them early at www.giants.jp/en.

Jingū Baseball Stadium   Baseball
(神宮球場; Jingū Kyūjo; Map p246; ✆ 0180-993-589; www.jingu-stadium.com; 3-1 Kasumigaoka-machi, Shinjuku-ku; tickets ¥1600-4600; Ⓢ Ginza line to Gaienmae, exit 3) Jingū Baseball Stadium, built in 1926, is home to the Yakult Swallows, Tokyo's number-two team (but number-one when it comes to fan loyalty). Night games start at 6pm; weekend games start around 2pm. Pick up tickets from the

> *Japan's oldest amusement park has creaky old carnival rides and heaps of vintage charm.*

booth next to Gate 9, which is open 11am to 5pm (or until 20 minutes after the game starts).

🌐 Amusement Parks

Tokyo Dome City Attractions   Amusement Park
(東京ドームシティアトラクションズ; ✆ 03-3817-6001; www.tokyo-dome.co.jp/e/attractions; 1-3-61 Kōraku, Bunkyō-ku; day pass adult/child/teenager ¥3900/2100/3400; ⊙ 10am-9pm; 🚼; ℝ JR Chūō line to Suidōbashi, west exit) The top attraction at this amusement park next to Tokyo Dome is the 'Thunder Dolphin' (¥1030), a roller coaster that cuts a heart-in-your-throat course in and around the tightly packed buildings of downtown. You can buy individual-ride tickets, day passes, night passes (valid from 5pm) and a five-ride pass (¥2600).

Hanayashiki   Amusement Park
(花やしき; Map p254; ✆ 03-3842-8780; www.hanayashiki.net/index.html; 2-28-1 Asakusa, Taitō-ku; adult/child ¥1000/500; ⊙ 10am-6pm;

Hanayashiki Amusement Park

CDRW / SHUTTERSTOCK ©

S Ginza line to Asakusa, exit 1) Japan's oldest amusement park has creaky old carnival rides and heaps of vintage charm. Once you're inside, you can buy tickets for rides (which cost a few hundred yen each). A haunted-house attraction here allegedly housed a real ghost that is said to still appear on the grounds.

Purikura no Mecca   Arcade
(プリクラのメッカ; Map p246; 3rd fl, 29-1 Udagawa-chō, Shibuya-ku; purikura ¥400; ☺24hr; ℝ JR Yamanote line to Shibuya, Hachikō exit) It's easy to see why teens get sucked into the cult of *purikura* ('print club', aka photo booths): the digitally enhanced photos automatically airbrush away blemishes and add doe eyes and long lashes for good measure (so you come out looking like an anime version of yourself). After primping and posing, decorate the images on screen with touch pens. Note that all-guy groups aren't allowed in.

✪ Courses

Wanariya   Traditional Craft
(和なり屋; Map p254; ☎03-5603-9169; www.wanariya.jp; 1-8-10 Senzoku, Taitō-ku; indigo dyeing/weaving from ¥1920/1980; ☺10am-5pm Thu-Tue; S Hibiya line to Iriya, exit 1) A team of young and friendly Japanese runs this indigo dyeing and traditional hand-loom-weaving workshop where you can learn the crafts and have a go yourself in under an hour or so.

Buddha Bellies   Cooking
(http://buddhabelliestokyo.jimdo.com; 2nd fl, Uekuri Bldg, 22-4-3 Kanda-Jimbōchō, Chiyoda-ku; courses from ¥7500; S Shinjuku line to Jimbōchō, exit A2) Professional sushi chef and sake sommelier Ayuko leads small hands-on classes in sushi, *bentō* (boxed lunch) and udon making. Prices start at ¥7500 per person for a 2½-hour course.

T-Art Academy   Art & Crafts
(https://pigment.tokyo/academy; Terrada Harbor One Bldg, 2-5-5 Higashi-Shinagawa, Shinagawa-ku; per person from ¥4000; ℝ Rinkai line to

🏀🔍 Baseball in Japan

Even if you don't follow baseball, it's worth getting tickets to a game in Tokyo just to see the perfectly choreographed cheers (Swallows fans have a famous 7th-inning stretch routine). Baseball has a culture all its own here, as spectators chomp on dried squid and buy beer from *uriko*, the young women with kegs strapped to their backs, who work the aisles with tireless cheer. Within Tokyo, the Yomiuri Giants, who play at Tokyo Dome (p200), and Yakult Swallows, who play at Jingū Baseball Stadium (p200), are cross-town rivals.

Baseball at Jingū Baseball Stadium (p200)
MASAKATSU YAMAZAKI / GETTY IMAGES ©

Tennōzu Isle, exit B) Run in conjunction with art-supply store Pigment (p114), these artist-led workshops include topics such as 'intro to calligraphy' and 'how to mix traditional paints' (with mineral pigments and animal fat). Some are held in English (you can join the Japanese classes, too); if you've got a group you can request a workshop with a translator (at extra cost). Reservations necessary.

Mokuhankan   Traditional Craft
(木版館; Map p254; ☎070-5011-1418; http://mokuhankan.com/parties; 2nd fl, 1-41-8 Asakusa, Taitō-ku; per person ¥2000; ☺10am-5.30pm Wed-Mon; ℝ Tsukuba Express to Asakusa, exit 5) Try your hand at making *ukiyo-e* (woodblock prints) at this studio run by expat David Bull. Hour-long 'print parties' are great fun and take place daily; sign up

Cycling

Tokyo is by no means a bicycle-friendly city. Bike lanes are almost nonexistent and you'll see no-parking signs for bicycles everywhere (ignore these at your peril: your bike could get impounded, requiring a half-day excursion to the pound and a ¥3000 fee). Still, you'll see people cycling everywhere and it can be a really fun way to get around the city. Some hostels and ryokan have bikes to lend.

Hipster bicycle manufacturer **Tokyobike** (Map p254; ☎03-3827-4819; www.tokyobike.com/rental; 6-3-12 Yanaka, Taitō-ku; per day ¥2500; ⏰10am-7pm Wed-Sun; 🚉JR Yamanote line to Nippori, west exit) in Yanaka rents seven-speed city bikes. Reserve one in advance by sending an email with your name, desired day and height. There are free bicycle rentals on Sundays for a course around the Imperial Palace.

See Rentabike (www.rentabike.jp) for other places around town that rent bicycles.

online. There's a shop here too, where you can see Bull's and Jed Henry's humorous *Ukiyo-e Heroes* series – prints featuring video-game characters in traditional settings.

Tokyo Cooking Studio Cooking
(東京クッキングスタジオ; Map p250; http://tokyo.cookingstudio.org; Hins Minato #004, 3-18-14 Minato, Chūō-ku; classes for up to 3 people from ¥30,000; Ⓢ Yūrakuchō line to Shintomichō, exit 7) Genial English-speaking chef Inoue Akira is a master of soba – noodles made from nutty buckwheat flour. He's taught how to make and eat this classic Tokyo dish to chefs who have gone on to win Michelin stars for their cooking. Classes are held in a compact kitchen overlooking the Sumida River.

Ohara School of Ikebana Ikebana
(小原流いけばな; Map p246; ☎03-5774-5097; www.ohararyu.or.jp; 5-7-17 Minami-Aoyama, Minato-ku; per class ¥4000; Ⓢ Ginza line to Omote-sandō, exit B1) Every Thursday, from 10.30am to 12.30pm, this well-regarded, modern ikebana school teaches introductory flower-arrangement classes in English. Sign up via email by 3pm the Tuesday before.

Tokyo Cook Cooking
(Map p252; ☎03-5414-2727; www.tokyo-cook.com; 3rd fl, Roppongi Green Bldg, 6-1-8 Roppongi, Minato-ku; classes from ¥8640; Ⓢ Hibiya line to Roppongi, exit 3) Among the several types of cooking classes on offer here in English are ones focusing on making vegetarian dishes, the temple food *shojin-ryori* and soba noodles. It's held inside the restaurant Sougo (p126).

Tokyo Kitchen Cooking
(Map p254; ☎090-9104-4329; www.asakusa-tokyokitchen.com; 502 Ayumi Bldg, 1-11-1 Hanakawado, Taitō-ku; course from ¥7560; Ⓢ Ginza line to Asakusa, exit 4A) English-speaking Yoshimi is an Asakusa-based cook who teaches small groups of visitors how to make a range of Japanese dishes. Her menu list is broad and includes mosaic sushi rolls, tempura, ramen and *gyōza*. Vegetarians and those with gluten intolerance are catered for too. Yoshimi will also meet you at the subway exit and guide you to her kitchen.

Tours

Haunted Tokyo Tours Tours
(www.hauntedtokyotours.com; hauntedtokyotours@hotmail.com; per person from ¥4500) Fun and friendly English-speaking guides take

Boat cruise at Tokyo Bay

amblers to the scenes of some of the city's most notorious ghost haunts and urban legends. You'll never look at Tokyo the same way again.

Tokyo Bay Cruise Cruise
(Map p250; ☑03-5679-7311; www.ss3.jp; 1 Nihombashi, Chūō-ku; 45/60min cruises ¥1500/2000; ⑤Ginza line to Mitsukoshimae, exit B5 or B6) For a unique perspective on Tokyo, hop aboard one of these daily river cruises. Lasting either 45 minutes or an hour, they proceed along the Nihombashi-gawa towards the Sumida-gawa, or make a loop around Nihombashi-gawa to Kanda-gawa. The landing stage is next to Nihombashi.

You'll get to see beneath many historic bridges as well as the expressway built above the river.

SkyBus Bus
(Map p250; ☑03-3215-0008; www.skybus.jp; 2-5-2 Marunouchi, Chiyoda-ku; tours adult/child from ¥1600/700, Sky Hop Bus ¥2500/1200;

For a unique perspective on Tokyo, hop aboard one of these daily river cruises.

⊙ticket office 9am-6pm; ℝJR Yamanote line to Tokyo, Marunouchi south exit) Open-top double-decker buses cruise through different neighbourhoods of the city (for roughly 50 to 80 minutes); most have English-language audio guidance aboard. The Sky Hop Bus plan allows you to hop on and off buses on any of the three routes.

Gray Line Bus
(☑03-3595-5948; www.jgl.co.jp/inbound/index.htm; per person ¥4000-13,000) Offers half-day and full-day tours with stops, covering key downtown sights and also day trips to Mt Fuji and Hakone. Pick-up service from major hotels is available, otherwise most tours leave from in front of the Dai-Ichi Hotel in Shimbashi (near Ginza).

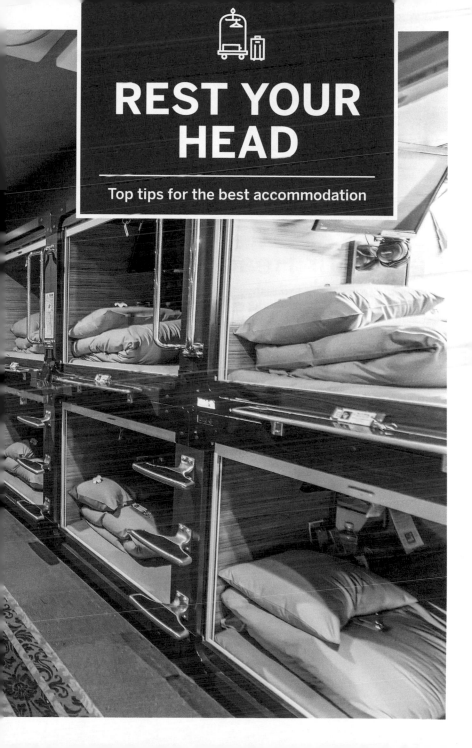

REST YOUR HEAD

Top tips for the best accommodation

Rest Your Head

Tokyo is known for being expensive; however, more attractive budget and midrange options are popping up every year. Business hotels are an economic, if institutional, option. While boutique hotels haven't really taken off, ryokan (traditional inns with Japanese-style bedding) fill the need for small, character-filled sleeping spaces. If it's luxury you're after, you can take your pick from Tokyo's astounding array of top-tier hotels, which provide oases of calm. For budget travellers, the best deals are on the east side of town, in neighbourhoods such as Ueno and Asakusa. Levels of cleanliness and service are generally high everywhere.

In This Section

Business Hotels 208

Capsule Hotels 208

Hostels 208

Luxury Hotels 208

Ryokan 208

Prices

Hostels and ryokan have fixed rates and often charge per person; for hotels of all classes, rates vary tremendously and discounts significantly below rack rates can be found online. Sales tax (8%) applies to hotel rates. There is also a city-wide 'accommodation tax' of ¥100 on rooms over ¥10,000 and ¥200 for rooms over ¥15,000.

Traditional-style hotel room

Reservations

Advanced booking is highly recommended as popular spots fill up. Walk-ins can fluster staff at smaller inns or ryokan (or staff might not be present). Busy periods include the first week of January, 'Golden Week' (29 April to 5 May) and August.

Useful Websites

Jalan (www.jalan.net) Popular discount accommodation site.

Japanese Inn Group (www.japaneseinngroup.com) Bookings for ryokan and other small inns.

Japanican (www.japanican.com) Accommodation site run by JTB, Japan's largest travel agency.

Lonely Planet (lonelyplanet.com/Japan/Tokyo/hotels) Reviews, recommendations and bookings.

🛎️ Apartment Rentals

Apartment rentals are a popular option in Tokyo, with a studio costing about the same as a double room in a business hotel (but with the added perks of a kitchen). Many hosts have portable wi-fi devices for guests to use – another money saver. However, short-term rental and apartment share sites currently operate in a grey zone in Tokyo. According to law, a unit may be rented for a minimum of 30 days. Ota-ku (where Haneda Airport is located) is an exception; here the minimum stay is seven nights. This may change, as the government plans to review legislation pertaining to vacation rentals (called *minpaku* in Japanese).

Accommodation Types

Business Hotels

Functional and economical, 'business hotels' are geared to the lone traveller on business. The compact rooms usually have semidouble beds (140cm across; roomy for one, a bit of a squeeze for two) and tiny en-suite bathrooms. They're famous for being deeply unfashionable, though many chains have updated their rooms in recent years. Expect to pay from ¥10,000 to ¥15,000 (or ¥14,000 to ¥19,000 for double occupancy). Most accept credit cards.

Capsule Hotels

Capsule hotels offer rooms the size of a single bed, with just enough headroom for you to sit up. Think of it like a bunk bed with more privacy (and a reading light, TV and alarm clock). Prices range from ¥3500 to ¥5000, which includes access to a large shared bath. Many are men-only; otherwise floors are gender-segregated. Most only accept cash and do not permit guests with visible tattoos.

Hostels

Tokyo hostels are clean and well-managed; many provide cultural activities and social events for guests. Most have a mixture of dorms and private rooms, and cooking and laundry facilities. Expect to pay about ¥3000 for a dorm and ¥8000 for a private room (double occupancy).

Luxury Hotels

Expect to find the amenities of deluxe hotels anywhere in the world: satellite TV, concierge service in fluent English and enough space to properly unwind. Many of Tokyo's luxury hotels are in high-rise buildings and offer fantastic city views. They also offer direct airport access, via the Limousine Bus. Prices vary wildly, with online deals possible.

Ryokan

Ryokan (Japanese-style inns) offer a traditional experience, with tatami (woven-mat floor) rooms and futons (traditional quilt-like mattresses) instead of beds. Exclusive establishments can charge upwards of ¥25,000; however, there are a number of relatively inexpensive ryokan in Tokyo, starting at around ¥8000 a night (for double occupancy).

Most ryokan have 'family rooms' that can sleep four or five – an economical choice if you're travelling as a group or with kids. Some offer rooms with private baths, but one of the pleasures of staying in a traditional inn is the communal bath. Many ryokan accept cash only.

Where to Stay

Tokyo is huge, so be sure to factor in travel time and costs when deciding where to stay. And while pricier neighbourhoods tend to have pricier bars and restaurants, you can always find cheap options.

Neighbourhood	Atmosphere
Marunouchi & Nihombashi	Convenient for all sights and for travel out of the city; business district with sky-high prices and quiet weekends.
Ginza & Tsukiji	Shops and restaurants at your doorstep; few inexpensive options.
Roppongi & Akasaka	Nightlife district with great eating and drinking options, plus art museum; noisy and hectic at night with some seedy pockets.
Ebisu & Meguro	Near major hubs with great bars and restaurants and fewer crowds; can feel removed from the city centre.
Shibuya & Shimo-Kitazawa	Convenient transport links and plenty of nightlife; extremely crowded; possible sensory overload.
Harajuku & Aoyama	Sights, restaurants and shops galore; very limited sleeping options.
Kōenji, Kichijōji & West Tokyo	Cheaper than central Tokyo and local vibe. Far from main sights; riding the crowded Chūō line everyday can be a drag.
Shinjuku & Ikebukuro	Superb transport links, food and nightlife options; very crowded around station areas and cheaper options near the red-light district.
Kagurazaka, Kanda & Akihabara	Central, reasonable prices and good transit links. Few budget options; many areas quiet at night.
Ueno & Yanesen	Lots of greenery, museums and easy airport access; good ryokan here tend to be isolated in residential neighbourhoods.
Asakusa & Ryogoku	Atmospheric old city feel, great budget options and backpacker vibe; can feel quiet at night and far from more central areas.
Odaiba & Tokyo Bay	Proximity to family-friendly attractions; otherwise inconvenient.

Shibuya Crossing (p108)

In Focus

Tokyo Today   **212**
The city has its sights on the 2020
Olympics and beyond. Can it pull
through in uncertain times?

History   **214**
How a fishing village became one of
the world's leading cities, despite
repeated destruction.

Arts   **219**
Tokyo's rich cultural offerings swing
from traditional woodblock prints to
avant-garde cinema.

Architecture   **222**
Tokyo is famous for its visionary contemporary buildings created by both
local and international names (but
there's more here, too).

Pop Culture   **224**
Manga, anime, fashion and robots:
Tokyo is the go-to place for all things
cutting edge (and cute).

Tokyo Today

Tokyo has reinvented itself countless times in the four centuries since its founding. With the 2020 Summer Olympic Games on the horizon, it hopes to do so again, with plans for a greener, friendlier city. Following decades of economic stagnation and a soon-to-be-shrinking workforce, the stakes are high. Does Tokyo still have what it takes to pull off another reincarnation?

Tokyo 2020

Since it was announced in 2013 that Tokyo would hold the 2020 Games, the city has gone into full preparation mode, enacting its 'Tokyo Vision 2020'. The 1964 Tokyo Summer Olympics – the first to be held in Asia – marked Tokyo's big comeback after the city was all but destroyed in WWII. The powers that be are hoping that the 2020 games will again be a symbolic stimulus. The most dramatic redevelopment is taking place around Tokyo Bay, where many of the events will be held. Already in the works is the Umi-no-Mori (Sea Forest), a vast green space on one of the bay's artificial landfill islands, overseen by architect Andō Tadao. Other positive changes that are already starting to happen: a more accessible Tokyo for people with disabilities, better English signage and tourist information, and expanded wi-fi networks.

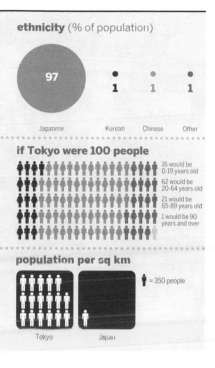

ethnicity (% of population)

97

1   1   1

Japanese   Korean   Chinese   Other

if Tokyo were 100 people

16 would be
0-19 years old

62 would be
20-64 years old

21 would be
65-89 years old

1 would be 90
years and over

population per sq km

≈ 350 people

Tokyo   Japan

Political Shake-up

Tokyo ran through two governors in four years. Both were pressured to resign after just two years in office, amid claims of misusing campaign funds (Inose Naoki) and government money (Masuzoe Yōichi). In 2016, with the sentiment that enough was enough, the city elected – by a landslide among a record turnout – its first female governor, Koike Yuriko. Once a member of the long-time ruling Liberal Democratic Party (LDP), Koike ran as an independent after the party chose to nominate someone else.

A former defence minister and fluent Arabic speaker, Koike has already enacted her campaign promise to rein in spending and increase transparency: with the budget for Olympic construction projects spiralling out of control she has sent more plans back to the discussion table – and possibly the chopping block. (Even before Koike took over, the Olympic budget had become a sore point; in 2015 the central government scrapped the plan for a stadium designed by the late Iraqi-British architect Zaha Hadid after construction costs had soared, replacing it with a more subdued and cheaper-to-make design by Kuma Kengo.) The new governor is also responsible for the abrupt decision to halt the move of Tsukiji Market to the newly constructed facility in Toyosu, after learning that contractors cut corners in carrying out decontamination of the site (where a gas refinery once stood).

City of the Future

The Olympics aren't the only noteworthy event slated to happen in 2020: while the population of Japan has been declining since the 2000s, it's predicted that Tokyo's population will peak in 2020 and then also begin to decline. The birth rate for the capital hovers at around 1.1, the lowest in the nation (the national average is 1.4), and the labour force is shrinking, but the country as a whole remains wary of immigration. The central government has campaigned for more women to enter the workforce to bolster numbers (though conservative sentiment against this lingers) and for families to have more children. Tokyoites who are vocal on social media say they can't win: the combination of the city's high cost of living, long working hours and long waiting lists for daycare means something has to give.

Tokyo is seen as a forerunner in facing the kinds of problems that major modern cities around the world will face as their populations begin a similar tapering off. The city's redevelopment initiatives also include provisions for making Tokyo a more attractive city in which to live and work – such as job centres for senior citizens, special economic zones for foreign companies and, yes, more childcare facilities. If it works, Tokyo could become a model for cities of the future. And the government's back-up plan? Trying to sell Tokyoites on moving to the countryside. And robots.

Meiji-jingū (p44)

History

Tokyo is one of the world's great cities. In the 400-plus years since its founding, the city has played many roles: samurai stronghold, imperial capital and modern metropolis. Its latest identity as a city of the future – as it is portrayed in manga (Japanese comics), anime (Japanese animation) and think pieces – is just another example of Tokyo's protean nature.

10,000 BC
Tokyo area inhabited by pottery-making people during late neolithic Jōmon period.

AD 710
Japan's first permanent capital established at Nara. The city is modelled on Chang'an, capital of Tang-dynasty China.

1457
Ōta Dōkan constructs the first Edo Castle. Under shogun Tokugawa Ieyasu in the 17th century, it becomes the world's largest fortress.

Imperial Palace (p98)

A City is Born

Before Tokyo there was Edo – literally 'Gate of the River' – named for its location at the mouth of the Sumida-gawa. For much of Japan's history, as governments rose and fell in the imperial capital of Kyoto, Edo was a sleepy fishing village. During the 14th and 15th centuries provincial warlords, called *daimyō*, began flexing their muscles and challenging the central powers. They built castles and fortresses around the country, carving Japan into a patchwork of fiefdoms. One such castle was constructed in the mid 15th century by a warrior poet named Ōta Dōkan in a place called Edo.

By the mid-16th century, the battle for supremacy among the *daimyō* had begun in earnest. A series of fearsome warlords made successive attempts to unite the country under one rule (theirs). The one who emerged victorious, in the legendary Battle of Sekigahara in 1600, was Tokugawa Ieyasu. Ieyasu had already consolidated considerable power in eastern Japan. When he claimed the title of shogun (generalissimo) he chose Edo as his

1600	**1638**	**1657**
Tokugawa Ieyasu establishes his capital in Edo, beginning 250 years of peace known as the Edo period.	*Sakoku* national isolation policy; Japan cuts off almost all contact with the outside world.	Great Meireki Fire devastates Edo, killing over 100,000 and destroying two-thirds of the city.

base. While the emperor in Kyoto remained the titular leader, it was Ieyasu who wielded the real power; Edo would become, if not in name, then in spirit, the capital city.

Life in Old Edo

Under Tokugawa rule, society was rigidly hierarchical. At the top were the *daimyō* (feudal lords) and their samurai (loyal warriors). Then came the peasants – the farmers and fishermen – and at the bottom were the *chōnin,* the townspeople, including merchants and artisans. The layout of Edo, too, was divided: on the elevated plain to the west of the castle was the *yamanote* (literally 'mountain's hand'), where the feudal elite built its estates. In the east, along the banks of the Sumida-gawa, the *chōnin* lived elbow to elbow in wooden tenement houses in *shitamachi* (the low-lying parts of Edo). These shanty towns were often swept by great conflagrations, which locals referred to as *Edo-no-hana*, or flowers of Edo.

Wealth, however, didn't follow such neat lines; in reality, some *chōnin* grew fabulously wealthy and enjoyed a lifestyle that thumbed its nose at the austerity prescribed by the ruling class. It was the *chōnin* who patronised the kabuki theatre, sumo tournaments and the pleasure district of Yoshiwara, to the north of Asakusa – generally enjoying a joie de vivre that the dour lords of Edo Castle frowned upon. Today, the best glimpses we have into that time come from *ukiyo-e* (woodblock prints).

The Meiji Restoration

For 250 years the Tokugawa shoguns kept Japan almost entirely isolated. Then, in 1853, the black ships under the command of US Navy Commodore Matthew Perry sailed into Tokyo Bay demanding that Japan open itself to foreign trade. The humiliating acquiescence that followed fanned existing flames of anti-government sentiment: a coalition of southern Japan *daimyō* (feudal lords) founded a movement (and army) to restore the emperor to power. In 1868, after months of civil war, the shogun stepped down and the 16-year-old Emperor Meiji was named head of state. Meiji moved the seat of imperial power from Kyoto to Edo, renaming the city Tokyo (Eastern Capital).

The Meiji Restoration had far-reaching social implications, as Japan opened up to the world and began to adopt technology as well as political and social ideas from the West. The caste-like social hierarchy was abolished, giving rise to a new sense of mobility. Tokyo's rapid industrialisation drew job seekers from around Japan, causing the population to grow rapidly.

Taishō Modernism

Around the start of the 1900s, old feudal-era loyalties finally buckled and party politics flourished for the first time, giving rise to the term Taishō Democracy – after the era of the short-lived Taishō emperor (1912–26). Western fashions and ideas, initially the domain

1721
Edo's population grows to 1.1 million, making it the world's largest city.

1853
Black ships of the US navy arrive under the command of Commodore Matthew Perry, forcing Japan open to US trade.

1868
Meiji Restoration; the imperial residence moves to Edo, which is renamed Tokyo.

of only the elite, began to trickle down to the middle class. More and more Tokyoites began adopting Western dress (which they most likely traded for kimonos as soon as they got home). Cafes and dance halls flourished.

Women began to work outside the home, in offices, department stores and factories, enjoying a new freedom and disposable income. Like women around the world in the 1920s, they cut their hair short and wore pants. These were the 'modern girls' – or *moga* for short – who walked arm in arm with their male counterparts, the *moba*, around Ginza, then the most fashionable district in the city.

The Great Kantō Earthquake

According to Japanese folklore, a giant catfish living underground causes earthquakes when it stirs. At noon on 1 September 1923 the catfish really jumped: the Great Kantō Earthquake, a magnitude 7.9 quake that struck south of Tokyo in Sagami Bay, caused unimaginable devastation in Tokyo. More than the quake itself, it was the subsequent fires, lasting some 40 hours, that laid waste to the city, including some 300,000 houses. A quarter of the quake's 142,000 fatalities occurred in one savage firestorm in a clothing depot.

World War II

Following the accession of Emperor Hirohito (*Shōwa tennō* to the Japanese) and the initiation of the Shōwa period in 1926, the democratic spirit of the last two decades was replaced by a quickening tide of nationalist fervour. In 1931 the Japanese invaded Manchuria and in 1937 embarked on full-scale hostilities with China. By 1940, a tripartite pact with Germany and Italy had been signed and a new order for all of Asia formulated: the Greater East Asia Co-Prosperity Sphere. On 7 December 1941, the Japanese attacked Pearl Harbor, bringing the US, Japan's principal rival in the Asia-Pacific region, into the war.

Despite initial successes, the war was disastrous for Japan. On 18 April 1942, US B-25 bombers carried out the first bombing and strafing raid on Tokyo. Incendiary bombing commenced in 1944, the most devastating of which took place over the nights of 9 and 10 March 1945, when some two-fifths of the city, mainly in the Shitamachi area, went up in smoke and tens of thousands of lives were lost. By the time Emperor Hirohito made his famous capitulation address to the Japanese people on 15 August 1945, much of Tokyo had been decimated – sections of it were almost completely depopulated, like the charred remains of Hiroshima and Nagasaki after they were devastated by atomic bombs.

The Postwar Miracle

Tokyo's phoenix-like rise from the ashes of WWII and its emergence as a major global city is something of a miracle. Still, during the US occupation in the early postwar years, Tokyo was something of a honky-tonk town. Now-respectable areas such as Yūrakuchō were the haunt of the so-called *pan-pan* girls (prostitutes).

1923
Great Kantō Earthquake kills over 140,000. An estimated 300,000 houses are destroyed.

1944–45
Allied air raids during WWII destroy large swaths of the city, including the Imperial Palace; casualties of more than 100,000 are reported.

1964
Tokyo Olympic Games held, marking Japan's postwar reintegration into the international community.

Marunouchi district

★ **Best Reads**

Low City, High City (Edward Seidensticker; 1970)

Tokyo Now & Then (Paul Waley; 1984)

Embracing Defeat (John Dower; 2000)

The Book of Tokyo: A City in Short Fiction (Edited by Michael Emmerich, Jim Hinks and Masashi Matsuie; 2015)

By the 1950s, with a boom in Japanese profits arising from the Korean War, Tokyo began to rapidly rebuild, especially the central business district. (Extravagant plans, which included a lush greenbelt around the city, existed, but pragmatism – and financial constraints – prevailed). Construction and modernisation continued at a breakneck pace peaking in the late 1980s, when wildly inflated real-estate prices and stock speculation fuelled what is now known as the 'bubble economy'. Based on the price paid for the most expensive real estate in the late '80s, the land value of Tokyo exceeded that of the entire US.

The Bubble & the Burst

When the bubble burst in 1991, the economy went into a protracted slump that was to continue, more or less, into the present. There were also other, more disturbing, troubles in Japanese society. In March 1995, members of the Aum Shinrikyō doomsday cult released sarin nerve gas on crowded Tokyo subways, killing 12 and injuring more than 5000. This, together with the devastating Kōbe earthquake of the same year, which killed more than 6000 people, signalled the end of Japan's feeling of omnipotence, born of the unlimited successes of the '80s.

On 11 March 2011, a magnitude 9.0 earthquake rocked northeastern Japan, resulting in a record-high tsunami that killed nearly 20,000 people and sparked a meltdown at the Dai-ichi nuclear plant in Fukushima-ken. Tokyo experienced little actual damage, but was shaken nonetheless. The capital itself is long overdue for a major earthquake and for a time the idea of decentralisation was bandied about – to mitigate the effects of a potential disaster.

With the announcement in 2013 that Tokyo would hold the 2020 Summer Olympics, however, all talk of decentralisation evaporated. With a renewed focus on turning the city into a showpiece, Tokyo is now focusing on what it does best: building.

1989
Death of Emperor Hirohito; Heisei era begins as Hirohito's son Akihito ascends the throne.

2013
Tokyo is awarded the 2020 Summer Olympics; plans are set in motion to revitalise and internationalise the city.

2016
Tokyo elects its first female governor, Koike Yuriko; Emperor Akihito (b 1933) announces his wish to retire.

Viewing Sunset over the Ryogoku Bridge from the Ommaya Embankment, by Katsushika Hokusai

Arts

Many outstanding Tokyo museums, both public and private, showcase Japan's long history of painting, sculpture, ceramics and more. Some forms, such as ukiyo-e (woodblock prints), have a special tie to the capital, having blossomed here during the Edo period. Tokyo is also the centre of Japan's contemporary art scene, with scores of galleries scattered around the city.

Ukiyo-e

Far from the nature scenes of classical paintings, *ukiyo-e* (literally 'pictures of the floating world') were for the common people, used in advertising or in much the same way posters are used today. The subjects of these woodblock prints were images of everyday life, characters in kabuki plays and scenes from the 'floating world', a term derived from a Buddhist metaphor for life's fleeting joys. Edo's particular 'floating world' revolved around pleasure districts such as the Yoshiwara. In this topsy-turvy kingdom, an inversion of the usual social hierarchies imposed by the Tokugawa shogunate, money meant more than rank, actors were the arbiters of style and courtesans elevated their art to such a level that their accomplishments matched those of the women of noble families.

Movie theatre in Shinjuku

TOSHIKI ONO / A COLLECTIONRF / GETTY IMAGES ©

★ **Best on Film**

Stray Dog (Kurosawa Akira; 1949)

Tokyo Story (Ozu Yasujirō; 1953)

When a Woman Ascends the Stairs (Naruse Mikio; 1960)

Lost in Translation (Sofia Coppola; 2003)

Adrift in Tokyo (Satoshi Miki; 2008)

The vivid colours, novel composition and flowing lines of *ukiyo-e* caused great excitement when they finally arrived in the West; the French came to dub it 'Japonisme'. *Ukiyo-e* was a key influence on Impressionists and post-Impressionists (including Toulouse-Lautrec, Manet and Degas).

Painting

Japan has a rich history of painting (though one heavily influenced by China). Traditionally, paintings consisted of black ink or mineral pigments on *washi* (Japanese handmade paper) and were sometimes decorated with gold leaf. These works adorned folding screens, sliding doors and hanging scrolls; never behind glass, they were a part of daily life. Throughout the Edo period, the nobility patronised artists such as those of the Kanō school, who depicted Confucian subjects, mythical Chinese creatures or scenes from nature.

With the Meiji Restoration (1868) – when artists and ideas were sent back and forth between Europe and Japan – painting necessarily became either a rejection or an embracement of Western influence. Two terms were coined: *yōga* for Western-style works and *nihonga* for works in the traditional Japanese style. In reality, though, many *nihonga* artists incorporate shading and perspective into their works, while using techniques from all the major traditional Japanese painting schools.

'Superflat' & Conceptual Art

The '90s were a big decade for Japanese contemporary art; love him or hate him, Murakami Takashi brought Japan back into an international spotlight it hadn't enjoyed since 19th-century collectors went wild for *ukiyo-e*. His work makes fantastic use of the flat planes, clear lines and decorative techniques associated with *nihonga*, while lifting motifs from the lowbrow subculture of manga (Japanese comics). As much an artist as a clever theorist, Murakami proclaimed in his 'Superflat' manifesto that his work picked up where Japanese artists left off after the Meiji Restoration – and that it might just be the future of painting, given that most of us now view the world through the portals of two-dimensional screens.

Naturally, younger artists have had trouble defining themselves in the wake of 'Tokyo Pop', as the highly exportable art of the '90s came to be known. Just as artists were looking to move past questions of Japanese-ness, the March 2011 earthquake, tsunami and nuclear meltdown caused another wave of soul searching about the role of art in contemporary (and contemporary Japanese) society. Some artists addressing this include conceptual artist Tanaka Koki (named Deutsche Bank's Artist of the Year in 2015) and the collection of irreverent pranksters known as ChimPom, who run a gallery space in Kōenji.

Cinema

Japan's golden age of cinema in the 1950s – the era of international acclaimed auteurs Ozu Yasujirō, Mizoguchi Kenji and Kurosawa Akira – is responsible for a whole generation of Japanophiles. Ozu (1903–63) was the first great Japanese director, known for his piercing, at times heartbreaking, family dramas. Mizoguchi (1898–1956) began by shooting social realist works in the 1930s, but found critical acclaim with his reimagining of stories from Japanese history and folklore. Kurosawa (1910–98) is an oft-cited influence for film-makers around the world. His films are intense and psychological; the director favoured strong leading men and worked often with the actor Mifune Toshirō. Kurosawa won the Golden Lion at the Venice International Film Festival and an honorary Oscar for the haunting *Rashōmon* (1950), based on the short story of the same name by Ryūnosuke Akutagawa and staring Mifune as a bandit.

Murakami Haruki

Among contemporary novelists, Murakami Haruki (b 1949) is the biggest star, both at home and internationally. The release of his latest novel, *Kishidancho Goroshi* (Killing Commendatore; 2017), created a media frenzy and fans lined up early outside bookstores to snag a copy. The book is the first in a volume of two (no word yet one when it will be released in English). Of all his books, the one most Japanese people are likely to mention as their favourite is the one that established his reputation, *Norwegian Wood* (1987). It's a wistful story of students in 1960s Tokyo trying to find themselves and each other. Like the main character, Murakami once worked at a record store; the university in the novel is modelled after his Alma Mater, Waseda University.

Japanese cinema continues to produce directors of merit, but has not emerged as the influential cultural force that its heyday seemed to foreshadow. Among the most widely recognised Japanese directors today is Kitano Takeshi (b 1947), long known in Japan as the comedian Beat Takeshi. Among the directors currently active on the festival circuit, two to watch include Hirokazu Koreeda (b 1962), auteur of delicate but unflinching family dramas, and the provocateur Sion Sono (b 1961).

Modern Literature

Japan's most important writer of the modern era, Sōseki Natsume (1867–1916) was one of the first generation of scholars to be sent abroad – he studied English literature in London. His ability to convey Japanese subtlety and wit through the lines of the then newly imported Western-style novel, while taking a critical look at modernising Japan and its morals, has endeared him to generations of Japanese readers. Nobel Prize winner Kawabata Yasunari (1899–1972) spent his 20s living in Asakusa – then Tokyo's equivalent of Paris' Montmartre. His novel *Asakusa Kurenaidan* (The Scarlet Gang of Asakusa; 1930), about the neighbourhood's demi-monde, was inspired by his time there.

Japan's other Nobel Laureate, Ōe Kenzaburo (b 1935), confronts modern Japan head-on, using the individual as a stand-in for society in disturbing works such as *Kojinteki na taiken* (A Personal Matter; 1964). Meanwhile, Japan's most controversial literary figure is Mishima Yukio (1925–70), who wrote essays in addition to dense, psychological novels. His growing obsession with *bushidō* (the samurai code) eventually led to a bizarre, failed takeover of the Tokyo headquarters of the Japanese Self-Defense Forces that ended with Mishima committing *seppuku* (ritual suicide). *Death in Midsummer and Other Stories* (1956) is a good introduction to his work.

Edo-Tokyo Museum (p80)

MARTIN MOOS / GETTY IMAGES ©

Architecture

Japan's traditional design aesthetic of clean lines, natural materials, heightened spatial awareness and subtle enhancement – still found in the modern city today – has long been an inspiration to creators around the world. Meanwhile, the country's contemporary architects are among the most internationally acclaimed.

Traditional Designs

Until the 20th century, the city's houses and shops were almost entirely constructed of wood, paper and tile, and early photos show a remarkable visual harmony in the old skyline. Unfortunately, such structures were also highly flammable and few survived the twin conflagrations of the first half of the 20th century – the Great Kantō Earthquake and WWII. However, traditional elements are still worked into contemporary structures. These include tatami (reed mat) floors and *shōji* (sliding rice-paper screen doors), which you'll encounter if you stay in a ryokan (traditional inn) or eat at a traditional restaurant. Temples and shrines, though almost all modern reconstructions, more often than not mimic their earlier incarnations.

Foreign Influences

When Japan opened its doors to Western influence following the Meiji Restoration (1868), the city's urban planners sought to remake downtown Tokyo in the image of a European city. A century-long push and pull ensued between enthusiasts and detractors: architects who embraced the new styles and materials and those who rejected them. Tokyo Station, with its brick facade and domes looking very much like a European terminus, went up in 1914. Meanwhile, the Tokyo National Museum (1938) was done in what was called the Imperial Style, a sturdy, modern rendering of traditional design.

Modern Icons

Modern Japanese architecture really came into its own in the 1960s. The most influential architect of the age was Tange Kenzō (1913–2005), who was in turn influenced by traditional Japanese forms as well as the aggressively sculptural works of French architect Le Corbusier. Tange's landmark structures include the National Gymnasium (1964) in Yoyogi-kōen and the Tokyo Metropolitan Government Building (1991). Among his contemporaries were the Metabolists Kurokawa Kishō, Kikutake Kiyonori and Maki Fumihiko, whose design philosophy championed flexible spaces over fixed form.

Kikutake went on to design the Edo-Tokyo Museum (1992). This enormous structure encompasses almost 50,000 sq metres of built space and reaches 62.2m (the height of Edo Castle) at its peak. Meanwhile, Maki's Spiral Building (1985) is a favourite with Tokyo residents for its user-friendly design, gallery space, cafe and shops. Tange and Maki have both been recipients of the prestigious Pritzker Architecture Prize, in 1987 and 1993 respectively.

Temple or Shrine?

Buddhist temples and Shintō shrines were historically intertwined and centuries of coexistence means the two resemble each other architecturally; you'll also often find small temples within shrines and vice versa. The easiest way to tell the two apart though is to check the gate. The main entrance of a shrine is a *torii* (gate), usually composed of two upright pillars, joined at the top by two horizontal crossbars, the upper of which is normally slightly curved. *Torii* are often painted a bright vermilion. In contrast, the *mon* (main entrance gate) of a temple is often a much more substantial affair, constructed of several pillars or casements, joined at the top by a multitiered roof. Temple gates often contain guardian figures, usually *Niō* (deva kings).

Contemporary Architects

Since the 1980s a new generation of Japanese architects have emerged who continue to explore modernism and postmodernism, while incorporating a renewed interest in Japan's architectural heritage. Names to know include Pritzker Prize winners Andō Tadao, who creates monumental works in concrete; SANAA (Sejima Kazuyo and Nishizawa Ryūe), known for their luminous form-follows-function spaces; Itō Toyō, whose designs are light and conceptual; and Shigeru Ban, who makes fantastic use of low-cost and recycled materials. Kengo Kuma, meanwhile, is Tange's successor in terms of impact on Tokyo, having received a number of high-profile commissions lately, including the 2020 Olympic stadium.

MICHAEL H / GETTY IMAGES ©

Pop Culture

Tokyo is a master at crafting pop-cultural products that catch the attention of the world. Here more people read manga (comics) than newspapers, street fashion is more dynamic than that on the catwalk, robots are the stars of anime (Japanese animation) as well as real-life marvels of technology, and everyone, including the police, has a kawaii (cute) cartoon mascot.

Manga

Walk into any Tokyo convenience store and you can pick up several phone-directory-sized weekly manga anthologies. Inside you'll find about 25 comic narratives spanning everything from gangster sagas and teen romance to bicycle racing and *shōgi* (Japanese chess), often with generous helpings of sex and violence. The more successful series are collected in volumes *(tankōbon),* which occupy major sections of bookshops.

As Japan's publishing industry faces a severe decline in sales across the board, manga is the one bright hope, with sales of *tankōbon* clocking up over 500 million volumes in 2015, and the market booming for *keitai* manga – comics read on smart phones. Top seller *One Piece* shifts over 14 million units a year alone. Major publishers, including Kodansha and

Pop culture in Akihabara (p102)

Kadokawa, are based in Tokyo and this is where many *mangaka* (manga artists) get their start in the industry.

Anime

Anime can mean anything from the highly polished hand-drawn output of Studio Ghibli to the low-budget series churned out each season for Japanese TV. It is created for all ages and social groups, encompassing genres from sci-fi and action-adventure to romance and historical drama.

The medium includes deep explorations of philosophical questions and social issues, humorous entertainment aimed at kids and bizarre fantasies. Many popular manga are later serialised as anime. Some works offer breathtakingly realistic visuals, exquisite attention to detail, complex and expressive characters, and elaborate plots.

Studio Ghibli (www.ghibli.jp) is Japan's most critically acclaimed and commercially successful producer of animated movies. Its films include classics such as *Nausicaä of the Valley of the Wind* (1984), *My Neighbor Totoro* (1988) and the Oscar-winning *Spirited Away* (2001), directed by Miyazaki Hayao. In 2016 Miyazaki announced he was coming out of retirement to direct a full-length version of *Kemushi no Boro* (Boro the Caterpillar), a short movie he had previously made for the Ghibli Museum (p96).

Among the best-known anime is *Akira* (1988), Ōtomo Katsuhiro's psychedelic fantasy set in a future Tokyo inhabited by speed-popping biker gangs and psychic children. *Ghost in the Shell* (1995) is an Ōshii Mamoru film with a sci-fi plot worthy of Philip K Dick involving

Astro Boy figurines

★ **Classic Manga**

Astro Boy (Tezuka Osamu; 1952–68)

Doraemon (Fujio Fujiko; 1969–96)

Rose of Versailles (Ikeda Riyoko; 1972–3)

Barefoot Gen (Nakazawa Keiji; 1973–4)

Black Jack (Tezuka Osamu; 1973–83)

cyborgs, hackers and the mother of all computer networks. The works of Kon Satoshi (1963–2010), including the Hitchcockian *Perfect Blue* (1997), the charming *Tokyo Godfathers* (2003) and the sci-fi thriller *Paprika* (2006), are also classics.

One new director to watch is Shinkai Makoto: his 2016 *Kimi no Na wa* (Your Name) was both a critical and box-office smash – the second highest-grossing domestic film ever, after *Spirited Away*. It's scheduled for world release in 2017. Also look out for movies by Hosoda Mamoru, including *Toki o Kakeru Shōjo* (The Girl Who Leapt Through Time; 2009) and *Bakemono no Ko* (Boy and the Beast; 2015).

Hyperfashion

Visitors are often in awe of Tokyo's incredible sense of style and its broad range of sub-cultures. It's not uncommon to see Japanese wearing kimonos for special occasions and *yukata* (light summer kimonos) for fireworks shows and festivals in summer.

Tokyo's fashion designers who have become international superstars include Issey Miyake, Yohji Yamamoto and, more recently, Rei Kawakubo of Comme des Garçons. Other designers include Fujiwara Hiroshi, a renowned street-wear fashion arbiter, who has a huge impact on what Japanese youth wear.

Fashion trends come and go in the blink of a heavily made-up eye in Tokyo. The streets of Harajuku and Shibuya remain the best places to view the latest looks such as *guro-kawaii* (somewhat grotesque cuteness). An icon of the scene is Kyary Pamyu Pamyu (http://kyary.asobisystem.com). A runaway success since her musical debut in 2011 with PonPonPon, Kyary (whose real name is Takemura Kiriko) has been compared to Lady Gaga for her outrageous fashions and self-promotion.

Pop Culture Districts

Akihabara should be the first stop on any pop-culture Tokyo tour. With its multitude of stores selling anime- and manga-related goods, not to mention maid cafes and all the electronic gizmos imaginable, Akiba (as it's known to locals) is peak geek territory. Fans of Tezuka Osamu should hop off the JR Yamanote line at Takadanobaba to view a fabulous mural homage to his characters under the railway tracks there. Further north, Ikebukuro is home to a cluster of anime- and manga-related shops and businesses, including butler cafes (cosplay theme cafes aimed at geek gals) and the world's largest Pokemon store (p162).

J-Pop

Japanese pop music, commonly shortened to J-pop, is a major driver of the country's fashion industry. Avex is one of Japan's biggest recording labels and one of its brightest stars is Hamasaki Ayumi (http://avex.jp/ayu). Noted for her chameleon style and high-concept videos, Ayu – as she is known to her adoring fans – has shifted more than 50 million records since her debut in 1998.

There was consternation from fans in 2016 as SMAP, a 'boy band' who have sold 35 million-plus records over a 25-year career, announced they would be quitting the scene. However, in this multi-billion-yen industry, there is no shortage of wannabes waiting to fill their shoes.

Robots

Long before fantasy *mecha* (a manga/anime term for robot technology) caught on with the likes of Go Nagai's *Mazinger Z* (an anime featuring a flying robot) and the video series *Patlabor*, the Japanese had an affinity for robotic devices. During the Edo period (1603–1868), small mechanical dolls known as *karakuri ningyō* were used by feudal lords to serve tea and entertain guests.

Fast forward to 21st-century Tokyo and human-scale robots are still entertaining people. There's the over-the-top cabaret, Robot Restaurant (p37), where the robots star alongside bikini-clad dancers. At the National Museum of Emerging Science & Innovation (p112), ASIMO, the world's most advanced humanoid robot bows, jogs and poses for visitors. At Aqua City, the realistic, multilingual android ChihiraJunco (p113) acts as a concierge, while the Henn-na Hotel (www.h n-h.jp) next to Tokyo Disney Resort in nearby Chiba Prefecture is staffed by robots.

Godzilla

Godzilla, the legendary star of Japanese cinema, has been experiencing a revival in Tokyo following a major US-movie reboot in 2014. Of course, as true fans know, this pop-culture icon has never really gone away, starring in 29 movies produced by studio Toho in Japan alone. The latest, *Shin Godzilla,* directed by anime supremos Anno Hideaki and Higuchi Shinji, was a local box-office smash in 2016.

A mash-up of the Japanese words for gorilla *(gorira)* and whale *(kujira)*, Godzilla first stomped his way out of Tokyo Bay in 1954, blasting everything in his path with his atomic breath. Recreating something of that moment for a contemporary audience is an installation of the monster's head and claws on the 8th floor of the Hotel Gracery Shinjuku. On the hour from noon to 8pm, the giant artwork comes to life with flashing red eyes, laser lights and steam ejected from its roaring mouth. Die-hard fans can cuddle up with Godzilla in the hotel's themed room. Other Godzilla pilgrimage locations in Tokyo include Hibiya's Chanter Sq, where there's a 2.5m-tall statue of the monster on a plinth; and the Yamanote line platform at Shinagawa Station, where his silhouette appears in a floor tile marking the spot from where distances on the line are calculated.

Autumn leaves at Koishikawa Kōrakuen (p16)

TAKASHI IMAGES / SHUTTERSTOCK ©

Survival Guide

DIRECTORY A–Z 229

Customs Regulations 229
Discount Cards 229
Electricity 229
Emergency 229
Health 229
Insurance 230
Internet Access 230
Legal Matters 230
LGBT Travellers 230

Money 231
Opening Hours 231
Public Holidays 231
Safe Travel 232
Telephone 232
Time 232
Toilets 232
Tourist Information 233
Travellers
with Disabilities 233

Visas 233
Women Travellers 233

TRANSPORT 234

Arriving in Tokyo 234
Getting Around 236

LANGUAGE 238

Directory A–Z

Customs Regulations

○ Japan has typical customs allowances for duty-free items; see Visit Japan Customs (www.customs.go.jp) for more information.

○ Stimulant drugs, which include the ADHD medication Adderall, are strictly prohibited in Japan. To bring in certain narcotics (such as codeine), you need to prepare a 'yakkan shomei' – an import certificate for pharmaceuticals. See the Ministry of Health, Labour & Welfare's website (www.mhlw.go.jp/english/policy/health-medical/pharmaceuticals/01.html) for more details about which medications are classified and how to prepare the form.

Discount Cards

Grutto Pass (¥2000; www.rekibun.or.jp/grutto) gives you free or discounted admission to 79 attractions around town within two months. If you plan on visiting more than a few museums, it's excellent value. All participating venues sell them.

Electricity

Type A
100V/50Hz/60Hz

Emergency

English-speaking operators at Japan Helpline (☎0570-000-911) are available 24 hours a day to help you negotiate tricky situations. If you don't have access to mobile service, use the contact form on the website (http://jhelp.com/english/index.html).

Ambulance & Fire	☎119
Police	☎110
Non-emergency police hotline for foreigners (☻8.30am-5.15pm Mon-Fri)	☎03-3503-8484
Emergency medical interpretation (☻9am-8pm)	☎03-5285-8181

Health

Tokyo enjoys a high level of medical services, but few hospitals and clinics have doctors and nurses who speak English. Larger hospitals are your best bet. Expect to pay about ¥3000 for a simple visit to an outpatient clinic and from around ¥20,000 and upwards for emergency care.

Clinics

Primary Care Tokyo (プライマリーケア東京; ☎03-5432-7177; http://pctclinic.com; 3rd fl, 2-1-16 Kitazawa, Setagaya-ku; ☻9am-12.30pm Mon-Sat, 2.30-6pm Mon-Fri; ᐧKeiō Inokashira line to Shimo Kitazawa, south exit) Fluent English-speaking, American-trained doctor who can address common health complaints.

Tokyo Medical & Surgical Clinic (東京メディカルアンドサージカルクリニック; ☎03-3436-3028; www.tmsc.jp; 2nd fl, 32 Shiba-kōen Bldg, 3-4-30 Shiba-kōen, Minato-ku; ☻8.30am-5pm Mon-Fri, to noon Sat; ᔆHibiya line to Kamiyachō, exit 1) Staffed with English-speaking Japanese and foreign physicians. Twenty-four-hour emergency consultation is also available. Note: prices here are steep.

Emergency Rooms

Seibo International Catholic Hospital (聖母病院; ☎03-3951-1111; www.seibokai.or.jp; 2-5-1 Nakaochiai, Shinjuku-ku; ᐧJR Yamanote

Japanese Years

In addition to the typical Western calendar, Japan also counts years by the reigns of its emperors. The current era is called Heisei (pronounced hay-say) after the ceremonial name bestowed on the current emperor, Akihito. He ascended to the throne in 1989 (Heisei 1); thus 2018 is Heisei 30 (and with talk of possible retirement, a new era may soon begin).

line to Mejiro, main exit) and **St Luke's International Hospital** (聖路加国際病院; Seiroka Kokusai Byōin; Map p250; ☎03-3541-5151; http://hospital.luke.ac.jp; 9-1 Akashi-chō, Chūō-ku; Ⓢ Hibiya line to Tsukiji, exits 3 & 4) both have some English-speaking doctors.

Medications

Pharmacies in Japan do not carry foreign medications, so it's a good idea to bring your own. In a pinch, reasonable substitutes can be found, but the dosage may be less than what you're used to.

Insurance

Basic emergency coverage is adequate. Note that Japanese hospitals only take Japanese health insurance, so you will need to pay in full and get reimbursed. Worldwide travel insurance is available at www.lonelyplanet.com/travel-insurance. You can buy, extend and claim online any time – even if you're already on the road.

Internet Access

❂ Free wi-fi can be found on subway platforms, at convenience stores, major attractions and shopping centres – though signals are often weak. Look for the sticker that says 'Japan Wi-Fi'. Download the Japan Connected (www.ntt-bp.net/jcfw/en.html) app to avoid having to log in to individual networks; if you are unable to connect, try clearing your cache.

❂ Pocket wi-fi devices, which can be used by multiple devices, can be rented from the airport. Some services, such as Japan Wireless (www.japan-wireless.com), will ship to your hotel.

Legal Matters

❂ Japanese police have extraordinary powers compared with their Western counterparts. If you find yourself in police custody, insist that you will not cooperate in any way until allowed to make a call to your embassy. Police will speak almost no English; insist that a *tsuyakusha* (interpreter) be summoned; police are legally bound to provide one before proceeding with any questioning.

❂ It is a legal requirement to have your passport on you at all times. Though checks are not common, if you are stopped by police and caught without it, you could be hauled off to a police station to wait until someone fetches it for you.

❂ Japan takes a hard-line approach to narcotics possession, with long sentences and fines even for first-time offenders.

LGBT Travellers

❂ Gay and lesbian travellers are unlikely to encounter problems in Tokyo. There are no legal restraints on same-sex sexual activities in Japan apart from the usual age restrictions. Some travellers have reported being turned away or grossly overcharged when checking into love hotels with a partner of the same sex. Otherwise, discrimination is unusual. One note: Japanese people, regardless of their sexual orientation, do not typically engage in public displays of affection.

❂ Tokyo has a small but very lively gay quarter, Shinjuku-nichōme; outside this and a handful of other places, however, the gay scene is all but invisible. For more advice on travelling in Tokyo, have a look at Utopia Asia (www.utopia-asia.com).

Money

o More and more places in Tokyo accept credit cards, but it's still a good idea to always keep at least several thousand yen on hand. Businesses that do take credit cards will often display the logo for the cards they accept. Visa is the most widely accepted, followed by MasterCard, American Express and Diners Club. Foreign-issued cards should work fine.

o Most Japanese-bank ATMs do not accept foreign-issued cards. Seven Bank ATMs at 7-Eleven convenience stores and Japan Post Bank ATMs at post offices accept most overseas cards and have instructions in English. Seven Bank ATMs are accessible 24 hours a day. Be aware that many banks place a limit on the amount of cash you can withdraw in one day (often around US$300).

o With a passport, you can change cash or travellers cheques at any Authorised Foreign Exchange Bank (signs are displayed in English), major post offices, some large hotels and most big department stores. Note that you receive a better exchange rate when withdrawing cash from ATMs than when exchanging cash or travellers cheques in Tokyo.

Opening Hours

Note that some outdoor attractions (such as gardens) may close earlier in the winter. Standard opening hours:

Banks 9am–3pm (some to 5pm) Monday to Friday

Bars around 6pm–late

Boutiques noon–8pm, irregularly closed

Cafes vary enormously; chains 7am–10pm

Department stores 10am–8pm

Museums 9am or 10am–5pm; often closed Monday

Post offices 9am–5pm Monday to Friday; larger ones have longer hours and open Saturday

Restaurants lunch 11.30am–2pm, dinner 6–10pm; last orders taken about half an hour before closing

Public Holidays

If a national holiday falls on a Monday, most museums and restaurants that normally close on Mondays will remain open and close the next day instead.

New Year's Day (Ganjitsu) 1 January

Coming-of-Age Day (Seijin-no-hi) second Monday in January

National Foundation Day (Kenkoku Kinen-bi) 11 February

Spring Equinox (Shunbun-no-hi) 20 or 21 March

Shōwa Day (Shōwa-no-hi) 29 April

Constitution Day (Kenpō Kinen bi) 3 May

Green Day (Midori-no-hi) 4 May

Children's Day (Kodomo-no-hi) 5 May

Marine Day (Umi-no-hi) third Monday in July

Mountain Day (Yama-no-hi) 11 August

Practicalities

o **Magazines** Time Out Tokyo (www.timeout.com/tokyo) and Metropolis (www.metropolisjapan.com) are two free English-language mags with city info.

o **Newspapers** Japan Times (www.japantimes.co.jp) is a long-running English-language daily.

o **Smoking** Tokyo has a curious policy: smoking is banned in public spaces but allowed inside bars and restaurants (though nonsmoking bars and restaurants exist, too). Designated smoking areas are set up around train stations.

o **Weights & Measures** The metric system is used along with some traditional Japanese measurements, especially for area (eg jō is the size of a tatami mat).

Tokyo Addresses

Tokyo is difficult to navigate even for locals. Only the biggest streets have names and they don't figure into addresses; instead, addresses are derived from districts (*ku*), blocks (*chōme*, pronounced cho-may) and building numbers. Smartphones with navigation apps have been a real boon. Many restaurants and venues have useful maps on their websites.

Respect-for-the-Aged Day (Keirō-no-hi) third Monday in September

Autumn Equinox (Shūbun-no-hi) 23 or 24 September

Health & Sports Day (Taiiku-no-hi) second Monday in October

Culture Day (Bunka-no-hi) 3 November

Labour Thanksgiving Day (Kinrō Kansha-no-hi) 23 November

Emperor's Birthday (Tennō-no-Tanjōbi) 23 December

Safe Travel

o The biggest threat to travellers in Tokyo is the city's general aura of safety. It's wise to keep up the same level of caution and common sense that you would back home. Of special note are reports that

drink-spiking continues to be a problem in Roppongi (resulting in robbery, extortion and, in extreme cases, physical assault).

o Twenty-four-hour staffed *kōban* (police boxes) are located near most major train stations.

Telephone

The country code for Japan is 📞81; Tokyo's area code is 📞03, although some outer suburbs have different area codes.

Mobile Phones

o Japan operates on the 3-G network, so overseas phones with 3-G technology should work in Tokyo.

o Data-only SIM cards for unlocked smartphones are available at kiosks at both Narita and Haneda airports and at large electronics stores (such as Bic Camera, Yodobashi Camera etc). To work, they may require some fiddling with settings, so make sure you've got a connection before you leave the shop. Staff usually speak some English. B-Mobile's Visitor SIM (www.bmobile.ne.jp/english/index.html), which offers 14 days of unlimited data (the speed will be reduced for heavy users) for ¥2380, is a good choice.

o For visitors who anticipate needing to make voice calls, a rental pay-as-you-go

phone is a better option. Rentafone Japan (www.rentafonejapan.com) offers rentals for ¥3900 a week (plus ¥300 for each additional day) and domestic calls cost a reasonable ¥35 per minute (overseas calls start at ¥45 per minute).

Public Phones

o Public phones do still exist and they work almost 100% of the time; look for them around train stations. Ordinary public phones are green; those that allow you to call abroad are grey and are usually marked 'International & Domestic Card/Coin Phone'.

o Local calls cost ¥10 per minute; note that you won't get change on a ¥100 coin. The minimum charge for international calls is ¥100, which buys you a fraction of a minute. Reverse-charge (collect) international calls can be made by dialling 📞0051.

Time

Tokyo local time is nine hours ahead of Greenwich Mean Time (GMT). Japan does not observe daylight saving time.

Toilets

o Public toilets, free, typically clean and with toilet

paper, can be found in most train stations; convenience stores often have toilets you can use, too. The most common words for toilet in Japanese are トイレ (pronounced 'toire') and お手洗い ('o-te-arai'); 女 (female) and 男 (male) will also come in handy.

○ Some restrooms still have squat toilets; Western-style toilets are often marked with the characters 洋式 (yōshiki) on the stall door. 'Washlets', increasingly common, are heated-seat thrones that wash and dry your intimate areas at the touch of a button.

○ Separate toilet slippers are usually provided in homes and restaurants where you take off your shoes at the entrance; they are typically just inside the toilet door.

Tourist Information

Note that Tourist Information Centers (TICs) cannot make accommodation bookings.

Tokyo Tourist Information Center (Map p253; 03-5321-3077; 1st fl, Tokyo Metropolitan Government bldg 1, 2-8-1 Nishi-Shinjuku, Shinjuku-ku; 9.30am-6.30pm; Ōedo line to Tochōmae, exit A4) Booking counters for tours, money-exchange machines, wi-fi, and a shop with a range of souvenirs. Additional branches

in Keisei Ueno Station, Haneda Airport and Shinjuku Bus Terminal.

JNTO Tourist Information Center (Map p250; 03-3201-3331; www.jnto.go.jp; 1st fl, Shin-Tokyo Bldg, 3-3-1 Marunouchi, Chiyoda-ku; 9am-5pm; Chiyoda line to Nijūbashimae, exit 1) Run by the Japan National Tourism Organisation, this TIC has information on Tokyo and beyond. There are also branches in Narita Airport terminals 1 and 2.

Travellers with Disabilities

○ Tokyo is making steps to improve universal access (called 'barrier free' here), but still gets mixed reviews from travellers. Newer buildings have wheelchair access ramps, and more and more subway stations have elevators (look for signs on the platform, as not all exits have elevators). Hotels from the higher end of midrange and above usually have a 'barrier-free' room or two (book well in advance). Larger attractions and train stations, department stores and shopping malls should have wheelchair-accessible restrooms (which will have Western-style toilets).

○ Two good resources are Accessible Tokyo (http://accessible.jp.org/tokyo) and Japan Accessible Tourism Centre (www.

japan-accessible.com/city/tokyo.htm).

○ Download Lonely Planet's free *Accessible Travel* guide from http://lptravel.to/AccessibleTravel.

Visas

Citizens of 67 countries, including Australia, Canada, Hong Kong, Korea, New Zealand, Singapore, USA, UK and almost all European nations will be automatically issued a *tanki-taizai* (temporary visitor visa) on arrival. Typically this visa is good for 90 days.

For a complete list of visa-exempt countries, consult www.mofa.go.jp/j_info/visit/visa/short/novisa.html#list.

Women Travellers

○ Tokyo is a relatively safe city for women travellers, though basic common sense still rules. Foreign women are occasionally subjected to some forms of verbal harassment or prying questions. Physical attacks are very rare, but have occurred.

○ Note that some budget hotels that target foreign travellers are in areas where prostitution occurs (such as Kabukichō); women, especially solo travellers, are more likely to be harassed in such places.

○ Several train companies have introduced women-only cars during rush hour to protect female passengers from *chikan* (men who grope women and girls on packed trains). There are signs (usually in pink) on the platform indicating where you can board these cars.

Transport

Arriving in Tokyo

Tokyo has two international airports. Narita Airport, in neighbouring Chiba Prefecture, is the primary gateway to Tokyo; most budget flights end up here. Haneda Airport, closer to the city

centre, is now seeing an increasing number of international flights; this is also where most domestic flights arrive. Flying into Haneda means quicker and cheaper access to central Tokyo. Both airports have smooth, hassle-free entry procedures and are connected to the city centre by public transport.

Flights, tours and cars can be booked online at lonelyplanet.com/bookings.

Narita Airport

Narita Airport (NRT; 成田空港; ☏0476-34-8000; www.narita-airport.jp) has three terminals (the new Terminal 3 handles low-cost carriers). Note that only terminals 1 and 2 have train stations. Free shuttle buses run between all the terminals every 15 to 30 minutes (from 7am to 9.30pm). Another free shuttle runs between Terminal 2 and Terminal 3 every five to 12 minutes (4.30am to

11.20pm); otherwise it is a 15-minute walk between the two terminals. All terminals have tourist information desks.

Bus

Purchase tickets from kiosks in the arrivals hall (no advance reservations necessary).

Friendly Airport Limousine (www.limousinebus.co.jp/en) Scheduled, direct, reserved-seat buses (¥3100) depart from all Narita Airport terminals for major hotels and train stations in Tokyo. The journey takes 1½ to two hours depending on traffic. At the time of writing, discount round-trip 'Welcome to Tokyo Limousine Bus Return Voucher' tickets (¥4500) were available for foreign tourists; ask at the ticket counter at the airport.

Keisei Tokyo Shuttle (www.keiseibus.co.jp) Discount buses connect all Narita Airport terminals and Tokyo Station (¥1000, approximately 90 minutes, every 20 minutes from 6am to 11pm). There are less frequent departures from Tokyo Station for Narita Airport terminals 2 and 3 between 11pm and 6am (¥2000), which are handy for budget flights at odd hours.

Train

Both Japan Railways (JR) and the independent Keisei line run between central Tokyo and Narita Airport terminals 1 and 2. For Terminal 3, take a train to Terminal 2 and then walk or take the free shuttle bus to Terminal 3 (and budget an

---

Climate Change & Travel

Every form of transport that relies on carbon-based fuel generates CO_2, the main cause of human-induced climate change. Modern travel is dependent on aeroplanes, which might use less fuel per kilometre per person than most cars but travel much greater distances. The altitude at which aircraft emit gases (including CO_2) and particles also contributes to their climate-change impact. Many websites offer 'carbon calculators' that allow people to estimate the carbon emissions generated by their journey and, for those who wish to do so, to offset the impact of the greenhouse gases emitted with contributions to portfolios of climate-friendly initiatives throughout the world. Lonely Planet offsets the carbon footprint of all staff and author travel.

extra 15 minutes). Tickets can be purchased in the basement of either terminal, where the entrances to the train stations are located.

Keisei Skyliner (www.keisei.co.jp/keisei/tetudou/skyliner/us) The quickest service into Tokyo runs nonstop to Nippori (¥2470, 36 minutes) and Ueno (¥2470, 41 minutes) stations, on the city's northeast side, where you can connect to the JR Yamanote line or the subway (Ueno Station only). Trains run twice an hour, 8am to 10pm. Foreign nationals can purchase advance tickets online for slightly less (¥2200). The Skyliner & Tokyo Subway Ticket, which combines a one-way or round-trip ticket on the Skyliner and a one-, two- or three-day subway pass, is a good deal.

Keisei Main Line Limited-express trains (*kaisoku kyūkō*; ¥1030, 71 minutes to Ueno) follow the same route as the Skyliner, but make stops. This is a good budget option. Trains run every 20 minutes during peak hours.

Narita Express (www.jreast.co.jp/e/nex) N'EX trains depart Narita approximately every half-hour between 7am and 10pm for Tokyo Station (¥3020, 53 minutes) and Shinjuku (¥3190, 80 minutes); the latter also stops at Shibuya (¥3190; 75 minutes). At the time of writing, foreign tourists could purchase return N'EX tickets for ¥4000 (valid for 14 days; ¥2000 for under 12s). Check online or enquire at the JR East Travel Service Centers at Narita Airport for the latest deals.

Baggage Shipment

Baggage couriers provide next-day delivery of your large luggage from Narita and Haneda airports to any address in Tokyo (around ¥2000 per large bag) or beyond, so you don't have to haul it on the trains. Look for kiosks in the arrival terminals. If you plan on taking advantage of this service, make sure to put the essentials you'll need for the next 24 hours in a small bag.

Taxi

Fixed-fare taxis run ¥20,000 to ¥22,000 for most destinations in central Tokyo.

Haneda Airport

Haneda Airport (HND; 羽田空港; ☑ international terminal 03-6428-0888; www.tokyo-airport-bldg.co.jp/en) has two domestic terminals and one international terminal. Note that some international flights arrive at awkward night-time hours, between midnight and 5am, when only sporadic buses to central Tokyo will be running.

Bus

Purchase tickets at the kiosks at the arrivals hall.

Friendly Airport Limousine (www.limousinebus.co.jp/en) Coaches connect Haneda with major train stations and hotels in Shibuya (¥1030), Shinjuku (¥1230), Roppongi (¥1130), Ginza (¥930) and others; fares double between midnight and 5am. Travel times vary wildly, taking anywhere from 30 to 90 minutes depending on traffic. Night buses depart for Shibuya Station at 12.15am, 12.50am and 2.20am and Shinjuku Bus Terminal at 12.20am and 1am.

Train & Monorail

Note that the international and domestic terminals have their own stations; when traveling to the airport, the international terminal is the second to last stop.

Keikyū Airport Express (www.haneda-tokyo-access.com/en) Trains depart several times an hour (5.30am to midnight) for Shinagawa (¥410, 12 minutes), where you can connect to the JR Yamanote line. From Shinagawa, some trains continue along the Asakusa subway line, which serves Higashi-Ginza, Nihombashi and Asakusa stations.

Tokyo Monorail (www.tokyo-monorail.co.jp/english) Leaves approximately every 10 minutes (5am to midnight) for Hamamatsuchō Station (¥490, 15 minutes), which is a stop on the JR Yamanote line. Good for travellers staying near Ginza or Roppongi.

Taxi

Fixed fares include Ginza (¥5600), Shibuya (¥6400), Shinjuku (¥6800), Ikebukuro (¥8500) and Asakusa (¥6900).

Train & Subway Passes

Prepaid rechargeable Suica and Pasmo cards (they're essentially the same; JR issues Suica and the subway issues Pasmo) work on all city trains and subways and allow you to breeze through the ticket gates without having to work out fares or transfer tickets.

Purchase one from any touch-screen ticket-vending machine in Tokyo (including those at Haneda and Narita airports). A ¥500 deposit and a minimum charge of ¥2000 is required (¥1000 for Pasmo); the deposit is refunded when you return the pass to any ticket window.

The only reason not to get a Suica or Pasmo is to take advantage of Tokyo Metro's 24-hour unlimited ride pass (adult/child ¥600/300). Note that this is only good on the nine subway lines operated by Tokyo Metro.

Getting Around

Boat

Tokyo Cruise (水上バス, Suijō Bus; ☎0120-977-311; http://suijobus.co.jp) Water buses run up and down the Sumida-gawa (Sumida River) roughly twice an hour between 10am and 6pm connecting Asakusa with Hama-rikyū Onshi-teien (¥980, 35 minutes) and Odaiba (¥1260, 70 minutes). Tickets can be purchased immediately before departure, if available, at any pier.

Tokyo Mizube Cruising Line (東京水辺ライン; ☎03-5608-8869; www.tokyo-park.or.jp/waterbus) Water buses head down the Sumida-gawa from Asakusa to Ryōgoku (¥310), Hama-rikyū Onshi-teien (¥620) and Odaiba (¥1130), and then back up again. Schedules are seasonal and infrequent in winter. Tickets don't have to be reserved in advance but can be purchased just before departure.

Taxi

• Taxis in Tokyo feature white-gloved drivers, seats covered with lace doilies and doors that magically open and close – an experience in itself. They rarely make economic sense though, unless you have a group of four.

• All cabs run by the meter. Fares start at ¥730 for the first 2km, then rise by ¥90 for every 280m you travel (or for every 105 seconds spent in traffic). There's a surcharge of 20% between 10pm and 5am (including fixed-fare taxis from the airport). Most (but not all) taxis take credit cards.

• Drivers rarely speak English, though fortunately most taxis now have navigation systems. It's a good idea to have your destination written down in Japanese, or better yet, a business card with an address.

• Train stations and hotels have taxi stands where you are expected to queue. Otherwise, you can hail a cab from the street, by standing on the curb and sticking your arm out. A red light means the taxi is free and a green light means it's taken.

Train & Subway

• Tokyo's extensive rail network includes JR (Japan Rail) lines, a subway system and private commuter lines that depart in every direction for the suburbs, like spokes on a wheel. Major transit hubs include Tokyo, Shinagawa, Shibuya, Shinjuku, Ikebukuro and Ueno stations. Trains and subways run 5am to midnight.

• Tokyo has 13 subway lines, nine of which are operated by Tokyo Metro (www.tokyometro.jp) and four by Toei (www.kotsu.metro.tokyo.jp). The lines are colour-coded, making navigation fairly simple. Unfortunately, journeys that require transfers between lines run by different operators cost more than journeys that use only one operator's lines.

• Figure out the best route to your destination with the Japan Travel app (www.navitimejapan.com); you can download routes to be used offline, too.

• Most train and subway stations have several different exits. Try to get your bearings and decide where to exit while still on the platform; look for the yellow signs that indicate which stairs lead to which exits. If you're not sure which exit to take, look for street maps of the area usually posted near the ticket gates, which show the locations of the exits.

Tickets

Fares start at ¥133/170/180 for JR/Tokyo Metro/Toei and go up depending on how far you travel.

o Purchase paper tickets or top up train passes at the touch-screen ticket-vending machines outside station ticket gates. These have an English function.

o To purchase a paper ticket, you'll need to work out the correct fare from the chart above the machines. If you can't work it out, just buy a ticket for the cheapest fare.

o All ticket gates have card readers for Suica and Pasmo train passes; simply wave your card over the reader.

o If you're using a paper ticket or a one-day pass, you'll need to use a ticket gate with a slot for inserting

a ticket. Make sure to pick it up when it pops out again.

o You'll need your ticket or pass to exit the station as well. If your ticket or pass does not have sufficient charge to cover your journey, insert it into one of the 'fare adjustment' machines near the exit gates.

Key Routes

Ginza subway line Shibuya to Asakusa, via Ginza and Ueno. Colour-coded orange.

Hibiya subway line Naka-Meguro to Ebisu, Roppongi, Ginza, Akihabara and Ueno. Colour-coded grey.

JR Yamanote line Loop line stopping at many sightseeing destinations, such as Shibuya, Harajuku, Shinjuku, Tokyo and Ueno. Colour-coded light green.

JR Chūō line Tokyo Station to points in west Tokyo, via Shinjuku. Colour-coded reddish-orange.

JR Sōbu line Runs across the city centre, connecting Shinjuku with Iidabashi, Ryōgoku and Akihabara. Colour-coded yellow.

Yurikamome line Elevated train running from Shimbashi to points around Tokyo Bay.

When to Travel

o Trains and subways run 5am to midnight.

o The morning rush (7am to 9.30am) for trains going towards central Tokyo (from all directions) is the worst, when 'packed in like sardines' is an understatement.

o Until 9.30am women (and children) can ride in women-only cars, which tend to be less crowded.

o The evening rush (around 5pm to 8pm) hits trains going out of central Tokyo – though as many work late or stay out, it's not as bad as the morning commute.

o The last train of the night heading out of the city (around midnight) is also usually packed – with drunk people. Friday night is the worst.

o Trains going the opposite directions during peak hours (towards central Tokyo in the evening, for example) are uncrowded, as are trains in the middle of the day.

Language

Japanese pronunciation is easy for English speakers, as most of its sounds are also found in English. Note though that it's important to make the distinction between short and long vowels, as vowel length can change the meaning of a word. The long vowels (ā, ē, ī, ō, ū) should be held twice as long as the short ones. All syllables in a word are pronounced fairly evenly in Japanese. If you read our pronunciation guides as if they were English, you'll be understood.

To enhance your trip with a phrasebook, visit **lonelyplanet.com**.

Basics

Hello.	こんにちは。	kon·ni·chi·wa
Goodbye.	さようなら。	sa·yō·na·ra
Yes.	はい。	hai
No.	いいえ。	ī·e
Please.	ください。	ku·da·sai
Thank you.	ありがとう。	a·ri·ga·tō
Excuse me.	すみません。	su·mi·ma·sen
Sorry.	ごめんなさい。	go·men·na·sai

What's your name?

お名前は 何ですか?	o·na·ma·e wa nan des ka

My name is ...

私の 名前は…です。	wa·ta·shi no na·ma·e wa...des

Do you speak English?

英語が 話せますか?	ē·go ga ha·na·se·mas ka

I don't understand.

わかりません。	wa·ka·ri·ma·sen

Accommodation

Where's a ...?	…はど こですか?	... wa do·ko des ka
campsite	キャンプ場	kyam·pu·jō
guesthouse	民宿	min·shu·ku
hotel	ホテル	ho·te·ru
inn	旅館	ryo·kan
Do you have a ... room?	…ルームは ありますか?	...rū·mu wa a·ri·mas ka
single	シングル	shin·gu·ru
double	ダブル	da·bu·ru

How much is it per ...?	…いくら ですか?	... i·ku·ra des ka
night	1泊	ip·pa·ku
person	1人	hi·to·ri

air-con	エアコン	air·kon
bathroom	風呂場	fu·ro·ba
window	窓	ma·do

Eating & Drinking

I'd like to reserve a table for (two).

(2人)の 予約をお 願いします。	(fu·ta·ri) no yo·ya·ku o o·ne·gai shi·mas

I'd like (the menu).

(メニュー) をお願いします。	(me·nyū) o o·ne·gai shi·mas

I don't eat (red meat).

(赤身の肉) は食べません。	(a·ka·mi no ni·ku) wa ta·be·ma·sen

That was delicious!

おいしかった。	oy·shi·kat·ta

Please bring the bill.

お勘定 をください。	o·kan·jō o ku·da·sai

Emergencies

Help!	たすけて!	tas·ke·te
Go away!	離れろ!	ha·na·re·ro
Call the police!	警察を呼んで!	kē·sa·tsu o yon·de
Call a doctor!	医者を呼んで!	i·sha o yon·de
I'm lost.	迷いました。	ma·yoy·mash·ta

I'm ill.

私は病 気です。	wa·ta·shi wa byō·ki des

Where are the toilets?

トイレは どこですか?	toy·re wa do·ko des ka

Transport & Directions

Where's the ...?

…はどこ ですか?	... wa do·ko des ka

What's the address?

住所は何 ですか?	jū·sho wa nan des ka

Can you show me (on the map)?

(地図で)教えて くれませんか?	(chi·zu de) o·shi·e·te ku·re·ma·sen ka

When's the next (bus)?

次の(バス)は 何時ですか?	tsu·gi no (bas) wa nan·ji des ka

Behind the Scenes

Writer Thanks

Rebecca Milner

Much gratitude as always to my family and friends for their support, company (on many a research excursion) and patience (especially when deadlines loom). Thank you to Simon and Laura for being there with spot-on tips, suggestions, advice (and patience). To Tomoko, the coolest Tokyo city bureaucrat, and Will, for his input on the arts and theatre scene.

Simon Richmond

My thanks to Hollie Mantle, Will Andrews, Yoshizawa Tomoko, Toshiko, Kenichi, Chris, Giles, Steve and Emiko, and my co-author Rebecca.

Acknowledgements

Climate map data adapted from Peel MC, Finlayson BL & McMahon TA (2007) 'Updated World Map of the Köppen-Geiger Climate Classification', Hydrology and Earth System Sciences, 11, 1633–44.
Illustrations p60–61 by Michael Weldon

This Book

This guidebook was researched and written by Rebecca Milner and Simon Richmond.
Destination Editor Laura Crawford
Product Editor Grace Dobell
Senior Cartographer Diana Von Holdt
Book Designer Wibowo Rusli
Assisting Editors Michelle Bennett, Melanie Dankel, Saralinda Turner, Maja Vatrić, Simon Williamson
Cartographer Julie Dodkins
Assisting Book Designers Ania Bartoszek, Katherine Marsh
Cover Researcher Wibowo Rusli
Thanks to Naoko Akamatsu, Bridget Blair, Liz Heynes, Lauren O'Connell, Mazzy Prinsep, Kirsten Rawlings, Alison Ridgway, Lyahna Spencer, Tony Wheeler

Send Us Your Feedback

We love to hear from travellers – your comments keep us on our toes and help make our books better. Our well-travelled team reads every word on what you loved or loathed about this book. Although we cannot reply individually to postal submissions, we always guarantee that your feedback goes straight to the appropriate authors, in time for the next edition. Each person who sends us information is thanked in the next edition, the most useful submissions are rewarded with a selection of digital PDF chapters.

Visit lonelyplanet.com/contact to submit your updates and suggestions or to ask for help. Our award-winning website also features inspirational travel stories, news and discussions.

Note: We may edit, reproduce and incorporate your comments in Lonely Planet products such as guidebooks, websites and digital products, so let us know if you don't want your comments reproduced or your name acknowledged. For a copy of our privacy policy visit lonelyplanet.com/privacy.

Index

A

accommodation 205-9, **209**
  apartment rentals 208
  budget 206
  capsule hotels 208
  language 238
  reservations 207
activities 197-203, *see also
  individual activities*
air travel 234-5
Akasaka **252**
  drinking 175-6
  entertainment 189
  food 126-7
  nightlife 175-6
  shopping 155-7
Akihabara 102-5, 226, **254-5**
  entertainment 105
  food 104-5, 138-40
  itineraries 27
  shopping 27, 104, 164-6
amusement parks
  Hanayashiki 200-1
  Tokyo Disney Resort 115
  Tokyo Joypolis 113
anime 8, 225-6
antiques 151
Aoyama **246-7**
  drinking 181
  entertainment 191-2
  food 133-5
  nightlife 181
  shopping 159-60
arcades 105, 201
architecture 20, 74-5, 222-3
area codes 232

000 Map pages

art galleries, *see* museums &
  galleries
arts 219-21, *see also* literature,
  music, painting
  Art Fair Tokyo 8
  Design Festa 10
  Japan Media Arts Festival 14
  Roppongi Art Night 15
  Sancha de Daidogei 15
Asakusa **254-5**
  drinking 182-3
  entertainment 25, 195
  food 143-5
  itineraries 24-5
  nightlife 182-3
ATMs 18, 231

B

baggage couriers 235
bars, *see* nightlife
baseball 200, 201
bathrooms 232-3
beer gardens 182
bicycle travel 100, 202
boat cruises 114-15, 203
boat travel 236
books 151, 163, 218, 221
budget 18
bus travel 234, 235
business hours, *see* opening
  hours
butō 195

C

cafes 30, 131, 132
calendar 230
cell phones 18, 232
cemeteries
  Aoyama Rei-en 67
  Yanaka-reien 65
cherry blossoms 9, 66-7
children, travel with 32-3

climate 4-17, 19, 234
clubs 172
costs 18, 171
courses 199, 201-2
  cooking 57, 201-2
  ikebana 202
  traditional crafts 201-2
credit cards 18, 231
culture 28, 212-13
currency 18
customs regulations 229
cycling 100, 202

D

daimyō 215-16
dance
  butō 195
  kabuki 88-91
  nō 190, 192-3
dangers 232
disabilities, travellers with 233
discount cards 31, 229
drinking, *see* nightlife
drinks
  cocktails 172
  craft beer 172
  sake 180
  shōchū 181

E

earthquakes 217, 218
Ebisu **246-7**
  drinking 176
  entertainment 189-90
  food 127-9
  nightlife 176
  shopping 157, 159
economy 212-13
Edo 215-16
electricity 229
emergencies 229, 238

entertainment 28, 184-95, *see also* dance
  internet resources 186
  jazz clubs 187
  live music 173, 189
  theatre 187
  tickets 186
ethnicity 213
etiquette 85, 123, 127
events 4-17, 31

F

family travel 32-3
fashion 150, 226
festivals 4-17, 31
film 220, 221
  Tokyo Filmex 16
  Tokyo International Film Festival 15
fireflies 11
flea markets 153
food 29, 117-45, **119**
  blogs 119
  budgeting 118
  cafes 131, 132
  cooking courses 57, 201-2
  etiquette 123, 127
  food alleys 141
  food halls 138
  highlights 120-1
  izakaya 120, 124, 125
  kissaten 132
  language 238
  monja-yaki 128
  ramen 136
  seafood 121
  shokudō 143
  shopping 150
  sushi 54-7
  sweets 144
  tempura 119
  tonkatsu 119
  toshikoshi soba 17
  vegan 134

  vegetarian 134
  yakitori 119
fortune telling 79
free attractions 31
Fuji Five Lakes 72-3

G

galleries, *see* museums & galleries
gardens, *see* parks & gardens
gay travellers 230-1
Ginza **250-1**
  drinking 174-5
  entertainment 188
  food 23, 57, 123-4, 136
  itineraries 22
  nightlife 174-5
  shopping 30, 153-5
Godzilla 227
go-karting 30, 105

H

Harajuku **246-7**
  drinking 181
  entertainment 191-2
  food 133-5
  itineraries 20-1, 26
  nightlife 181
  shopping 26, 46-9, 159-60
Haruki, Murakami 221
Hatsu-mōde 6
health 229-30
hiking
  Kawaguchi-ko Trail 70-1
  tours 72
history 29, 214-18
holidays 231-2
hostels 208

I

ikebana 202
Ikebukuro
  food 137-8
  shopping 161-2, 164

insurance 230
internet access 230
internet resources 18
  accommodation 207
  entertainment 186
  food 119
  nightlife 171
itineraries 20-7
  Omote-sandō 74-5, **74-5**
  Yanaka 64-5, **64-5**
izakaya 120, 124, 125

J

Japanese language 238
Jimbōchō 163
J-pop 227

K

kabuki 88-91
Kabukiza Theatre 88-91
Kagurazaka
  food 138-40
  shopping 164-6
Kanda **254-5**
  entertainment 194-5
  food 138-40
  shopping 164-6
Kantō earthquake 217
Kappabashi 166
karaoke 110-11
Kichijōji
  entertainment 192-3
  food 135, 137
  shopping 160-1
kimonos 156
kissaten 132
Kōenji
  drinking 182
  entertainment 192-3
  food 135, 137
  nightlife 182
  shopping 160-1
Kōenji Awa Odori 13
Kuramae 30, 165, **254-5**

L

language 18, 238
legal matters 230
lesbian travellers 230-1
LGBT travellers 230-1
  Tokyo Rainbow Pride 10
literature 218, 221, *see also*
  books
live music 173, 189

M

magazines 231
manga 224-5, 226
markets 31
  Ameya-yokochō 62-3
  flea markets 153
  Setagaya Boro-ichi 6
  Tsukiji Outer Market 22, 30,
    40-3
Marunouchi **250-1**
  drinking 174
  entertainment 188
  food 122-3
  itineraries 22
  nightlife 174
  shopping 152-3
measures 231
medical services 229-30
medications 230
Meguro **246-7**
  drinking 176
  entertainment 189-90
  food 127-9
  nightlife 176
  shopping 157, 159
Meguro-gawa 67
Meiji Restoration 216
mobile phones 18, 232
money 18, 231
monja-yaki 128
Mt Fuji 70-3

museums & galleries
  21_21 Design Sight 52
  Archi-Depot 113-14
  Asakura Museum of
    Sculpture, Taitō 63
  Complex 665 52-3
  Crafts Gallery 101
  Edokoro 64
  Edo-Tokyo Museum 80
  Gallery of Hōryū-ji Treasures
    58
  Ghibli Museum 26, 96-7
  Heiseikan 59
  Intermediatheque 101
  Kabuki-za Gallery 91
  Mori Art Museum 27, 51
  National Art Center Tokyo 52
  National Museum of
    Emerging Science &
    Innovation (Miraikan) 112-13
  National Museum of Modern
    Art (MOMAT) 100-1
  SCAI the Bathhouse 63
  ShugoArts 52
  Sumida Hokusai Museum
    30, 80
  Sumo Museum 69
  Suntory Museum of Art 51
  Taka Ishii 52
  Tokyo National Museum 24,
    58-63
  Tomio Koyama Gallery 52
  Tōyōkan 59
music
  festivals 8, 14
  live music 173, 189

N

newspapers 231
nightlife 169-83, **171**
  beer gardens 182
  blogs 171
  budgeting 171
  clubs 172

  highlights 172-3
  live music 173
  opening hours 170
  tipping 171
Nihombashi **250-1**
  drinking 174
  entertainment 188
  food 122-3
  nightlife 174
  shopping 152-3
nō 190, 192-3

O

Odaiba 112-13
Olympics 212-13, 218
Omote-sandō 74-5, **74-5**
onsen 82-7
opening hours 231
  nightlife 170
  shopping 149

P

packing list 19
painting 220
palaces
  Imperial Palace 6, 23, 98-101
parks & gardens 31
  Canadian Embassy Stone
    Garden 53
  Hama-rikyū Onshi-teien 22
  Hotel New Ōtani Gardens 53
  Imperial Palace East Garden 99
  Imperial Palace Plaza 99
  Inokashira-kōen 97
  Kitanomaru-kōen 100
  Meiji-jingū Gyoen 45
  Mohri Garden 53
  Rikugi-en 106-7
  Shinjuku-gyoen 67
  Sumida Park 67
  Tokyo Garden Terrace 53
  Ueno-kōen 24, 59
  Yoyogi-kōen 66

planning 18-19
  budgeting 31, 206
  calendar of events 4-17
  children, travel with 32-3
  festivals & events 4-17, 31
  internet resources 18, 119, 171, 186, 207
  itineraries 20-7
  repeat visitors 30
  Tokyo basics 18-19
  Tokyo neighbourhoods **2-3**
  travel seasons 4-17, 19
politics 212-13
pop culture 102-5, 158, 224-7
population 213
public holidays 231-2
public phones 232

R

ramen 136
robots 113, 227
Roppongi **252**
  drinking 175-6
  entertainment 189
  food 27, 126-7, 136
  itineraries 27
  nightlife 27, 175-6
  shopping 155-7
Roppongi Art Triangle 50-3
Ryōgoku **254-5**
  drinking 182-3
  food 143-5
  nightlife 182-3
Ryōgoku Kokugikan 68-9
ryokan 208

S

safety 232
sake 180
sales 149
Sanja Matsuri 10
sentō 82-7

Shibuya **246-7**
  drinking 176, 178-9, 181
  entertainment 190-1
  food 21, 129-32
  itineraries 20-1
  nightlife 111, 176, 178-9, 181
  shopping 159
Shibuya Center-gai 109
Shibuya Crossing 21, 108-9
Shimo-Kitazawa
  drinking 176-9, 181
  entertainment 190-1
  food 129-32
  nightlife 176-9, 181
  shopping 159
Shinjuku **253**
  drinking 95
  entertainment 194
  food 137-8
  itineraries 20-1
  nightlife 21, 175
  shopping 161-2, 164
Shinjuku Ni-chōme 175
shokudō 143
shopping 147-67, **149**
  antiques 151
  arts & crafts 150
  books 151, 163
  business hours 149
  department stores 23, 138, 154
  design 150, 158
  duty-free 148
  fashion 150
  flea markets 153
  food 150
  furoshiki 158
  highlights 150
  homewares 151
  kimonos 156
  kitchenware 158, 166
  opening hours 149
  sales 149
  souvenirs 158
  zakka-ten 162

shrines, see temples & shrines
SIM cards 232
smoking 231
souvenirs 158
spectator sports 199, 200
subway 236-7
Sumida-gawa Fireworks 12
sumo 68-9
Superflat art 220-1
sweets 144

T

Taishō Modernism 216-17
taxes 148
taxis 235, 236
teahouses 107, 120
telephone services 18, 232
temples & shrines 31, 223
  Asakusa-jinja 79
  Awashima-dō 80
  Chingo-dō 81
  Enju-ji 64
  Five-Storey Pagoda 79
  Kiyōmizu Kannon-dō 62
  Meiji-jingū 20, 44-5
  Nezu-jinja 63
  Sensō-ji 25, 76-81
  Ueno Tōshō-gū 62
tempura 119
Tennōzu Isle 30, 113-14
theatre 187
time 232
time zones 18
tipping 171
toilets 232-3
Tokyo Bay 112-15, 183
Tokyo City View 95
Tokyo Metropolitan Government Building 94
Tokyo Midtown 51
Tokyo Sky Tree 94
tonkatsu 119
tourist information 18, 233

tours 202-3
  boat 203
  bus 203
  hiking 72
  markets 43
  palaces 98
  walking 31, 64-5, 74-5, **64-5, 74-5**
train passes 236
train travel 234-7
travel to/from Tokyo 19, 234-5
travel within Tokyo 19, 236-7
trekking, *see* hiking
Tsukiji **250-1**
  drinking 174-5
  entertainment 188
  food 40-3, 123-4
  itineraries 22
  nightlife 174-5
  shopping 153-5

U

Ueno **254-5**
  drinking 182
  entertainment 195

  food 25, 142-3
  itineraries 24-5
  nightlife 182
  shopping 166-7
ukiyo-e 219-20

V

vacations 231-2
vegan travellers 134
vegetarian travellers 134
views 21, 92-5, 173
visas 18, 233

W

walking tours 31
  Omote-sandō 74-5, **74-5**
  Yanaka 64-5, **64-5**
weather 4-17, 19
websites, *see* internet resources
weights 231
West Tokyo
  drinking 182
  entertainment 192-3
  food 135, 137

  nightlife 182
  shopping 160-1
wi-fi 230
women travellers 233-4
World War II 217

Y

yakitori 119, 120
Yanaka 24-5, **24-5**, **254-5**
Yanaka Ginza 63, 64
Yanesen
  drinking 182
  food 142-3
  nightlife 182
  shopping 166
Yuriko, Koike 213

Z

zoos
  Ueno Zoo 59

Shibuya Center-gai (p109)

Tokyo Maps

Harajuku, Aoyama, Shibuya & Ebisu 246

Marunouchi, Nihombashi, Ginza & Tsukiji 250

Roppongi & Akasaka 252

Shinjuku 253

Ueno, Yanaka & Asakusa 254

Harajuku, Aoyama, Shibuya & Ebisu

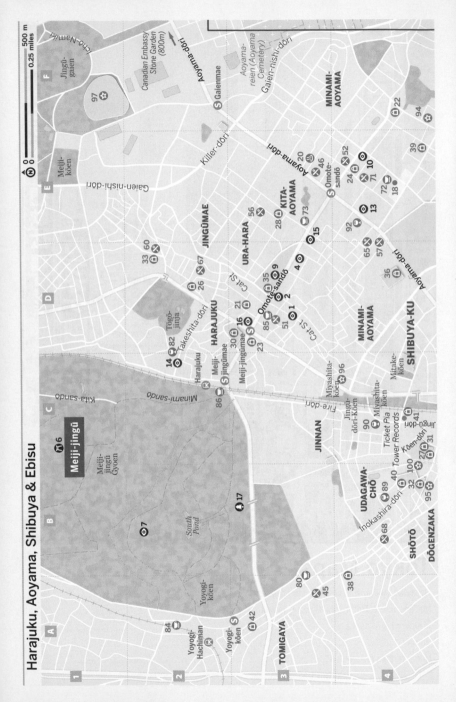

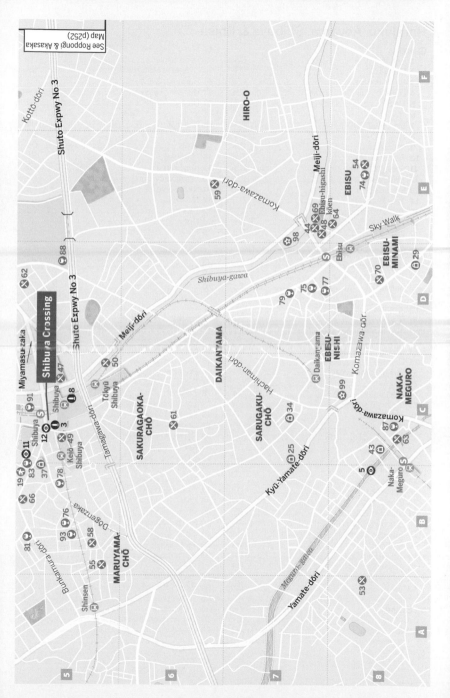

See Roppongi & Akasaka
Map (p252)

Kotto-dōri

Shuto Expwy No 3

HIRO-O

Meiji-dōri

Komazawa-dōri

59

EBISU

54

74

44 69

Ebisu-higashi

48

64

kōen

98

Sky Walk

Shibuya-gawa

Ebisu

S

77

70

EBISU-
MINAMI

29

75

79

88

62

Shuto Expwy No 3

Miyamasu-zaka

Shibuya Crossing

47

50

Meiji-dōri

DAIKANYAMA

Daikanyama

EBISU-
NISHI

Komazawa-dōri

91

Shibuya

Tōkyū
Shibuya

8

Hachiman-dōri

99

NAKA-
MEGURO

Shibuya

S

3

12

1

61

SARUGAKU-
CHŌ

34

87

63

Tamagawa-dōri

11

19

83

37

49

Keiō
Shibuya

78

Kyū-Yamate-dōri

25

43

5

Naka-
Meguro

S

66

Dōgenzaka

76

93

58

SAKURAGAOKA-
CHŌ

81

Bunkamura-dōri

55

MARUYAMA-
CHŌ

Shinsen

Meguri-gawa

Yamate-dōri

53

Harajuku, Aoyama, Shibuya & Ebisu

◉ Sights
1 Cat Street.......................... D3
2 Dior Omote-sandō D3
3 Hachikō Statue...................C5
4 Louis Vuitton Omote-sandō...... D3
5 Meguro-gawa B8
6 Meiji-jingū........................C1
7 Meiji-jingū Gyoen B2
8 Myth of Tomorrow C5
9 Omotesandō Hills D3
10 Prada Aoyama....................E4
11 Shibuya Center-gai...............C5
12 Shibuya Crossing.................C5
13 Spiral Building E4
14 Takeshita-dōri.................... C2
15 Tod's Omote-sandō...............E3
16 Tōkyū Plaza D3
17 Yoyogi-kōen.......................B3

◔ Activities, Courses & Tours
18 Ohara School of Ikebana..........E4
19 Purikura no Mecca................B5
20 Shimizu-yu.........................E3

ⓐ Shopping
21 6% Doki Doki D3
22 Arts & Science....................F4
Bedrock.......................(see 9)
23 Chicago Thrift Store.............. D3
24 Comme des Garçons...............E4
25 Daikanyama T-Site C7
26 Dog................................ D2
27 Fake Tokyo C4
28 Gallery Kawano...................E3
29 Kapital D8
KiddyLand....................(see 85)
30 Laforet........................... D3
31 Loft............................... C4
32 Mandarake........................ B4
33 Musubi............................ D2
34 Okura.............................C7
35 Pass the Baton D3
36 Raw Tokyo D4
37 Shibuya 109.......................B5
Shibuya Hikarie................(see 47)
38 Shibuya Publishing Booksellers A4
39 Sou-Sou E4
40 Tokyu Hands B4
41 Tower Records....................C4
42 Tsukikageya.......................A3
43 Vase C8

✖ Eating
44 Afuri E7
45 Ahiru Store.......................A3
Camelback....................(see 45)
46 Commune 246 ....E3
47 d47 Shokudō......................C5

48 Ebisu-yokochō.....................E7
49 Food Show C5
50 Gyūkatsu Motomura...............C5
51 Harajuku Gyōza-rō D3
52 Higashiya Man E4
53 Higashi-Yama A8
54 Ippo E8
55 Kaikaya B5
56 Maisen E3
57 Maru..............................D4
58 Matsukiya B5
59 Megutama E6
60 Mominoki House D2
61 Nagi Shokudō C6
62 Narukiyo D5
63 Ōtaru C8
64 Ouca E8
65 Pariya D4
66 Sagatani B5
67 Sakura-tei......................... D2
68 Tabela B4
69 Udon Yamachō E7
70 Yakiniku Champion D8
71 Yanmo............................. E4

⚆ Drinking & Nightlife
72 A to Z Cafe........................ E4
73 Anniversaire Café................. E3
74 Bar Martha E8
75 Bar Trench D7
76 Beat Cafe......................... B5
77 Buri...............................D7
78 Contact........................... B5
79 Enjoy House D7
80 Fuglen Tokyo A3
81 Good Beer Faucets B5
82 Harajuku Taproom................. D2
83 Karaoke-kan....................... B5
84 Little Nap Coffee Stand........... A2
85 Montoak D3
86 Mori no Terrace C2
87 Nakame Takkyū Lounge C8
88 Oath D5
89 Rhythm Cafe...................... B4
90 Shidax Village C4
91 Tight C5
92 Two Rooms E4
93 Womb B5

⚡ Entertainment
94 Blue Note Tokyo....................F4
95 Club Quattro B4
96 Crocodile C4
97 Jingū Baseball Stadium............ F1
98 Liquid Room.......................E7
99 Unit...............................C8
Uplink.........................(see 68)
100 WWW B4

Marunouchi, Nihombashi, Ginza & Tsukiji

◎ Sights

1 Crafts Gallery A2
2 Fushimi-yagura A4
3 Hama-rikyū Onshi-teien C8
4 Imperial Palace..A3
5 Imperial Palace East Garden....................B3
6 Imperial Palace Plaza............................. B4
7 Intermediatheque....................................C4
  Kabukiza Gallery ....(see 72)
8 Kikyō-mon...B3
9 Kitanomaru-kōen (Kitanomaru
  Park)..A1
10 National Museum of Modern Art
  (MOMAT)...B2
11 Seafood Intermediate
  Wholesalers' Area..................................D8
12 Tayasu-mon A1
13 Tokyo International Forum.......................C5
14 Tokyo Station.. D4
15 Tokyo Station Gallery............................. D4
16 Tsukiji Outer Market................................D7

◆ Activities, Courses & Tours

17 Imperial Palace Cycling Course...............C4
18 SkyBus C4
19 Tokyo Bay Cruise......................................E3
20 Tokyo Cooking Studio...............................F7
21 Tokyo Sushi Academy D7
  Tsukiji Market Information
  Centre.. (see 21)

◉ Shopping

22 Akomeya..D5
23 Antique Mall Ginza....................................D5
24 Bic Camera...C5
25 Coredo Muromachi.....................................E3
26 Daimaru... D4
  Dover Street Market Ginza.............(see 64)
27 Ginza Six C6
28 Itōya..D6
29 KITTE D4
30 Mitsukoshi D6
31 Muji C5
32 Natsuno..C6
33 Ōedo Antique Market................................C5
34 Sanrioworld Ginza C6
35 Starnet F1

36 Takashimaya E4
37 Takumi..C6
38 Tokyo Character Street..............................D4
39 Tsukiji Hitachiya D7
  Uniqlo...(see 27)

◆ Eating

40 Apollo..C6
41 Bird Land..C6
42 Hōnen Manpuku..E3
43 Kagari...D6
44 Kikanbō..E1
45 Kyūbey..C7
46 Maru..C6
47 Monja Kondō..F8
48 Nihonbashi Dashi Bar............................... E3
49 Rose Bakery Marunouchi..........................C4
50 Sanokiya..D7
51 Sushikuni...D7
52 Taimeiken.. E3
53 Trattoria Tsukiji Paradiso! D8
54 Tsukugon...E7
55 Yamachō D7
56 Yūrakuchō Sanchoku Inshokugai C6

◎ Drinking & Nightlife

57 100% Chocolate Cafe................................ D5
58 Aux Amis Des Vins.................................... D5
59 Bamboo Cafe..C6
60 Bistro Marx...C6
61 Cafe de l'Ambre...C7
62 Cha Ginza...C6
  Jugetsudo ....(see 72)
63 Kagaya B7
64 Komatsu Bar...C6
65 Manpuku Shokudō......................................C5
66 Nihonbashi Toyama E3
67 Peter: the Bar...C5
68 Sake Plaza... A6
69 So Tired..C3
70 Turret Coffee..E7

✪ Entertainment

71 Cotton Club...C4
72 Kabukiza Theatre....................................... D6
73 Nippon Budōkan..A1
74 Tokyo Takarazuka Theatre.......................B6

Marunouchi, Nihombashi, Ginza & Tsukiji

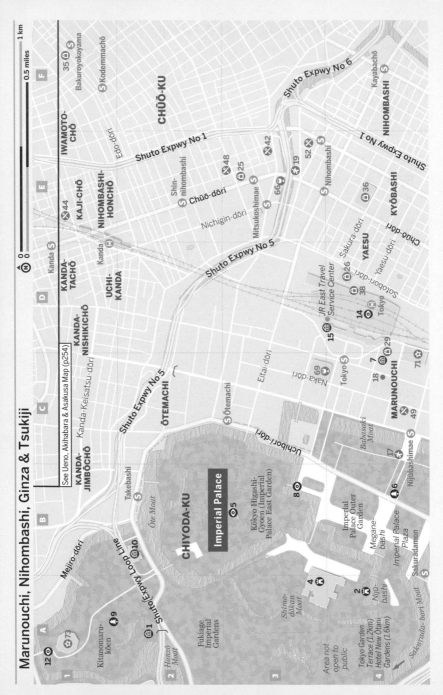

1 km
0.5 miles

F
35 ⑤ Bakuroyokoyama
⑤ Kodemmachō
CHŪŌ-KU
Shuto Expwy No 6
Kayabachō ⑤
NIHOMBASHI
Shuto Expwy No 1

E
IWAMOTO-CHŌ
Edo-dōri
Shuto Expwy No 1
44 ✕
KAJI-CHŌ
NIHOMBASHI-HONCHŌ
Shin-nihombashi
Chūō-dōri ⑤
Nichigin-dōri
48 ✕
25 🏛
52 ✕ 42 ✕
19 🏨
66 ⑤
Mitsukoshimae ⑤
Nihombashi ⑤
36 🏛
KYŌBASHI
Chūō-dōri

D
Kanda ⑤
KANDA-TACHŌ
Kanda ⑤
UCHI-KANDA
Shuto Expwy No 5
JR East Travel Service Center
26 🏛
38 🏛
YAESU
Sotobori-dōri
Yaesu-dōri
Sakura-dōri
14 🏛
15 🏛
Tokyo ⑤
29 🏛
7
71 ✹

C
See Ueno, Akihabara & Asakusa Map (p254)
KANDA-NISHIKICHŌ
Kanda-Keisatsu-dōri
Eitai-dōri
Tokyo ⑤
68 ⑤
Naka-dōri
18
MARUNOUCHI
49 ✕

B
KANDA-JIMBŌCHŌ
Shuto Expwy No 5
Takebashi ⑤
Ōte Moat
ŌTEMACHI
Ōtemachi ⑤
Uchibori-dōri
CHIYODA-KU
Imperial Palace
5 ◉
Kōkyo Higashi-Gyoen (Imperial Palace East Garden)
8 ◉
Babasaki Moat
Megane-bashi
17 ✹
Imperial Palace Outer Garden
Imperial Palace Plaza
Nijūbashimae ⑤
6
Sakuradamon ⑤

A
Mejiro-dōri
Kitanomaru-kōen
73 ✹
9
1 🏛
Shuto Expwy Loop Line
12 ◉
Hanzō Moat
Fukiage Imperial Gardens
Shimo-dōkan Moat
4 🔶
2 🔶
Niju-bashi
Area not open to public
Tokyo Garden Terrace (1.2km);
Hotel New Otani Gardens (1.6km);
Sakurada-bori Moat

N 0 0

1
2
3
4

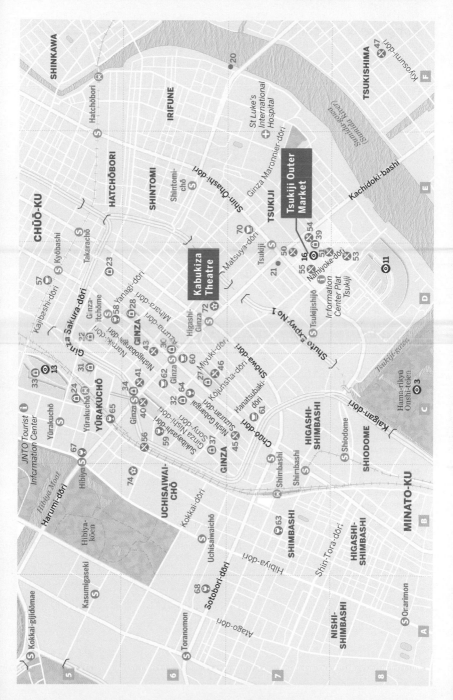

Roppongi & Akasaka

◎ **Sights**
1 21_21 Design Sight..B1
2 Aoyama Rei-en..A1
3 Complex 665..B3
4 Mohri Garden...B3
5 Mori Art Museum..B3
6 National Art Center Tokyo..........................B2
7 Roppongi Hills...B3
8 Suntory Museum of Art..............................B2
9 Tokyo City View...B3
10 Tokyo Midtown..B2

◉ **Activities, Courses & Tours**
11 Tokyo Cook...C2

🏠 **Shopping**
12 Axis Design...C3
   Living Motif..(see 12)
   Nuno...(see 12)
13 Souvenir from Tokyo....................................B2

✖ **Eating**
14 Gogyō...A2
15 Honmura-An...B2
16 Jōmon..C3
17 Kikunoi..C1
18 Lauderdale..B3
   Sougo..(see 11)

🍷 **Drinking & Nightlife**
19 Agave...B2
20 Brewdog..C2
21 SuperDeluxe...B3
22 The Garden...C3
23 These...A3

🎭 **Entertainment**
24 Billboard Live...B2
25 Suntory Hall...D1

Shinjuku

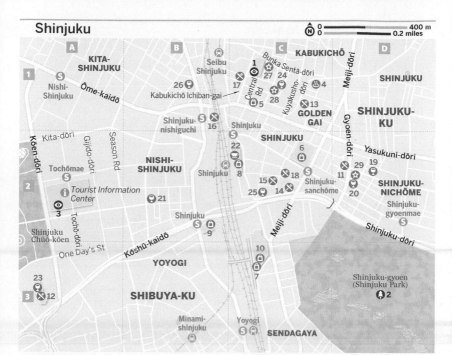

N 0 ————— 400 m
   0 ————— 0.2 miles

⊚ Sights

1 Kabukichō C1
2 Shinjuku-gyoen D3
3 Tokyo Metropolitan Government
   Building A2

✪ Activities, Courses & Tours

4 Thermae-yu C1

⊟ Shopping

Beams .... (see 14)
Disk Union .... (see 18)
5 Don Quijote C1
6 Isetan C2
7 Kinokuniya C3
8 Lumine Est C2
9 NEWoMan B2
10 Tokyu Hands C3

⊗ Eating

11 Donjaca D2
12 Kozue A3

13 Nagi C1
14 Nakajima C2
15 Numazukō C2
16 Omoide-yokochō B1
17 Shinjuku Asia-yokochō C1
18 Tsunahachi C2

⊝ Drinking & Nightlife

19 Aiiro Cafe D2
20 Arty Farty D2
21 BenFiddich B2
22 Berg C2
23 New York Bar A3
24 Ren C1
25 Samurai C2
26 Zoetrope B1

✪ Entertainment

27 Loft C1
28 Robot Restaurant C1
29 Shinjuku Pit Inn D2

Ueno, Akihabara & Asakusa

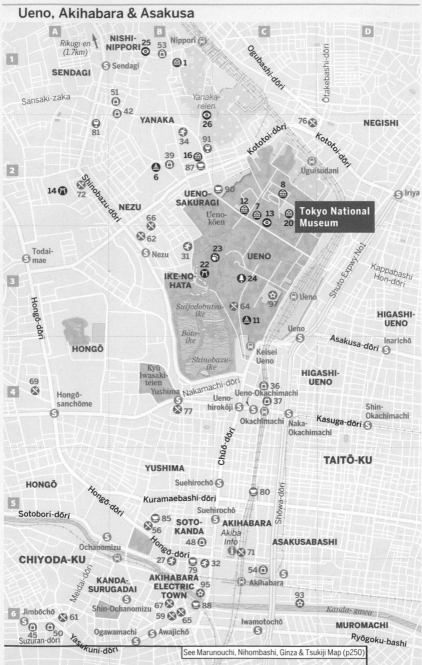

A

B

C

D

1

Rikugi-en → NISHI-NIPPORI **25** 53 Nippori

(1.7km)

Sendagi **1**

SENDAGI

Sansaki-zaka **51**

42

YANAKA

Yanaka-reien

81

26

NEGISHI

76

Kototoi-dōri

Kototoi-dōri

Ogubashi-dōri

Ōtakebashi-dōri

34 **91**

39 **16**

6 **87**

UENO-SAKURAGI **90**

8

Uguisudani

Iriya

2

14 **72**

Shinobazu-dōri

NEZU

Ueno-kōen

12 **7**

13

20

Tokyo National Museum

66

62

Todai-mae

Nezu **31**

23

22

24

UENO

Kappabashi Hon-dōri

Shuto Expwy No.1

3

Hongō-dōri

IKE-NO-HATA

Suijodobutsu-ike

64

97

Ueno

11

HIGASHI-UENO

Inarichō

HONGŌ

Bōto-ike

Shinobazu-ike

Keisei Ueno

Ueno

Asakusa-dōri

4

69

Hongō-sanchōme

Kyū Iwasaki-teien Yushima

Nakamachi-dōri

Ueno-hirokōji

77

36

Ueno-Okachimachi **37**

HIGASHI-UENO

Shin-Okachimachi

Okachimachi

Naka-Okachimachi

Kasuga-dōri

YUSHIMA

Chūō-dōri

TAITŌ-KU

5

HONGŌ

Hongō-dōri

Suehirochō

Kuramaebashi-dōri

Suehirochō

80

Showa-dōri

Sotobori-dōri

85

56

SOTO-KANDA

AKIHABARA

Akiba Info **48**

ASAKUSABASHI

Ochanomizu

Hongō-dōri

71

CHIYODA-KU

27 **79**

32

54

Akihabara

KANDA-SURUGADAI

AKIHABARA ELECTRIC TOWN

95

93

6

Jimbōchō **61**

Shin-Ochanomizu

67

59 **65**

88

Iwamotochō

MUROMACHI

Kanda-gawa

Ryōgoku-bashi

45 **50**

Suzuran-dōri

Ogawamachi

Awajichō

Yasukuni-dōri

Meidai-dōri

See Marunouchi, Nihombashi, Ginza & Tsukiji Map (p250)

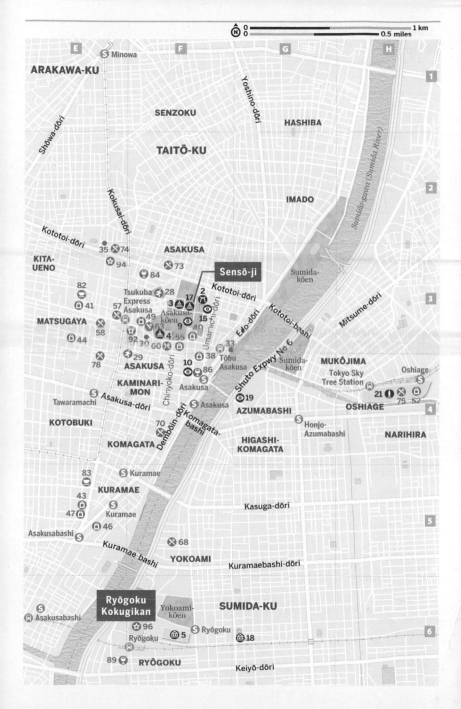

Ueno, Akihabara & Asakusa

⊙ **Sights**
1 Asakura Museum of Sculpture,
    Taitō..B1
2 Asakusa-jinja.....................................F3
3 Awashima-dō.....................................F3
4 Chingo-dō...F3
5 Edo-Tokyo Museum..........................F6
6 Enju-ji...B2
    Five-Storey Pagoda.....................(see 3)
7 Gallery of Hōryū-ji Treasures...........C2
8 Heiseikan..C2
9 Hōzō-mon...F3
10 Kaminari-mon.....................................F4
11 Kiyōmizu Kannon-dō..........................C3
12 Kuroda Memorial Hall........................C2
13 Kuro-mon...C2
14 Nezu-jinja...A2
15 Niten-mon...F3
16 SCAI the Bathhouse...........................B2
17 Sensō-ji...F3
18 Sumida Hokusai Museum...................G6
19 Super Dry Hall....................................G4
20 Tokyo National Museum.....................C2
21 Tokyo Sky Tree...................................H4
22 Ueno Tōshō-gū....................................B3
23 Ueno Zoo...C3
24 Ueno-kōen...C3
25 Yanaka Ginza......................................B1
26 Yanaka-reien.......................................B2

⊕ **Activities, Courses & Tours**
27 Akiba Kart..B6
28 Hanayashiki.......................................F3
29 Jakotsu-yu..F4
30 Mokuhankan..F3
31 Rokuryu Kōsen....................................B3
32 Super Potato Retro-kan.....................B6
33 Tokyo Kitchen.....................................F3
34 Tokyobike Rental Service...................B2
35 Wanariya...E3

⊙ **Shopping**
    2k540 Aki-Oka Artisan.................(see 80)
36 Ameya-yokochō...................................C4
37 Ameyoko Rizumu................................C4
38 Bengara...F4
    Chabara...(see 71)
39 Edokoro Allan West............................B2
40 Fujiya..F3
41 Ganso Shokuhin Sample-ya...............E3
42 Isetatsu...B1
43 Kakimori..E5
44 Kappabashi-dōri..................................E3
45 Komiyama Shoten...............................A6
46 Koncent...E5
    Kurodaya.......................................(see 10)
    mAAch ecute..................................(see 88)
47 Maito..E5
48 Mandarake Complex...........................B5

49 Marugoto Nippon................................F3
50 Ohya Shobō...A6
51 Shokichi...B1
    Solamachi.....................................(see 75)
52 Sumida City Point...............................H4
    Tokyo Hotarudo.............................(see 30)
53 Yanaka Matsunoya..............................B1
54 Yodobashi Akiba.................................C6
55 Yonoya Kushiho..................................F3

⊗ **Eating**
56 Amanoya...B5
57 Asakusa Imahan.................................E3
58 Asakusa Unagi Sansho.......................E3
59 Botan...B6
60 Daikokuya...F3
61 Ethiopia...A6
62 Hantei..B3
63 Hoppy-dōri..F3
64 Innsyoutei...C3
65 Isegen..B6
66 Kamachiku...B3
67 Kanda Yabu Soba................................B6
68 Kappō Yoshiba....................................F5
69 Kingyozaka..A4
70 Komagata Dozeu..................................F4
71 Komaki Shokudō..................................C5
72 Nezu no Taiyaki...................................A2
73 Onigiri Yadoroku.................................F3
74 Otafuku...E3
75 Rokurinsha..H4
76 Sasa-no-Yuki.......................................C2
77 Shinsuke..B4
78 Sometarō...E4

⊙ **Drinking & Nightlife**
79 @Home Cafe..B6
    Asahi Sky Room............................(see 19)
80 Boo...C5
81 Bousingot..A2
82 Café Otonova.......................................E3
83 Camera...E5
84 'Cuzn Homeground.............................F3
85 Imasa...B5
86 Kamiya Bar..F4
87 Kayaba Coffee.....................................B2
88 N3331..B6
89 Popeye...E6
90 Torindō..C2
91 Yanaka Beer Hall................................B2

⊙ **Entertainment**
92 Asakusa Engei Hall.............................F3
93 Club Goodman.....................................C6
94 Oiwake...E3
95 P.A.R.M.S...B6
96 Ryōgoku Kokugikan............................F6
97 Tokyo Bunka Kaikan...........................C3

Symbols & Map Key

Look for these symbols to quickly identify listings:

- ◎ Sights
- ✪ Activities
- ✪ Courses
- ✪ Tours
- ✪ Festivals & Events
- ✪ Eating
- ✪ Drinking
- ✪ Entertainment
- ✪ Shopping
- ✪ Information & Transport

These symbols and abbreviations give vital information for each listing:

- 🌿 Sustainable or green recommendation
- FREE No payment required

- ☏ Telephone number
- ☺ Opening hours
- P Parking
- ☺ Nonsmoking
- ❄ Air-conditioning
- @ Internet access
- 🛜 Wi-fi access
- ☲ Swimming pool
- ☐ Bus
- ☐ Ferry
- ☐ Tram
- ☐ Train
- ☐ English-language menu
- ☑ Vegetarian selection
- 👪 Family-friendly

Find your best experiences with these Great For... icons.

- Art & Culture
- Beaches
- Budget
- Cafe/Coffee
- Cycling
- Detour
- Drinking
- Entertainment
- Events
- Family Travel
- Food & Drink
- History
- Local Life
- Nature & Wildlife
- Photo Op
- Scenery
- Shopping
- Short Trip
- Sport
- Walking
- Winter Travel

Sights
- 🏖 Beach
- 🐦 Bird Sanctuary
- ☸ Buddhist
- 🏰 Castle/Palace
- ✝ Christian
- 卍 Confucian
- 🕉 Hindu
- ☪ Islamic
- 卐 Jain
- ✡ Jewish
- ❶ Monument
- 🏛 Museum/Gallery/Historic Building
- Ⓡ Ruin
- ⛩ Shinto
- ☬ Sikh
- ☯ Taoist
- 🍷 Winery/Vineyard
- 🦁 Zoo/Wildlife Sanctuary
- ◎ Other Sight

Points of Interest
- Bodysurfing
- Camping
- Cafe
- Canoeing/Kayaking
- Course/Tour
- Diving
- Drinking & Nightlife
- Eating
- Entertainment
- Sento Hot Baths/Onsen
- Shopping
- Skiing
- Sleeping
- Snorkelling
- Surfing
- Swimming/Pool
- Walking
- Windsurfing
- Other Activity

Information
- Bank
- Embassy/Consulate
- Hospital/Medical
- @ Internet
- Police
- Post Office
- Telephone
- Toilet
- Tourist Information
- ● Other Information

Geographic
- Beach
- Gate
- Hut/Shelter
- Lighthouse
- Lookout
- Mountain/Volcano
- Oasis
- Park
-)(Pass
- Picnic Area
- Waterfall

Transport
- Airport
- BART station
- Border crossing
- Boston T station
- Bus
- Cable car/Funicular
- Cycling
- Ferry
- Metro/MRT station
- Monorail
- P Parking
- Petrol station
- Subway/S-Bahn/Skytrain station
- Taxi
- Train station/Railway
- Tram
- Tube Station
- Underground/U-Bahn station
- ● Other Transport

...e pocket and a sense of ... Tony and Maureen Wheeler needed ... for the trip of a lifetime – across Europe and Asia overland to Australia. It took several months, and at the end – broke but inspired – they sat at their kitchen table writing and stapling together their first travel guide, *Across Asia on the Cheap*. Within a week they'd sold 1500 copies. Lonely Planet was born. Today, Lonely Planet has offices in Franklin, London, Melbourne, Oakland, Dublin, Beijing, and Delhi, with more than 600 staff and writers. We share Tony's belief that 'a great guidebook should do three things: inform, educate and amuse'.

Our Writers

Rebecca Milner

California born and longtime Tokyo resident (14 years and counting!), Rebecca has co-authored Lonely Planet guides to *Tokyo, Japan, Korea* and *China*. A freelance writer covering travel, food and culture, Rebecca has been published in the *Guardian, Independent, Sunday Times Travel Magazine, Japan Times* and more. After spending the better part of her twenties working to travel – doing odd jobs in Tokyo to make money so she could spend months at a time backpacking around Asia – Rebecca joined the Lonely Planet team of freelance authors in 2010.

Simon Richmond

Journalist and photographer Simon Richmond has specialised as a travel writer since the early 1990s and first worked for Lonely Planet in 1999 on the *Central Asia* guide. He's long since stopped counting the number of guidebooks he's researched and written for the company, but countries covered include Australia, China, India, Iran, Japan, Korea, Malaysia, Mongolia, Myanmar (Burma), Russia, Singapore, South Africa and Turkey. For Lonely Planet's website he's penned features on topics from the world's best swimming pools to the joys of Urban Sketching. His travel features have been published in newspapers and magazines around the world, including in the UK's *Independent, Guardian, Times, Daily Telegraph* and *Royal Geographical Society Magazine;* and Australia's *Sydney Morning Herald* and *Australian* newspapers and *Australian Financial Review Magazine*.

STAY IN TOUCH LONELYPLANET.COM/CONTACT

AUSTRALIA The Malt Store, Level 3, 551 Swanston St, Carlton, Victoria 3053
☑ 03 8379 8000, fax 03 8379 8111

IRELAND Unit E, Digital Court. The Digital Hub, Rainsford St, Dublin 8, Ireland

USA 124 Linden Street, Oakland, CA 94607
☑ 510 250 6400, toll free 800 275 8555, fax 510 893 8572

UK 240 Blackfriars Road, London SE1 8NW
☑ 020 3771 5100, fax 020 3771 5101

 twitter.com/lonelyplanet

 facebook.com/lonelyplanet

instagram.com/lonelyplanet

youtube.com/lonelyplanet

lonelyplanet.com/newsletter